"This very worthy book shines histori[...] s-old contributions of Black and Brown pec[...] tion-ship between Christian faith and social [...] which organizers and faith communities sometimes seem desperate for new models in the name of innovation, the authors plumb our collective history and make the case that some strategies are timeless and have merit in an array of cultural circumstances—including today's. Inasmuch as I subscribe personally to the principle of *sankofa*, I'm especially grateful for the authors' willingness to look back in order to move forward."

—**Paul Roberts Sr.**, Johnson C. Smith Theological Seminary

"As you read *Buried Seeds*, your knowledge of base ecclesial communities (CEBs in Latin America and the Philippines) and hush harbors (US antebellum South) will be deepened, you will gain wisdom concerning our own social challenges, and you will benefit from practices the authors present. What's more, as you enter the worlds of Salvatierra and Wrencher, if you dwell there with heart and mind and if you bring these worlds into conversations, then as you reenter your own world, your awareness and imagination will be changed. You will be more apt to see the Spirit of Jesus ahead of you and around you, calling you and your community toward participation."

—**Mark Lau Branson**, Fuller Theological Seminary; coauthor (with Juan Martínez) of *Churches, Cultures, and Leadership*

"*Buried Seeds* pays homage to the critical course of liberationist growth and process: freedom is embedded in the miracle of life's happenings; and no matter the circumstances, life will always spring up where there is potential for flourishing. Salvatierra and Wrencher have gifted us all a book that feels like a garden!"

—**Oluwatomisin Olayinka Oredein**, Brite Divinity School

"Beginning with the challenging but hopeful admonition, 'The Church has to be so much more,' this timely and significant work offers real-life examples of churches and Christian communities that are so much more. Drawing inspiration and examples from the oppressed and the poor, this book provides the hope that renewal can truly come from the margins. *Buried Seeds* exemplifies the best of what the church can be and offers a much-needed antidote for an ailing church."

—**Soong-Chan Rah**, Fuller Theological Seminary

"If you're about to close the door on Christianity for good, wait, and read this book first! *Buried Seeds* is the dose of hope we've needed in an age where it's hard to tell the difference between ecclesia and empire. Salvatierra and

Wrencher draw on decades of lived experience to remind us that for generations Black and Brown peoples have shown us The Way, forging a rich faith out of exile and struggle. Packed with pertinent research, rigorous theological analysis, and vivid stories, this book is a manual for leaders who seek to provoke the Christian church into resurrected life. *Buried Seeds* made me commit anew to 'the assembling of ourselves together.'"

—**Rev. Naomi Washington-Leapheart**, curator, Salt | Yeast | Light

"*Buried Seeds* is a sacred gift to a church in crisis. The authors take us on a journey and help us recover the radical and unsung roots of the Christian faith by introducing us to transformational ministry models. For those who take seriously the call to Christian community and to putting faith into action, Salvatierra and Wrencher will provide guidance and wisdom through their Spirit-filled words."

—**Karen González**, author of *The God Who Sees* and *Beyond Welcome*

BURIED SEEDS

BURIED SEEDS

LEARNING from the VIBRANT RESILIENCE
of MARGINALIZED CHRISTIAN COMMUNITIES

ALEXIA SALVATIERRA
and BRANDON WRENCHER

Foreword by ROBERT CHAO ROMERO
Afterword by WILLIE JAMES JENNINGS

Baker Academic
a division of Baker Publishing Group
Grand Rapids, Michigan

© 2022 by Alexia Salvatierra and Brandon Wrencher

Published by Baker Academic
a division of Baker Publishing Group
PO Box 6287, Grand Rapids, MI 49516-6287
www.bakeracademic.com

Printed in the United States of America

Library of Congress Cataloging-in-Publication Data
Names: Salvatierra, Alexia, 1956– author. | Wrencher, Brandon, 1985– author.
Title: Buried seeds : learning from the vibrant resilience of marginalized Christian communities / Alexia Salvatierra and Brandon Wrencher ; foreword by Robert Chao Romero ; afterword by Willie James Jennings.
Description: Grand Rapids : Baker Academic, a division of Baker Publishing Group, [2022] | Includes bibliographical references and index.
Identifiers: LCCN 2021050966 | ISBN 9781540964649 (paperback) | ISBN 9781540965677 (casebound) | ISBN 9781493435029 (pdf) | ISBN 9781493435012 (ebook)
Subjects: LCSH: Christian communities—Case studies. | Basic Christian communities—Case studies. | African Americans—Religious life—Case studies.
Classification: LCC BV4405 .S235 2022 | DDC 262--dc23/eng/20211118
LC record available at https://lccn.loc.gov/2021050966

The following texts are quoted from extensively throughout. The authors thank the publishers for permission to reprint the material: Ernesto Cardenal. 1976. *The Gospel in Solentiname*. Maryknoll, NY: Orbis Books. All rights reserved. Reprinted by permission of Orbis Books; Pablo Galdámez. 1983. *Faith of a People*. Maryknoll, NY: Orbis Books. All rights reserved. Reprinted by permission of Orbis Books; and Niall O'Brien. 1987. *Revolution from the Heart*. Oxford: Oxford University Press. Reproduced with permission of the Licensor through PLSclear.

Baker Publishing Group publications use paper produced from sustainable forestry practices and post-consumer waste whenever possible.

22 23 24 25 26 27 28   7 6 5 4 3 2 1

Contents

Foreword

ROBERT CHAO ROMERO

When God came incarnate as a human being to launch a kingdom movement of global redemption, God came as a Galilean. Jesus was raised in Galilee, focused his ministry in Galilee, selected his first apostles from Galilee, and after rising from the dead, commanded his disciples to meet him there as well. Latine and Black theologians such as Virgilio Elizondo, Elizabeth Conde-Frazier, and Howard Thurman have shown us that Galilee was the quintessential marginalized community, or "hood," of Jesus's day. Owing to Roman imperialism, Galileans lived as a colonized people in their own historic lands. Most were peasant farmers who faced economic insecurity on account of excessive rents, Roman tribute, and temple tithes and taxes. Jews from Galilee were also looked down on by their southern compatriots in Judea because they lived in a borderlands region, and their frequent contact with gentiles threatened standards of cultural and religious purity. And if Galilee was the hood, then Jesus's hometown of Nazareth was "the hood of the hood." As one of his early disciples famously quipped, "Nazareth! Can anything good come from there?" (John 1:46).

As Latines and African Americans in the United States, we are all Galileans. We share a common history of segregation in housing, education, and public spaces, as well as discrimination in voting rights, employment, public health, and the criminal justice system. Today, we live together in many of the Galilees that still persist and that continue to bear the uneven weight of socioeconomic and political inequality. In the prophetic words of Howard Thurman, we have lived "as standing with our backs against the wall" (Thurman 1976, 11). As faithful peoples, however, we have journeyed collectively through such racial challenges with Jesus, and we have struggled to recover the Galilean roots of Christianity as the Brown and Black church. In this book, Rev. Dr. Alexia Salvatierra and Rev. Brandon Wrencher document two compelling case studies of this struggle as reflected in the base ecclesial community (BEC) movement of Latin America and the Philippines and the hush harbors of enslaved Africans in the antebellum South.

As a reflection of the early church, BECs emerged between the 1960s and the 1990s as widespread networks of small groups of poor and marginalized people who were committed to a holistic vision of spiritual, personal, and communal transformation in Christ. In places such as Brazil, El Salvador, and the Philippines, BECs fought for social goals such as the recovery of land rights, the provision of basic necessities such as electricity and water, the nonviolent overthrow of terrorizing dictatorships, and also for the personal restoration of marriages and deliverance from addiction. Centuries before, hush harbors were clandestine gathering places where enslaved Africans would "steal away" to worship the God of the oppressed, care for mutual needs, and plot for the abolition of slavery. Hush harbors functioned as alternative religious spaces in contrast to separate and unequal plantation churches and segregated gatherings that developed under the gaze and supervision of white ministers and slaveholding Christians. Like the history of the primitive church, the history of BECs and hush harbors is messy and contested; and yet, similar to the early church, and contrary to much popular perception, BECs and hush harbors were grassroots-led movements centered on commitment to Jesus, sacred Scripture, and the empowerment of the Holy Spirit. Where BECs lost such spiritual focus (as discussed by Salvatierra, a personal participant in the BEC movement), they did not survive.

As a professor of ethnic studies at UCLA and a pastor among justice-minded Christians over many years, I have witnessed, with great sadness, the exodus of thousands of students and young adults from the US church because of the apathy toward and opposition to contemporary issues of racial justice expressed by large swaths of evangelicalism. As noted by Salvatierra and Wrencher, increasingly the church is not seen as a place to find holistic spiritual community. Based on rigorous academic research and more than six decades of combined grassroots ministry experience on the part of the authors, this book offers a treasure of indigenous strategies of transformation for those who are willing to seriously engage the heritage and legacy of the BEC and hush harbor movements. *Buried Seeds* is a critical read both for scholars of missiology and church planting and for young Christian leaders of color around the world who wish to recover the radical Galilean roots of global Christianity.

Introduction

Longing for More

The Church has to be so much more. The Church has to be the light. The Church has to be the salt. We have to be the difference. We have to bring hope. We have to bring love. We have to show them that God is out there . . . actually practice what we preach. . . . "Hey, I didn't see you last Sunday. How are you doing?" or "Hey, I heard you got a promotion, let's go celebrate you" or "Hey, I heard you need a gallon of milk. Can I buy your groceries for the week?" (Research subject, "Latinx Millennials in the U.S. and Theological Education," by Alexia Salvatierra 2019)

Belonging is a fragrance of change. Millennials and other emerging generations particularly value community, from socializing to community service to public policies that support the well-being of communities. They also value authenticity; young adults do not hunger for the pretense of community. They are not the only generation with the longing to connect; many of us in our fragmented and divided society wish for a deeper experience of community. At the same time, we ideally want our community to also satisfy our souls. The hunger for community is often connected to a deep desire for communion with God as well as with other human beings. Millennials, according to a 2015 Pew study, are also spiritually oriented, with 80 percent believing in God and increasing numbers identifying with statements like "I feel a deep sense of spiritual peace and well-being" or "I experience a deep sense of wonder about the universe" (Pew Research Center 2019).

Yet congregational participation, membership, and leadership are declining, particularly among younger generations. According to the Pew Research Center, the number of Christians in the US is projected to drop over twelve percentage points from 2010 to 2050, while the population of the unaffiliated is expected to double (Pew Research Center 2019). In 2010 the average age for a Christian was thirty-nine years old in comparison to thirty years old for an unaffiliated person. Increasingly, the church is not seen as a place to find holistic spiritual community.

During the same period, we have also seen an ethnic and racial transition in the United States. In the 2013 census, 72 percent of boomers were non-Hispanic whites in comparison to 57 percent of millennials and 53 percent of Generation Z; by 2045, the majority of the US will belong to an ethnic minority (Frey 2018). Both younger generations and ethnic minorities tend toward a greater commitment to social justice than the general population on multiple indexes. Without encouraging the integration of personal and social transformation, the church will not meet the need young people of color have for holistic spiritual community.

On the one hand, most young people of color are not looking to older white people to provide the inspiration or guidance they need in order to create the kind of community they seek. On the other hand, they long for mentors and models. In our recent study of Latinx millennials at the Centro Latino of Fuller Theological Seminary, we found that roughly half of the subjects explicitly articulated that one of their most important needs was for a mentor from their community (Salvatierra 2019).

The base ecclesial communities[1] in Latin America and the Philippines in the late twentieth century and the hush harbors of the US Deep South during the antebellum era offer two models of vital Christian community created by ancestors and elders from Black and Brown communities. Both were grassroots models of church, an organized and vibrant network of dedicated disciples engaged in worship and justice. Both models arose at times of great cultural transition, were designed for religious and social transformation, and were led by Black and Brown poor laity.

The Gospel in Solentiname (Cardenal 1976), a collection of transcripts of Bible studies that took place in a base ecclesial community in Nicaragua, shares a group reflection on the miracle of the loaves and fishes in the Gospel of Luke that encapsulates the spirit and flavor of the movement.

> PANCHO: I'm just catching on to what this means here! They didn't have enough—right?—to feed the five thousand people. But then [Jesus] says to them:

1. A number of terms are commonly used to describe this movement, including *base communities*, *base Christian communities*, and *base ecclesial communities*. We have chosen the latter (abbreviated as BEC) as our general language because it is the most common term used in Latin America. However, when the sources use BCC or CEB (the abbreviation in Spanish), we use their terms. The word *base* refers to the majority of the people who reside in a community. In Latin America and the Philippines, the majority of the people were (and continue to be) economically poor and politically marginalized. In the base ecclesial community movement, the word *base* began to be used as a synonym for the poor.

It doesn't matter, share it. And they shared it, and with his power he made it stretch out. The lesson is that no matter how little we have we always have to give.

FELIPE: The teaching is also that if we come together to hear the message we're not going to be hungry, because with a united people, there are no problems. Maybe I won't have food, but my neighbor will. If we're together, something can happen to us like what happened to those people with Jesus Christ. If we're together it doesn't hurt to share. And then we're practicing the message of God.

OLIVIA: Here [Jesus] shows that we must all do the sharing and make the increase of the five loaves that were so few and that is to share love. Food and medicine are abundant in the underdeveloped countries but in the hands of the poor, nothing is abundant, and that's because love is lacking. The first thing is the education of the people. . . . And I see now if we have that knowledge with love, then there is food, there are medicines for everyone. When there is brotherhood among everybody, it seems to me that the miracle will occur, and then nobody will be in need of anything, because the people will be giving things through love. And that's what Christ wants, that is the kingdom of God. (Cardenal 1976, 222)

In the documented narratives of enslaved Africans and in other oral tradition, we see the powerful worship and witness of hush harbors:

The folks would sing and pray and testify and clap their hands, just as if God was right there in the midst of them. He wasn't way off in the sky. He was a-seeing everybody and a-listening to every word and a-promising to let His love come down. (Faulkner 1993, 54).

Aunts and mothers were all part of a network of slave women that helped to provide stability and support for the entire slave community. One of the significant contributions of these Christian slave women was playing an active role in the formation of secret prayer meetings. Slaves would "steal away" or "turn the pot down" in secret meetings and to keep their activities quiet. These prayer meetings constituted an important aspect of African American Christianity. . . . Prayer meetings would occur in private . . . away from the supervision of white people. Often meetings happened in brush arbors or "hush harbors" which were private, secluded areas that slaves designated for worship. (Abbott 2003, 48)

The excitement and hope that exude from the words of the *campesinos* (tenant farmers) in Solentiname and the oral tradition of enslaved Africans testify to the possibility of the kind of vibrant, holistic, and authentic Christian community that many of us long for.

In this book, we look closely and deeply at the principles and practices that undergirded and built these communities. We have identified five key themes: kinship (*familia en comunión*), leader-full (*participación*), conscious-ness (*concientización* and *el mensaje de liberación*), spirit-uality (*sanidad* and *la teología de las abuelas*), and faith-full organizing (*alma y fermenta de la sociedad*). We reflect together as coauthors on how to use these principles and practices to cultivate vibrant, resilient, integral Christian communities led by marginalized people, the contextualization of base ecclesial communities and hush harbors for the twenty-first century.

As we explore these principles and practices in the experiences of BECs and hush harbors, we use a methodology that was a core element of the process of *concientización* (which involved analyzing the structures and systems that impacted the lives of BEC members and their neighbors)[2] in light of *el mensaje de liberación* (the message of liberation): *ver*, *juzgar*, and *actuar*. *Ver* means "to see." A BEC would start out by seeing its reality. *Juzgar* means "to judge" or "to interpret." A BEC then had to interpret its reality, allowing the lies of society to be exposed by divine truth. Last, *actuar* means "to act on what you have understood," especially in the context of an ongoing circle or spiral of action and reflection. A modern-day version of this BEC process involves asking the questions "What?," "So what?," and "Now what?"

The following chapters begin by describing how BECs and hush harbors carried out a certain practice, under headings "*Ver* (See) / What?" Then we move to an interpretation of that practice for the modern era, comparing it with similar practices and exploring relevant theory, under headings "*Juzgar* (Judge) / So What?" Last, we focus on practical recommendations, under headings "*Actuar* (Act) / Now What?"

We recognize that these movements were essentially for and led by mar-ginalized, oppressed, and poor people. In the antebellum period and in the 1970s and 1980s, at the height of these movements, it was crystal clear whether that description fit a potential member or leader of those communities. In the US in the twenty-first century, our economic, racial, social, and political boundaries are complex and contested. Still, we believe that the legacy of BECs and hush harbors is relevant for us all, but relevant in different ways depending on social location and background.

We offer three sets of recommendations for adapting the insights and prac-tices of the BECs and hush harbors to the modern context. For people who ex-perience and define themselves as marginalized, oppressed, and economically

---

2. This process was both encouraged and used in the Second Vatican Council in Medellín in 1968. According to Laurel Potter, twenty-first-century BECs in El Salvador have continued to use this process while adding "evaluate" and "celebrate" to the traditional triad "see," "judge," and "act" (Potter 2021).

poor and who live and worship in a community that shares that identity, there is one set of recommendations. These people fall into the Amos category, and their experience of oppression and marginalization is profound and formative. In the Bible, Amos, a prophet and shepherd, is a homegrown leader who shares the perspective and background of those he leads. Shepherds were among the poorest and most marginal members of the community in ancient Israel.

Some who interacted with BECs and hush harbors came from a place of greater privilege but wanted to be part of and help build communities in which a critical mass of oppressed people were in leadership. In BECs, pastoral agents—those who helped to start BECs—were often from a different class or had risen to a certain level of economic and social status (priests, nuns, college students). For these people, their privileges formed their perspectives and decisions. They fall into the Lydia category, named after the business-woman who was a key leader in the early church, as she used her money and power to support the ministry.

The differences between an Amos and a Lydia are not hard-and-fast but rather reflect a complex continuum; you decide what ideas are most relevant for you. We are also aware that Lydias may offer support at different distances. Some Lydias may intend to integrate into a community that is marginalized and oppressed, others may want to partner, and still others may merely want to learn from the vital Christianity created by those communities. We hope to offer useful insights to all of you.

We also offer a third category of recommendations to people referred to as Ruths. When we are first introduced to Ruth in the biblical narrative, she is a widow, a gentile, and an immigrant—three groups with little to no societal power in ancient Israel. By the end of the story, she is married to an Israelite landowner and in the process of becoming the ancestor of King David. She experiences both sides on the continuum from oppression to privilege. The Ruth group contains people who are in-between—who have had real and formative experiences of both oppression and privilege. In the hush harbors, these oppressed yet more privileged persons tended to be clergy and any enslaved Africans who gained access to reading and writing. Perhaps you were born or raised in a marginalized community, but you have been able to move into wider circles and exercise more social power than your family has. Maybe you are mixed—one parent more privileged and one more oppressed. You may have been born into privilege but lost your status and found yourself pushed to the margins. Being a Ruth involves both a different set of burdens and a different set of gifts. In our "*Actuar* (Act) / Now What?" sections, we speak to Amos, Lydia, and Ruth.[3]

3. The Christian Community Development Association uses similar categories, phrased a little differently: relocators (those who come from outside to be part of a community), remainers

In the final chapter, we lift up modern-day examples of Christian faith communities that use similar principles and practices. In the postludes, two of the leaders of these communities reflect on the meaning of this book for their ministries. Reverend Marcos Canales is the lead pastor of La Fuente Ministries, a bilingual, intercultural, and intergenerational ministry in Los Angeles County, California. La Fuente Ministries' purpose is to "connect with Christ through Worship and Word, grow with Christ through a nurturing sense of *familia*, and serve with Christ through our vocations and community organizations" (La Fuente Ministries 2021). La Fuente Ministries is committed to the integration of evangelism and justice and to bilingualism (Spanish/English) as a catalyst for spiritual, congregational, and missional formation.

Reverend Anthony Smith is the lead co-pastor of Mission House Church, an African American–centered multicultural church in Salisbury, North Carolina. Mission House's mission is to "mobilize an army of love for the good of our neighborhoods and city." Missioners—what members are called—are committed to a DNA of incarnation (being sent into the community), mission (joining the Spirit's work of renewal in the community), and reconciliation (being agents of peace in a divided world) ("Our Mission" 2021).

Most members of both churches are millennials of color, but all generations and multiple cultures are well represented. We are deeply grateful for the witness of Anthony, Marcos, and their communities, and for the contribution they've made to the book. This book would also not have been possible without the support of Rose Archer—pastor, chaplain, and doctoral student in sociology—for her role as a research assistant for this project. I (Brandon) want to express appreciation to Rev. Nelson Johnson and Mrs. Joyce Johnson, and Bishop Tonyia Rawls for their affirmation and support of this project. And I am deeply grateful for Rev. Wesley Morris, Dr. Oluwatomisin "Tomi" Oredein, and Greg Jarrell for being readers and giving feedback on the project!

Before we jump in, we would like to share a little about who we are as authors and how we came to write this book.

Our Stories

Rev. Dr. Alexia Salvatierra

I was born to a family of semisocialist immigrants from Mexico and Russia and grew up in a working-class neighborhood in Los Angeles, made up of

---

(those who are of and from the community), and returners (those from the community who have increased their personal prosperity and opportunities and have moved out of the community but who come back to rejoin and serve). People in the final category may experience themselves as insiders or as outsiders.

Hispanic pre–Vatican II Catholics and white Baptist fundamentalists; I was consciously on strike against God from the age of nine. I came to accept Jesus as my personal Lord and Savior in the Jesus Movement of the early 1970s when I was introduced to the God on the cross who suffered with us and for us, ultimately uniting love and power. The Jesus Movement built on the base of the hippie movement; young people in those movements felt a strong sense of community with each other. We experimented with profoundly vulnerable worship, sharing life together, and acts of radical generosity, but we had little to no knowledge of the broader picture of Christian community. Shortly afterward, I encountered the Catholic Worker, an intentional community movement started by Dorothy Day and Peter Marin in the 1930s. I volunteered with the Catholic Worker on skid row in Los Angeles and was a full member of the Oakland Catholic Worker from 1991 to 1996, when its focus and constituency were asylum seekers from Central America. I had previously been involved with the Central American Sanctuary movement and with the peace process in Central America. The BEC movement in El Salvador informed our work in Oakland, and many of our members had been part of a base community. Years later, I also built a program for low-wage immigrant workers in Los Angeles's Inland Empire with a colleague who had been taught to lead base communities by the Jesuits, whose murders were a major turning point in the civil war in El Salvador in the 1980s and early 1990s.

However, my deepest experience of base communities took place in the Philippines from 1984 to 1987. As a missionary, I became part of the pro-democracy movement and participated on a regular basis in a BEC. Coming back to the United States from that experience, I sought to incorporate the insights and practices of that movement into a variety of contexts, starting with a peer chaplaincy program that built a BEC-style community among homeless people and continuing in my work as a pastor and a nonprofit ministry director with Hispanic farmworkers, with an African American church in an increasingly Central American neighborhood, and with a statewide organization engaging faith leaders and congregations in broader initiatives for economic justice and immigrant rights (which led to a book on faith-rooted organizing). Along the way, I became a leader in the Christian Community Development Association, which trains primarily evangelical Christians in a multiracial model for intentional communities that work to transform their neighborhoods. Over the past decade, I have been teaching, practicing, and training others in Christian community development, faith-full organizing, and the development of base ecclesial communities around the world. In the process, I have become the *madrina* (godmother) to a network of *puentes* (bridges)—Latinx millennial Christian leaders. (I am also the actual mother of a puente.) In my work as a professor at the Centro Latino and School of

Intercultural Studies at Fuller Theological Seminary, I have been the primary investigator for a study of Latinx millennials and theological education, which has served as a more objective test of my intuitive sense of how important the BEC heritage could be for their vocation and vision.

Rev. Brandon Wrencher

I came to faith in the 1990s as an adolescent in Black Holiness-Pentecostal and small, working-class Baptist churches in the rural South. I come from a long lineage of ministers and community workers in both of these traditions. Passionate, expressive worship; dynamic preaching; pride in African American culture; and service in community were central to my spiritual formation. I carry my daddy's name and the sense of duty and responsibility to your people that he instilled in me. I was also formed by a freethinking, Jesus-following Black mother whose critical consciousness of oppression enabled her to survive as a single mother of three children in a world that put targets on all our backs. My mom inspired and encouraged my questions about the world. Many of those questions were theological and moral. Why is there so much evil in the world? Why are so many people poor and so few rich? How is God loving if God also sends people to hell? Do my friends who dress and talk differently and who aren't like "us" have to change before being welcome at church? Where is God in the midst of all this? Most of what I learned about faith from the churches of my youth satisfied my curiosity and deeply shaped my character. But I was very unsatisfied with how my youthful faith failed to help me grapple with these questions. I married a Black woman who is also a freethinker and creative rebel in her own right. Together we have sought to be faithful to the internal dissidence, to follow the questions, the longings, even when it takes us off the beaten path of traditional ministry.

Grappling with these tensions and questions animated my call to seminary and ministry in parachurch, nonprofit, higher education, and local church contexts. My ministry has also included local leadership, organizing, and activism with many groups for social and spiritual change, such as the Christian Community Development Association, the Movement for Black Lives, the Carolina Federation, the Historic Thousands on Jones Street (HKonJ), and People's Assembly Coalition. Over the last fourteen years in North Carolina and Chicago as a pastor, teacher, and prophetic catalyst, I have formed communities and fought for justice with the spiritually and socially marginalized. In service to my experiences in grassroots ministry and my upbringing, I rediscovered and claimed the antebellum hush harbors as a revolutionary model of church and missional engagement.

More recently, in 2016 hush harbors became a direct inspiration for me in catalyzing two projects: *Liberating Church* and the Good Neighbor Movement. Funded by the Louisville Institute, *Liberating Church* is a book project I co-edited with my friend Venneikia Williams and a team of clergy activist contributors who researched how the antebellum hush harbors can inform vitality in Black-centered faith communities in the twenty-first century. The project entailed generating eight marks of a hush harbor church:

1. Steal Away—hidden in plain sight
2. North Star—building a new world
3. Joy Unspeakable—Holy Spirit power and mysticism
4. Talking Book—communal biblical interpretation through the lens of Jesus's teachings and ministry, the exodus, and the Spirit
5. *Sankofa*—rooted, embodied, and ancestral practices
6. *Ubuntu*—intimacy, healing, and trust among an intergenerational village
7. All God's Children Got Shoes—egalitarian leadership
8. Stay Woke—a practice of remembering and re-membering

We used these marks to produce questions to survey and interview six Black-centered faith start-ups (Wrencher 2022). With neighbors, family, and friends, I founded Good Neighbor Movement, a faith justice start-up that is a network of multiracial, queer-affirming, Black-centered contemplative activist groups in neighborhoods across Greensboro, North Carolina, engaged in liberationist worship and activism. Shaped by hush harbors, each contemplative activist group is laity-led, and sacred texts and artistic expression are engaged dialogically for personal and social transformation in local neighborhoods.

Conclusion

Black and Brown communities have often been in tension in the United States. In 1992, I (Alexia) was the pastor of a primarily African American church in East Oakland. It was a community in transition, with recent Central American arrivals joining Mexican residents to make Hispanics the most populous ethnic group in the area, displacing the previously dominant Black population. When the Los Angeles riots/uprising started in 1992, our church (St. John's Lutheran in East Oakland, CA) called the neighborhood together to try to unite around a more constructive response to racial injustice. At one point during the meeting, African American and Hispanic residents began to exchange barbed comments; we thought that violence might kick off right there in our church hall. Then Moses Walker, council president of our church, said in his deep bass voice, "The Man has us fighting over crumbs." Everything changed. We laughed. We breathed. We realized that we were called together to do a great work that neither group could do alone.

In the midst of the COVID-19 pandemic, police violence captivated the attention of the US and communities across the globe like never before. A video went viral of a Black man, George Floyd, being choked to death by a Minneapolis police officer. Black Lives Matter uprisings sparked across the US and around the globe. Young leaders of color protesting in the streets were asking, "Where is the church?" With sanctuaries closed due to the pandemic, most churches were limited to pastoral leadership. The needs of local uprisings required more than what most pastors could offer on their own. The distributed network of small contemplative activist groups that I (Brandon) co-lead with a multiracial laity team in Greensboro, North Carolina, was poised for this moment. I remember looking at them and saying, "We are essential workers for this movement." We deployed our leaders and their groups to meet multiple needs of local uprisings, from canvassing and logistics to leading rituals and music. Many of us organized healing stations at demonstrations to accompany people experiencing racialized trauma, grief, and conflict. In response to the vital presence of our faith community, local secular activists asked us to help organize thousands of people who were new to activism into long-term commitment beyond the moment. Our faith community organized four learning groups that studied liberation theology and abolitionist politics to welcome nearly one hundred people from diverse backgrounds to deepen the soul of their action for Black lives.

These glimpses of creative unity often fade when tensions rise, resources feel scarce, or justice is no longer a popular headline. Our hope for you as you read this book is that it offers you a solid framework on which you can build BIPOC-led,[4] vibrant, resilient, integral Christian communities that will fulfill the dream of our ancestors and slake the longing of our young people.

> In the last days, God says, I will pour out my Spirit on all people. Your sons and daughters will prophesy, your young men will see visions, your old men will dream dreams. (Acts 2:17)

---

4. BIPOC stands for Black, Indigenous, and People of Color.

1

Base Ecclesial Communities

The Lord Hears the Cry of the Poor

We learned that we have been called to serve and live collectively, searching for the common good. We learned to be "us." The participants were
all very poor but we saw that God was calling the people. (Ana Ortiz [a
longtime leader of a base ecclesial community in El Salvador], October 8,
2020)

Small Christian communities have existed since the church began. One
could say that Jesus's initial band of apostles and friends had all the
characteristic features of a small Christian community. Small communities allow for intimacy and mutual responsibility, core components of
authentic and profound relationships. Vital churches provide their members
the option of belonging to a small Christian community and encourage their
participation.

This book is not about small Christian communities in general. Between
the 1960s and the 1990s, certain Latin American countries and the Philippines experienced the emergence and dramatic growth of a movement called
base ecclesial communities (BECs). This movement's core achievement was
the organization of widespread networks of small groups of poor and marginalized people whose spiritual, personal, and communal transformation

resulted in remarkable advances in peace and justice in their communities and societies. The objective impact of BECs ranged from immediate changes in poor communities—government provision of electricity and water, recovery of land rights, collective enterprises that raised families out of economic misery, protection from predators—to the support of broader social movements that threw off the yoke of dictators. At their best, BECs also lifted individuals and families out of despair and self-destruction through mutual care and radical power-sharing that was rooted in Scripture and prayer. This seamless integration of the spiritual, therapeutic, communal, economic, and political arenas by and for the benefit of a poor community has fascinated observers and provoked critics. In the foreword to Pablo Galdámez's book *Faith of a People*—a detailed account of ten years in the life of a BEC in El Salvador—well-known Salvadoran theologian Jon Sobrino describes the book as revealing a profound truth about the potential of oppressed communities:

> The truth about the poor appears in this book with their names, their lives, their problems, and yes, their shortcomings, their "booze" and their male chauvinism, their lottery and their moneylenders—all the demons that have to be expelled. But this is why the "other truth" about the poor is so resplendent in these pages—their creativity and solidarity, their dedication and heroism, their faith and hope, their commitment and charity. The most profound truth that this book has to communicate is that the poor have given of their best, and have embarked on an incredible adventure—the adventure of their own liberation and that of a whole people. (Galdámez 1986, xii)

While BECs established a legacy and a foundation that continue to impact the Catholic Church around the world, there is no question that the movement's size and power have diminished, in spite of recent efforts to revive it.[1] Yet the powerful insights and practices forged by the movement in the cauldron of the struggles of the time have enduring value for those who seek, in any time and place, to create a church that liberation theologian Leonardo Boff describes as "a Church of and with the poor" (Boff 2011, 9), a church that incarnates and achieves holistic justice.

BECs "erupted messily and painfully into the world at a precise moment in time, as a result of a particular combination of historical circumstances" (Hebblethwaite 1994, 3). To understand the universal significance of BECs, we must first understand them in their historical context.

---

1. As recently as 2016, the Bishops' Committee for the Accompaniment of the BECs at the Catholic Bishops Conference of Latin America and the Caribbean called for the strengthening and renewal of the movement. The Catholic Bishops Conference of the Philippines issued a similar call in 2007.

Los Principios[2]

In her comprehensive overview of the BEC movement, Margaret Hebblethwaite states that "they [BECs] are the church context from which liberation theology has sprung, and to which liberation theology in turn leads" (Hebblethwaite 1994, 2). While there are many interconnections between liberation theology and BECs, the roots of the BEC movement predate liberation theology by a decade. The stirring in the Catholic Church that troubled the waters of tradition and led to the Second Vatican Council (1962–65) was evident in Latin America in the 1950s. The lack of priests in rural Brazil (Barra do Piraí) in 1956 led to the formation of a network of lay catechists. Two years later, the Basic Education Program (MEB) in Brazil built on Paulo Freire's work by using radio programs and directing popular education to raise social issues and encourage engagement in addressing poverty and injustice. BECs in Brazil were first reported in 1960 (in the Rio Grande del Norte and Rio de Janeiro states). Simultaneously, pastoral experiments began in Central America. San Miguelito Church in Panama started its first base community with the support of three priests from Chicago who had been utilizing the methods of Brazilian educator Freire with urban, poor residents of informal barrios.[3] San Pablo Apóstol in Nicaragua sought advice from San Miguelito when it began in 1966.

The document on the role of the Catholic Church in the modern world (*Gaudium et spes*), which emerged from the Second Vatican Council in 1965, called for the Catholic Church to act as the soul and leaven of the society. This document articulated a profound shift in the formal doctrine of the Catholic Church toward a holistic, missional orientation and commitment, which fueled the growth of the BEC movement. Father Niall O'Brien, who accompanied and observed the birth of the BEC movement in the Philippines, describes his eagerness as a young missionary from the Irish Columban Fathers to put into practice in his ministry the changes of Vatican II: "In 1964, the Second Vatican Council was in full swing. Pope John had issued two startling encyclicals. Both had taken the side of the poor and were hopeful about doing something about poverty. I was excited about the changes and frustrated that I could not get any information on what was now happening at the Council" (O'Brien 1987, 5). While it took him several years to become a key leader in initiating and supporting BECs, the seeds sown by Vatican II were already beginning to bloom.

---

2. The word *principio* in Spanish means both "beginning" and "principle." Therefore, it is a good word to use for a section that examines both the historical beginnings of a movement and the principles it embodied.

3. In the Philippines and Latin America, *barrio* refers to a small town or village.

The two subsequent conferences of Latin American Bishops, at Medellín in 1968 and at Puebla in 1979, both resulted in documents that affirmed and further encouraged the growth and vitality of BECs. The document "Pastoral de Conjunto," produced by the Medellín conference, states that "the Christian base community is the first and fundamental ecclesial nucleus, which on its own level must make itself responsible for the richness and expansion of the faith, as well as of the cult which is its expression. This community, then, is the initial cell of the ecclesial structure and the focus of evangelization, and at present it is a fundamental factor in human promotion and development" (Hebblethwaite 1994, 180). It also refers to BECs as "a sign of the presence of God in the world." Conservative forces in the Catholic Church sought to utilize the Puebla conference as a vehicle for backing away from these sanctions and commitments. While the Puebla documents do include the concerns of Catholic leaders about the loss of BEC leaders to "ideologically radical" political social movements, they also continued the official affirmation of BECs: "Small communities, especially the CEBs [BECs], create more personal interrelations, acceptance of God's word, reexamination of one's life, and reflection on reality in the light of the gospel. They accentuate committed involvement in the family, one's work, the neighborhood, and the local community. We are happy to single out the multiplication of small communities as an important ecclesial event that is peculiarly ours, and as the 'hope of the church.'"

The Latin American Bishops Conferences (CELAM) did not lay out a specific program or a curriculum for BECs. While BECs exchanged tactics and instruments (e.g., certain popular education strategies and exercises—dinámicas, such as the Seven Steps Bible Study and leadership development modules created by the Lumko Institute of South Africa), they were rooted in the common commitment to creatively live out a set of core concepts and visions. BECs were committed to the preferential option for the poor, building the family of God, and becoming the soul and leaven of the society.

These principles led to a set of practices. To make the preferential option for the poor real, it was necessary to build the capacity of the poor to become subjects instead of objects, to become creative agents in their lives and world. The two practices that shaped the leadership of the poor were concientización and el mensaje de liberación. While the word concientización can be translated as "awareness" or "consciousness," in the BEC movement, it referred to the practice of fearless social, economic, and political analysis of the structures and systems that impacted the lives of BEC members and their neighbors. This practice drew on the liberating pedagogy of Paulo Freire as well as on the insights of the social sciences. The insights arising from the process of concientización were then analyzed using the Scriptures read from a liberation perspective. In this book, we refer to this practice as el mensaje de liberación (the message of liberation).[4]

The BEC movement was not a movement of individuals; each BEC had to become a microcosm of the family of God. This required two distinct practices. First, all the members of the community had to participate democratically in the life and work of the community, bringing all their gifts and wisdom and sharing responsibility for the tasks required to build their community and carry out their mission. In this book, we refer to this practice as *participación* (participation). Second, they had to take responsibility for caring for each other's needs, sharing their resources generously, and living in empathy with each other's hopes, joys, and sorrows. We call this practice *familia en comunión* (family in communion).

The mission of BECs always included going beyond merely caring for each other to working for the transformation of their communities. The founding documents of Medellín called for BECs to become the soul and leaven of their communities—organizing, advocating for justice and peace, and working for economic and social changes that increased the opportunity for all to flourish and experience abundant life. They used a reflection-action model that continually strengthened their capacity and commitment. We refer to this set of practices as *alma y fermenta de la sociedad* (soul and leaven of the society).

To carry out this mission, BECs needed spiritual fuel, the full integration of the spiritual and the material. The practice of el mensaje de liberación gave hope, comfort, and guidance as well as insight and empowerment. At their best, BECs were also vehicles for the movement of the Holy Spirit, conduits for personal and relational healing, places where members shared mystical joy in prayer, song, and ritual. They also re-formed rituals to highlight the essential sanctity of daily life activities of poor and marginalized people, including their cultural roots. We call the set of spiritual practices that sustained the movement *sanidad* (healing), and we call the integration of culture *la teología de las abuelas* (the theology of the grandmothers).

All these principles and practices were rooted, in the contemporary language of the BEC movement, in the foundational concept of the preferential option for the poor, a concept that was explicitly stated at both CELAM conferences.

The First Foundational Concept: The Preferential Option for the Poor

The preferential option for the poor was essentially the choice to prioritize the perspective and leadership of the marginalized in the name and Spirit of

---

4. The term *concientización* in the BEC movement incorporated the component/process of el mensaje de liberación. We are separating the two steps for greater clarity, as secular groups have used the first term without including the scriptural reflection.

Jesus for the ultimate benefit of the whole. Liberation theologian Gustavo Gutiérrez explains the concept:

> The gospel read from the viewpoint of the poor,[5] the exploited classes and their militant struggles for liberation, convokes a church of the people (iglesia popular). It calls for a church to be gathered from among the poor, the marginalized. It calls for the kind of church that is indicated in Jesus's predilection for those whom the great ones of this world despise and humiliate (see Matt. 22:1–10; Luke 4:16–24). In a word, it calls together a church that will be marked by the faithful response of the poor to the call of Jesus Christ. It will spring from the people, this church. And the people will snatch the gospel out of the hands of their dominators, never more to permit it to be utilized for the justification of a situation contrary to the will of the God who liberates. (Gutiérrez 1981, 111)

In this church of the poor, members were encouraged to see the world and the Word through their own eyes and to honor the full participation and gifts of all those whose contributions were not historically recognized (supported through the practices of el mensaje de liberación, concientización, and participación). Formal education or position was no longer the only standard for respect and authority; the historic wisdom of the grandmothers in the context of the culture of the community was also received and integrated.

The preferential option for the poor can be understood only in the context of the nature and impact of poverty in Latin America and other areas of the world affected by the legacy of colonialism. This includes the impact of the historical domination of the church by the wealthy and the relative objective and internalized powerlessness of the poor and marginalized in these contexts. "The Social Panorama of Latin America 2019" is a report by the United Nations Economic Commission for Latin America and the Caribbean (UNECLAC); it estimates that in 2018 almost 60 percent of Latin America still qualified as poor and another 21 percent met the standard for lower-middle income (at risk of falling back into poverty) (UNECLAC 2019). Of the 185 million poor Latin Americans in 2018, 66 million suffered extreme poverty. These figures were projected to rise to 191 million and 72 million in 2019. Statistics are insufficient to communicate the level of human misery that they represent. A common saying among liberation theologians is that poverty means an early and unjust death. The following is a vivid account from O'Brien, early in his time in the Philippines:

5. Gutiérrez clarifies on various occasions that poverty is not simply economic in Latin America. "The poor" is a category that includes different forms of oppression and marginalization, including race- and gender-based inequities.

I had taken shelter from a passing tropical shower in a shack several hours into my journey. In the hut were some adults and some children. The children were bloated from what I now know was lack of food and probably infestation with intestinal worms. The children had no clothes except for T-shirts.

I took out my food and thoughtlessly began to eat it when I noticed all eyes upon me. It dawned on me that they were all hungry and there was no food. I shared what I had, regretting that I had not brought more. The adults refused, allowing the children to take it, and the children wolfed down the little I had to offer, making me ashamed that I had begun to eat without thinking of them in the first place. When we finished I was still hungry. (O'Brien 1987, 17)

When I (Alexia) was a missionary in the Philippines from 1984 to 1987, I served as a chaplain in the National Children's Hospital, a job that included visiting the "Mal Ward," the room where they kept the malnourished children on intravenous feeding until they were ready to go back to their barrios— where they would then fall back into malnutrition.

The situation these children were in would have been painful enough if it had been due to natural causes. In Latin America and the Philippines, typically historic land inequities and modern illegal land grabs force the poor off their subsistence farms either onto plantations (including plantations operated by Dole and other multinational businesses), where they are paid "malnutrition wages," or into informal settlements in the city, which are regularly destroyed so the land can be used for commercial purposes. Court cases trying to recover land can last for many years, and the verdicts are not enforced because of public corruption and/or the private armies of the wealthy. At the National Children's Hospital, children who were allergic to penicillin died because it was the only antibiotic on hand, even though one mile away at a middle-class Christian hospital, over twenty antibiotics were available. (The discrepancy did not apparently provoke the Christian hospital or its denominational over-seers to explore a partnership in which their resources could be shared with the poorer medical providers.)

O'Brien tells many stories about rural areas with little to no access to health care where people died in transit to the nearest hospital. When I was in the Philippines, the structures of feudalism and plantation capitalism were reinforced by Ferdinand Marcos's regime, which also terrorized and assas-sinated those who tried to protest or seek justice. Marcos was able to stay in power for over twenty years largely because of the blind support of the US (see Bonner 1987).

While various armed revolutions have simmered in the Philippines since it was first conquered by the Spaniards in the sixteenth century, the average poor Filipino before Vatican II was consoled by a Christianity steeped in magic ritual and the mystical transcendence of suffering. Theologian Nancy

Bedford calls this phenomenon in the Latin American context "dolorismo"—the understanding that suffering is good and earns spiritual merit if borne patiently (Bedford 1998, 321). During the same period, the hierarchy of the Roman Catholic Church acted as chaplains to the elite classes of society, being supported by them and ignoring the suffering caused by systems that privileged them. Before the 1950s, the idea that God could see through the eyes of the poor or call the poor to become agents of change in the name and Spirit of Jesus would have been completely alien. This spiritual and social reality was characteristic of Latin America as well. How did such a deeply ingrained system open up for a new movement by and with the poor?

Samuel Escobar, in his book *In Search of Christ in Latin America*, points to two central provocations (Escobar 2019). First, the successful revolution in Cuba, which began in 1953 and attained victory in 1959, echoed throughout Latin America. The apparently invincible and ordained structures of feudalism and economic imperialism had been upended. "Armed guerrilla forces, representing the possibility of gaining power and transforming the world, suddenly became a highly attractive idea and practice. . . . As the theme of revolution came to dominate the cultural life of the continent, significant sectors of youth in various Latin American societies abandoned their normal life and embraced various revolutionary causes" (119). Second, at the same time, "the presence and growth of Protestantism were and continue to be an incentive and undoubtable stimulus that forced Catholics to seek self-critique and renewal" (147). Certainly, the break in support networks created by the move from rural areas to the informal settlements of the urban poor may also have made intentional community more attractive and thus an effective strategy for evangelization (although BECs were rural as well as urban). Yet there is still an element of the miraculous movement and power of the Holy Spirit in the transition. Powerful and well-established institutions do not typically transform under pressure; rather, they tend to rigidify and defend themselves. While sectors of the Roman Catholic Church certainly acted this way, from the pope to the poor, the church changed. Priests, nuns, and lay catechists refocused their energy from maintaining and indoctrinating traditional ritual to the spiritual and social empowerment of the most marginalized communities.

To understand how the preferential option for the poor operated on the ground, it is important to first face the common critique that BECs were a political movement in the guise of a spiritual movement. It is true that BECs in Chile grew rapidly when the coup closed political spaces for discussion and the only spaces available for working for justice were religious. However, this does not in itself negate the spiritual dimension of BECs. It is also true that when the Catholic hierarchy shifted to a position less affirming of the political dimension of the BECs' work, members left for the secular revolutionary social movements. However, the case can be made that BECs offered much more to their members than a secular social or political movement. It is important to examine the integration of the spiritual and the political in BECs, particularly for the sake of twenty-first-century church plants or renewal efforts that seek a similar integration.

Cecília Loreto Mariz carried out a comparative study of BECs, Pentecostal churches, and Afro-Brazilian spiritual communities in Brazil, published as *Coping with Poverty* (1994). She concluded that the BECs were losing in the competition with Pentecostals for the participation of the poor because (1) they were initiated by pastoral agents who were not poor, and their leadership was less poor than the bulk of the community, (2) their focus was on communal and societal change instead of on helping individuals in the group with their personal needs and lives, and (3) they were rational and secular in their approach, beliefs, and concerns rather than spiritual or mystical. By this last critique, Mariz does not mean that BECs were not spiritual communities. She notes that they were centered on Scripture study, prayer, and worship. However, she questions whether these activities were goals in themselves or instruments for social change. She also claims that other studies of BECs and literature about BECs were written either by "theologians and religiously committed people who tended to emphasize descriptions of CEB [BEC] projects, rather than the everyday reality of the CEBs," or by people who "had no practical experience in CEBs" (Mariz 1994, 16–17).

Mariz's description of the authors and content of BEC materials is not true of the two primary accounts of life in BECs: O'Brien's *Revolution from the Heart* and Galdámez's *Faith of a People*. Both of these texts give the intimate details of the twists and turns, successes and failures, struggles and accomplishments of BECs. O'Brien focuses on his deep and extended experience of BECs on the island of Negros in the Philippines over a twenty-year period (1964–84). Galdámez details the life of a BEC community in El Salvador over a decade (1970–80). Interviews of Salvadoran BEC leaders and my (Alexia's) personal experiences in the Philippines match the stories told by O'Brien and Galdámez. These accounts do not support the findings or conclusions of Mariz. It is possible that the movement in South America had significantly different characteristics than the movement in Central America or in the Philippines. A more recent account from a BEC leader in Bolivia, while including stories about personal and social transformation, reflects that BEC leaders "have not evaluated how the persistence of the community aspect might affect the personal aspects or how the social aspects can function to the detriment of ecclesial and the immediate loss of the eschatological" (quoted in Healey and Hinton 2005, 11). At the same time, although arriving at an accurate assessment of the number of BEC communities is difficult to impossible, the general understanding of researchers is that roughly half of BECs were in Brazil. As a result, we need to take seriously the variations between South and Central American experiences as we analyze the potential insights of the BEC movement for the future.

By examining Mariz's three conclusions in light of the detailed, long-term accounts of daily life in BECs, we can seek to determine whether her conclusions are correct. First, were BECs initiated by pastoral agents who were not poor and led by leaders who were less poor (Mariz 1994, 45, 50)? The pastoral agents who started the first BECs in both accounts (O'Brien's and Galdámez's) were religious professionals, primarily priests and nuns. However, both long-term accounts describe in detail the process through which the people took charge of their own communities and then went on to start new communities without any support from the original missionaries. O'Brien talks about going on furlough to Ireland for a year and leaving BECs to run the parish. He also relates a funny story about going to the home of a friend in the evening and completely forgetting that he was supposed to be leading an urgent and delicate all-night vigil focused on a critical community problem. When he remembered in the morning and ran to the church, he discovered that they had not missed him at all. BEC leaders had taken over. Galdámez shares about the multiplication of the communities: "A friend of Father Chepe's, a person who worked in a co-op, started meeting with some fellow workers of his. A new married couple found out about our groups and offered their home as the 'synagogue.' . . . On the south side was a slum we hardly knew about. A member of our community who worked in a clinic discovered it and started a little group there. . . . Another group started working twenty kilometers from the parish, directed by a member of our own community" (Galdámez 1983, 7).

Mariz paints the typical BEC member as someone who achieved significant gains in income on their own and then hit a ceiling based on societal structures. In comparison, a significant percentage of BEC leaders in El Salvador and the Philippines were living in extreme poverty when they joined. Galdámez and O'Brien tell stories about individual leaders who entered the BEC from a background of miserable poverty in which family members had died from malnutrition, illness, and lack of access to health care. Ana, a leader of a BEC in El Salvador for over twenty years, shares how they started in a *colonia* (a poor area on the outskirts of an urban area) of San Salvador and then worked with a group of urban, poor squatters to start a collective farming project. The BEC that ran the project was from the informal settlement. Reflecting on the different levels of poverty in her BEC, Ana says that they had to intentionally work on the self-esteem of those whose situation required constant assistance until it improved. She notes that while they lost some members because of their shame at their initial dependence in contrast with the relative economic status of other members, the majority of the poorest members stayed in the community and grew in their participation and leadership (Ortiz, October 8, 2020).

Second, did BECs focus on communal and societal change instead of on helping individuals in the group with their personal needs and lives? Mariz claims that while the Pentecostals saw their task as missionary work, BEC pastoral agents thought of their work as popular education. She says that "missionary work is basically religious. It emphasizes the transformation of values and moral assumptions. . . . Educational work, in contrast, places emphasis on the transformation of cognitive assumptions" (Mariz 1994, 63). She goes on to say that "the CEB view assumes the individual's dependence on his society or group and therefore does not emphasize personal morality or individual transformation in the process of working out God's plan in this world" (68). On the contrary, Galdámez describes the first phase of BEC work by likening it to an exorcism: "Hardened drunks were delivered from demon booze, men who had lost their feelings for their wives were freed from their machismo, women who had lost their dignity in prostitution were liberated from the misery that had driven them into the hands of this demon. The people, so many people, who had been under control of the demon of individualism, began to join hands with their neighbors. Their deliverance was at hand" (Galdámez 1983, 6). This new moral and spiritual power in their lives extended to their marriages and families: "Couples were finding that for their work to be credible they had to declare their fidelity before the community. They were discovering that not only were they wife and husband, but they were support for one another in the Christian task. And they wanted to be happy. What was soon to be loyalty to the people to the death, began by loyalty and fidelity in married life" (17).

Both O'Brien and Galdámez tell remarkable stories of violent criminals who were preying on the villages whose characters and lifestyles were transformed by conversions brought on by acts of nonviolent confrontation by their victims seeking reconciliation. The process of evangelism and discipleship in BECs (at least in certain contexts) integrated missionary work and popular education for personal and social transformation.

Mariz accurately writes that the improvements in the economic well-being of BEC members were not the result of individual achievement alone but rather of changes in the services and opportunities available to the community as a result of the activities of the BEC. However, as she notes in one case, many BEC members obtained new positions and/or paid employment as a result of these new opportunities. Here are a few examples from a BEC in Bolivia:

Abdias, an Ayamara farmer, 42 years old, married with three children, had to migrate from a rural area to the city. For many years, he lived as a small vendor. Later, as a result of his experience in the Community of Villa Pagador, he became a leader of the BCC as well as of the town. Today, he coordinates a trash collection and recycling enterprise. Amalia, fifty-four years old, married with seven children, wife of a construction worker. She says that her experience and formation within the BCC has opened her eyes and given her an opportunity to serve people like herself. Today, she is the coordinator of "Habitad" in Cochabamba. She coordinates, along with others, home construction projects for poor families. Ambrosio, nineteen years old, an orphan responsible for two younger brothers. The invitation he received to participate in the Community of Our Lady of Guadalupe was the beginning of a new life. Now he animates and accompanies youth who are struggling with alcoholism. (Healey and Hinton 2005, 14)

Third, were BECs rational and secular in their approach, beliefs, and concerns rather than spiritual or mystical? Mariz states that "the CEB view does not recognize miracles or supernatural occurrences in everyday lives, nor does it assume any relationship between miracles and God's plan. God does not use miracles to help human beings carry out his plan; instead he uses human beings and relies on their abilities" (Mariz 1994, 67). BECs in Central America and the Philippines clearly believed that God works through human beings. However, that does not mean that their faith lacked a mystical dimension. *The Gospel in Solentiname* is a collection of transcripts of BEC Bible studies facilitated by liberation theologian Ernesto Cardenal in Nicaragua before the fall of the dictator Somoza. These transcripts allow a glimpse into the inner spiritual life and practices of a BEC. Here is a comment from a member of a BEC in a Bible study on an apocalyptic passage in Luke:

MARCELINO: A lot of us folks would like to see those days, to see something at least close to those days. But now, it is a little different. We can see by means of the spirit, when the spirit of God enters us, we can see the days that Jesus walked, and we can see the miracles. Other than that, we can't see anything, we're blind. But someday, says Jesus, it's going to be like we see a lightning bolt, it's going to be bright and clear, it's not going to be seeing just with the spirit, as I was saying. Not then, we're going to see, with our own eyes, the things that are happening. Anybody that looks and sees things is going to say: it's clear. (Cardenal 1976, 456)

Ana, from a BEC in El Salvador, says that a key element that drew her to participate in the BEC was the experience of the Holy Spirit in the gatherings. She says that there was an atmosphere she had never experienced in more traditional religious settings, a spirit of happiness, celebration, and brotherhood/sisterhood. Both Moises (a Salvadoran immigrant to the US who visited El Salvador at several intervals during the war and participated actively in the BEC movement) and Ana talk about the inspiring music (Moises Escalante, October 10, 2020). Moises adds that he was impressed by the peace that leaders exuded in the midst of risk and danger, which he attributes to their living faith. Gutiérrez describes the integration of faith and action for justice as follows:

> We remain convinced—and the practice of the poor confirms this—that the truly fruitful and imaginative challenge lies in a "contemplation in action" that will transform history. It has to do with encountering God in the poor, in solidarity with the struggle of the oppressed, in a faith filled with hope and joy that is lived within a liberation process whose agent is the poor people. Proclamation of the Father's love is something to be done at every moment "in season and out of season" as St. Paul put it. And evangelizing means proclaiming the Lord with words of life and acts of solidarity from the world of the poor and their struggles. (Gutiérrez 1981, 115)

A core rationale that Mariz uses for describing BECs as rational in opposition to mystical is their alteration of traditional symbols in rituals. Mariz claims that this assumes that the ritual or symbol itself had no intrinsic power. O'Brien describes the process and meaning of changing rituals and symbols differently. He talks about aligning the rituals and symbols with their intrinsic meaning, cleansing them from insertions made by those who would maintain unjust systems. For example, he describes the expansion of the promises made at baptism or confirmation into holistic pledges with a social dimension (O'Brien 1987, 167). He notes the added inspiration experienced by the hearers when it became clear, as in the early church, that the promise implied a risk that required a living faith. The placing of farm implements and other work tools on the altar and the use of tortillas for the communion bread were common symbolic statements. The use of everyday items and cultural symbols in sacramental contexts did not represent secularization but rather a recognition of the sacramental quality of people's daily lives, which made sense in the broader context of their recognition of God's presence with the poor.

In these stories of BEC members and leaders, we can see that the practice of sanidad (healing)—personal and relational healing and joy in the Holy Spirit—was a core component of their BEC experience. While the integration of traditional cultural practices was a typical aspect of the evangelical strategy of the Catholic Church in Latin America and the Philippines, BECs shifted the focus to the aspects of culture that reflected the daily lives of marginalized people, symbolically lifting up their value in the process. As mentioned earlier, we call this practice la teología de las abuelas (the theology of the grandmothers).

The Second Foundational Concept: Building the Family of God

The preferential option for the poor was not merely a push for the prioritization of the perspective of the poor in general society. A central mission of BECs was to build a community in which the poor were valued in every way, as givers and as receivers in relationships of mutual care and as team members for mutual ministry.

> The man who cut the grass for this thatch—pointing to the roof of the convent—lives out in Na-Salayan. A few weeks ago, he walked in all the way from that place, which is about ten kilometers away, carrying his wife on his back. As he walked, his little child of three ran along beside him clinging to his trouser leg. And another child of eight carried the baby. His wife was so far gone with T.B. that she was only bones. He told me that for a year she has not been able to sleep well. They have no pillow, so at night when they lay down, he would stretch out his arm so that she would lie on it the whole night. If Na-Salayan had had a Christian community, that man would not have walked in alone. The men of the hamlet would have carried his wife in a baby's hammock, the women would have looked after the children and the community health committee would have looked for medicines for the sick woman and told us about her condition months ago. Now it is certainly too late. You have a Christian community when you can lie down at night knowing that in your village no one is sick who is not being attended to, no one is persecuted who is not being helped, no one is lonely who is not being visited. (O'Brien 1987, 128–29)

Mariz notes that mutual help among poor people is not unique to BECs, particularly in collective cultures: "The existence and esteem of mutual help among kin and neighbors, however, does not necessarily indicate the existence of a community of the poor, such as CEBs attempt to create. Poor people help one another because they have needs, not because they identify with one another. What CEBs do is reinforce this value and attribute religious meaning to it" (Mariz 1994, 71). While poor people's mutual insurance is a fact of life in low-income communities (I help you today, you help me tomorrow), desperation often also leads to stealing, abuse, sabotage, and betrayal. Commitments to mutual aid can also drain the resources that could provide capital for economic development. In BECs, in contrast, the mutual pledge of assistance became a holy pledge that built momentum over time. BECs incarnated the practice of familia en comunión; they became a family in communion with one another and God. Because mutual aid was an ongoing commitment, members of BECs also learned to work together to plan and implement broader and more effective solutions to common needs.

A related aspect of BECs was the fluid division of labor among the members of the community. Instead of allowing a few, better educated lay leaders to carry out a limited number of sacramental tasks, BECs distributed all the tasks necessary for the mission among members of the community. Any task that supported the well-being of the community was viewed as a holy task. Galdámez calls the community members who took on a variety of tasks an "order of acolytes" because they made the mission possible just as an acolyte makes the celebration of a Mass possible by babysitting or taking chairs where they are needed (Galdámez 1983, 9). Religious tasks, such as leading a Bible study, were interchangeably assigned with secular tasks depending on members' gifts and interests. The principle of participación describes this living out of shared responsibility in which definitions of leadership were broadened to include most of the members.

In congruence with the core beliefs and values of the movement, women were lifted up and given greater roles than in the broader society or other expressions of the church. This sometimes had the negative side effect of men withdrawing from the communities. Ana says that some men chose not to participate after a critical mass of women took positions of leadership. She tells one story of a man who was initially a leader and then pulled back after his wife became involved. While he left permanently, other men were able, over time and through intentional conversation, to come back. This principle of lifting up women, including the traditional wisdom of women, was part of the practice of la teología de las abuelas (Ortiz, October 10, 2020).

The Third Foundational Concept: Becoming the Soul and Leaven of the Society

BECs sought to embody *Gaudium et spes*'s call to the church to become the soul and leaven of the society. In addition to demonstrating an alternative community of radical democratization with accountable and principled leadership, this included two core tasks: analyzing the reality of the poor to learn the reasons for their suffering (the practice of concientización) and creating communal and systemic solutions to the problems of the poor (the practice of alma y fermenta de la sociedad). The analysis of the reality experienced by the poor involved intentional integration of Scripture, popular education methodologies, and the social sciences. The activities of BECs to address poverty included the following:

- community development strategies such as cooperative businesses, credit unions, or collective farms and land trusts as well as public health initiatives led by the people themselves
- collective struggles with local authorities for basic rights such as electricity and potable water, available and affordable health care, respect of land rights, timely and fair legal processes, and security from violence

- participation in broader national social movements seeking to create more just structures

Mariz states that BECs consistently demonstrated their capacity to mobilize and motivate the poor to organize themselves and to participate in social movements. The accounts of BECs, both during their heyday and more recently, are full of anecdotes about the concrete results of their organization. The following story from *Faith of a People* of "the miracle of the marketplace women" is a snapshot.

In early June, the "marketplace women" came to see me. They wanted me to celebrate a Mass in honor of the Sacred Heart of Jesus in the marketplace. These women are an institution in El Salvador. They are very poor, but their courage in the face of difficulties is proverbial. Often, they get involved with the usury mechanism, the loan sharks. The situation is extremely rough, and there seems to be no way out of it. I told the community about the case, and we all thought it would be very hard to do anything about the situation of injustice these persons were living in. But these were persons of faith. I came for Mass on the appointed day. A number of the members of the communities and I went to the little square in the middle of the market. A life-sized statue of the Sacred Heart stood there. In the homily I opened a dialogue with them—on their love for one another, on the big problems they had—and soon we were talking about the biggest things that bound them together: no money to send the kids to school, to take them to the hospital or even to feed them three meals a day. And up came the subject of the moneylenders. Some of the women expressed gratitude for their services, saying it made it possible for them to survive. Then timidly, somebody said "they only make things worse." Majestic on his makeshift pedestal, the Sacred Heart of Jesus presided over this decisive moment of conscientizacion when the poor had the floor, when the poor could speak out. Then one of the women shouted out "the interest sure is high!" Others seconded her, then quickly covered their faces with their shawls, reciting prayers, as if asking forgiveness for their rebelliousness. That was when the moneylender left in a huff. Then there was fear. Some of the women realized that they'd put their foot in it, that their business was done for if they didn't have the loan sharks help. And in the midst of the anguish, God's light shone. Couldn't they get together and form a co-op? The next day the women met with our community to start a new co-op. We were sure the moneylender would pressure the women now. We had to make sure we had enough in our emergency fund, we had to get in contact with people who knew more about co-ops then we did. But the next day, the co-op was on its feet, thanks to money collected from the community. (Galdámez 1983, 27–29, abbreviated)

Mariz also notes the positive psychological consequences to participating in these struggles: poor people experienced hope and power as they jointly improved their lives even when they did not attain their broader goals (Mariz 1994, 115–16). While it is clear that BECs were intimately intertwined with broader social movements for justice, it is not easy to analyze the impact of the BEC movement on broader social and economic structures. However, the famous nonviolent deposal of the Philippine dictator Ferdinand Marcos in February 1986 was arguably fueled by the nonviolent commitment and action of BECs.

What Happened to the BECs?

Both Galdámez and O'Brien emphasize that BECs require many years to reach maturity. The process of creating healing and liberating communities among marginalized people is neither fast nor easy. They also underscore that the process cannot be manipulated or forced; people have to grow out of internalized oppression and grow into their full capacity for positive change. In both the Philippines and El Salvador, BECs grew up in the context of civil wars[6] in which the people experienced intensifying repression and violent martyrdom. The sacred ground that BECs had carved out for nonviolent action for justice was gradually eaten up by the daily reality of war. This threatened the stability of BECs. Ana, from a BEC in El Salvador, stayed through the war and describes how the members who fled the country and those who were martyred affected the functioning of the community. However, the communities continued throughout these attacks and losses (Ortiz, October 12, 2020).

In truth, BECs continue today. While BECs experienced a time when the hierarchy treated them with suspicion, both Pope Francis and the Bishops' Councils in Latin America and the Philippines have verbally supported BECs over the past fifteen years. There are BECs throughout the Global South that are linked to Catholic small-group networks around the world. However, the movement is significantly smaller and weaker than it was in the 1970s and 1980s. The BEC movement has come into competition with increasingly popular and powerful Pentecostal movements, which have offered experiences of community and spiritual power with less risk and sacrifice. Secular

6. The profound economic inequities in both the Philippines and El Salvador resulting from the Spanish land grants and the economic exploitation or expulsion of tenant farmers gave rise in the twentieth century to wide social unrest. The lack of adequate government response to these concerns spawned both nonviolent protest and revolutionary movements. The cycle of repression and reaction led to ongoing struggles that erupted finally into full-blown civil wars. The war in El Salvador began in 1979 and ended with the peace agreements in 1992. The civil conflict in the Philippines began in 1969 and ended in the country as a whole with the ouster of dictator Ferdinand Marcos in 1986. (Islamic rebel forces have continued sporadic conflict with government forces on the island of Mindanao.)

social movements and left-leaning governments have proven unable to change profound structural realities while also guaranteeing human rights. Other Protestant and evangelical movements, such as the Misión Integral movement, pioneered by René Padilla and Samuel Escobar, and the Lutheran Church of El Salvador under Bishop Medardo Gomez,[7] have learned from the example of BECs and attempted to incorporate similar practices in their small-group and congregational contexts. They have added theological and spiritual perspectives from their faith traditions and adapted their strategies correspondingly. Guillermo Cook, a Protestant Latin American missiologist, has researched BECs from a Protestant perspective, identifying their similarities with and differences from Protestant movements. While these initiatives have not engaged most Latin American churches, in our analysis of BECs, we will include information about these parallel movements.

The heritage and legacy of the BEC movement and its parallel adaptations are full of indigenous strategies for transformation waiting to be translated and modified for young Christian leaders of color around the world.

Conclusion

The BEC movement arose at a particular point in time in the history of the Catholic Church and in the broader society in Latin America and the Philippines. BECs represented an unprecedented level of engagement by poor and marginalized people as protagonists in their common spiritual and social lives. While scholars have questioned whether BECs were fully representative of the poor and truly integrated spiritual and social dimensions, powerful evidence suggests they did create a new model of being church that has potential relevance for anyone seeking to integrate personal spiritual formation, communal care, power-sharing, and social transformation under the leadership of marginalized and oppressed people. As we seek to draw inspiration and guidance from this movement for Christian community today, we will build on the core BEC principles of the preferential option for the poor, the building of the family of God, and the mission of becoming the soul and leaven of the society.

7. Bishop Medardo Gomez was the only high-level Protestant leader directly targeted for government oppression. When the four Jesuits at the Central American University were murdered by members of a military battalion in 1989, the same soldiers proceeded to the Lutheran Cathedral to kill Bishop Gomez, who was fortunately in the US at the time (Gomez 2012). Lutheran churches in rural and urban areas often consisted of the poorest of the poor, many of whom were involved with popular movements.

2

Hush Harbors

The Invisible Black Prophetic Church

hristianity is not the white man's religion. A tradition of Christian faith and practice emerged from the underside of America, from enslaved Africans in the antebellum South. There were no steeples, stoles, or stained glass. This tradition had no such luxuries. The Christianity of enslaved Africans was not a religion of privilege and position. It was a religion of freedom and revolution. Deep in the wilderness of the plantation slavocracy, enslaved Africans would escape to practice a communal spirituality that challenged them to love their bodies and their heritage, and to refuse any conditions that said otherwise. Welcome to the hush harbors, the invisible gathering places where enslaved Africans met to praise the God of the oppressed, pay attention to one another's needs, and plot the abolition of slaveholding Christianity and the plantation economy. Hush harbors are a place to turn to refashion for our times a Christian community shaped by risky love.

The Terror of the Plantation Economy

The environment of chattel slavery was no walk in the park. Cultural artifacts like the film *Birth of a Nation* depict Africans as happy with being slaves. Such propaganda numbed and concealed what really took place in the plantation economy. Africans in America were legally and politically considered not fully human. They had no rights that white people were expected to respect and uphold. Any deference given to Black people was out of respect for them as the property of a white master. Black people were legally denied access to the kinds of privileges that uplifted and bettered white people, like government programs, economic self-determination, and voting. Without the honor of human dignity and any rights to ensure their well-being, as property of the plantation economy, enslaved Africans were treated for how they could meet white pleasures. Rape, forced "breeding," mutilation through beatings, and lynching were only some of the violent bodily tactics white people used to punish and control enslaved Africans. Even the mundane parts of enslaved Africans' lives were not respected. Enslaved Africans were forbidden to gather or assemble together except under the supervision of white folks. They had curfews to prevent their escape at night. Their leisure was policed to control as much of their time for work on the plantation and to ensure the leisure of the white master and his family. Even the term *plantation* does not do justice to the racialized economic exploitation Black people faced. Author Nikole Hannah-Jones in her book *1619* calls these Southern sites of oppression "labor camps" (Hannah-Jones et al. 2021). The terror of the plantation economy was a totalizing vision. Every part of the lives of enslaved Africans was expected to be under the gaze of white supremacist, patriarchal capitalism.

Theology and Worship on the Plantation

What enables a race of people to exploit the labor of another race? To see them as their property? To colonize the land of Natives and the consciousness of Africans? What must a people believe about themselves to enact terror on another people and on the planet? "Slaves, obey your earthly masters in everything . . . , with reverence for the Lord" (Col. 3:22). These words summarize the theology of slaveholding Christianity.[1] And from these few words emerged an entire culture and history of violent desecration of land and peoples. Enslaved Africans had regular opportunities to worship on the plantation in racially integrated churches led by white folks. These integrated plantation churches operated by a separate and unequal rule: Black people and white people sat in the same sanctuaries, but everything else about the worship experience was separated by race, from using dif-

---

1. Some key sources for learning more about the history and theology of Christianity on the plantation among white people and enslaved Africans are Boles 1988; Gates 2021; Harding 1981; Hopkins 2000; Jennings 2010; and Raboteau 2001.

ferent restrooms to separate seating, prayer and Communion rituals, and burial grounds and baptismal waters. Enslaved Africans could also attend segregated gatherings led by Black preachers under the supervision of a white minister and white religious customs (Harrison 2009, 134–35). Worship in both of these plantation churches accommodated the terror of the plantation economy and slaveholding Christianity.

The theology of the plantation said that God works through white men to bring the world into order and submission. Most white plantation owners used Christianity, especially the words of Paul, to make Africans docile and numb to their plight, to believe it was God's will for them to be slaves. Other white plantation owners forbade the enslaved to be taught Christianity because they were worried biblical themes would incite revolution. How can Christianity hold within it these two contradictory possibilities? Race was the theological myth used by wealthy, white, male plantation owners to uphold the chattel slavery economy with a whitewashed, domesticated, heretical Christianity. Only a small percentage of wealthy, white, male plantation owners were actually at the top of the caste. When the owner was not around to be in charge of the plantation economy, wealthy white women were in control. When the owner's wife was not there, either a poor white man or woman or an enslaved Black man was in charge. Black women and children were always at the bottom. All Black lives were disposable. Race is a powerful myth because the racial caste system has never been consistent. Myths are only as true as people give credence to them and as they function to maintain the status quo. From the beginning of the chattel experiment, poor and working-class white people have shared more in common with Black and Native people than with the white elite. The power of the slavocracy system was that it operated at the intersection of white supremacy, white patriarchy, racialized capitalism, and the theological heresy of slaveholding Christianity.

Hush Harbors and the Plantation

Even if only temporarily, enslaved Africans escaped the plantation economy and slaveholding Christianity by organizing hush harbors. Drawing especially from documented slave narratives, hush harbors have been a treasure trove of study for religion scholars and theologians. The literature on hush harbors has centered two rich debates. First, there is the debate of erasure versus retention of African cultures or Africanisms. Much of the early literature about the period of slavery in the US claimed that the psychic and bodily trauma of the Middle Passage—of Africans being violently forced from their homelands in Africa by European settler-terrorists on ships under the most inhumane of conditions—stripped the first generation of enslaved

Africans of much if not all of their memories of their African cultures and customs. Certainly, this cultural knowledge was not passed down to successive generations, the argument went. This psychological and cultural violence was strategic in making African peoples more susceptible to being chattel for white plantation owners. Other scholars contended that hush harbors provided evidence to oppose the erasure thesis. Hush harbors depicted a rich continuity of Africanisms—music, language, religion, stories, and more—that enslaved Africans disguised for their own safety when under white surveillance. Because of the need to disguise Africanisms, the unaware observer could not readily see how enslaved Africans did in fact retain a variety of African customs and practices.

The second debate is over the nature of the Christianity that enslaved Africans practiced. Did enslaved Africans practice the Christianity of the slaveholder, which accommodated their own oppression? Christianity was an empire religion that accommodated the status quo. For enslaved Africans, to accept Christianity was to accept their plight on earth as they awaited their true freedom in the afterlife. Again, by peering into hush harbors, this thesis has been contested. Through the testimonies of enslaved Africans themselves, scholars discovered that Africans in the Americas not only practiced an otherworldly Christian religion that accommodated their oppression; hush harbors that enslaved Africans organized were sites of protest against the dominant Christianity of the slaveholder. In hush harbors, enslaved Africans made plans for permanent escape to the northern parts of the US. Additionally, enslaved Africans carried a hush harbor mindset of freedom with them onto the plantation to both cope with daily terror and plot for abolition without being caught by white plantation owners. This mystical hush harbor was as much a site of interior protest as the material hush harbor was a site of physical protest. These protest actions and mindsets were rooted in particular Christian beliefs that enslaved Africans initially discovered from slaveholding Christianity and then reinterpreted toward revolutionary ends.[2]

These debates have unearthed a rich legacy of the genius of enslaved Africans' beliefs and practices. In recent times, however, Black prophetic leaders have grappled with the importance of hush harbors not only for their historical relevance but also as a site of contemporary reflection on a more radical model of church and activism. The eight marks of hush harbors from *Liberating Church* help to unveil even more of the distinctive characteristics of hush harbors.

---

2. For more on the history of hush harbors and the debates therein see Boles 1988; Erskine 2014; Gates 2021; Harding 1981; Hopkins 2000; Jennings 2010; Raboteau 2001; Raboteau 2004; and Wilmore 1998.

Eight Marks of Hush Harbors

Steal Away

Breaking the custom of permanent white supervision over Black bodies meant, at best, being whipped and, at worst, death. In the plantation fields, enslaved Africans sang Spirituals—like "Steal Away" ("Steal away, steal away to Jesus . . . I ain't got long to stay here")—as a code. An untrained hearer would think they were referring to the afterlife, but a trained hearer would know that they were talking about how they would have to take freedom, steal it away in the here and now, if they were ever to have it (Harrison 2009, 134–35). The metaphor of "stealing away" came to stand for a lifestyle of holy deception and fugitivity. Enslaved Africans bent and twisted lyrics and branches as clues leading down a path through the woods to hush harbors.

> From the abundant testimony of fugitive and freed slaves it is clear that the slave community had an extensive religious life of its own, hidden from the eyes of the master. In the . . . seclusion of the brush arbors ("hush harbors") the slaves made a Christianity truly their own. (Raboteau 2004, 212)

> Yes sir, there was no pretending in those [hush harbor] prayer meetings. There was a living faith in a just God who would one day answer the cries of His poor black children and deliver them from their enemies. But the slaves never said a word to their white folk about this kind of faith. (Faulkner 1993, 54)

Hush harbors were sites that liberated Christianity from the slaveholder religion so that it could serve enslaved Africans' well-being and dreams of freedom. Only enslaved Africans who were vetted and vouched for—who demonstrated commitment to the politics of abolition—entered hush harbors. Even children were tested for their allegiance. One formerly enslaved African comments, "My master used to ask us children, 'Do your folks pray at night?' We said 'No,' 'cause our folks had told us what to say. But the Lord have mercy, there was plenty of that going on. They'd pray, 'Lord, deliver us from bondage'" (Callahan 2008, 88). The integrity of hush harbors depended on a serious vow made by its members to betray the plantation culture and systems (Douglass 1994, 27–28; Jones 1990, 145). Enslaved Africans' very bodies and families were at stake should they be caught by the patrollers in the woods who hunted runaways or by the plantation master himself. The threats of being hanged, whipped, or raped or having family members sold off meant that the decision to steal away to hush harbors to worship and follow the God of justice was a matter of life or death. One formerly enslaved African preferred committing to be a hush harbor member over worshiping weekly in buildings that were made accessible after emancipation, saying, "[Hush

Harbor] Meetings back there meant more than [church services] do now.
Then everybody's heart was in tune, and when they called on God they made
heaven ring. It was more than just a Sunday meeting and then no godliness
for a week. They would steal off to the fields and in the thickets and there . . .
they called on God out of heavy hearts" (Callahan 2008, 217). To steal away,
then, was not only about running away or deceiving the plantation economy
and slaveholding Christianity. It was also about embodying a different path
of being a disciple, of being church. Stealing away into hush harbors was a
hidden-in-plain-sight alternative to the domination and death-dealing religion
and economy of the American colonial project.

North Star

> Follow the drinking gourd,
> Follow the drinking gourd,
> For the old man is awaiting for to carry you to freedom
> If you follow the drinking gourd. (American Spiritual Ensemble 2006)

This Spiritual contained a coded message signaling the plan of enslaved
Africans to run away, to escape slavery permanently. The drinking gourd
represented a tool enslaved Africans used to dip water. In the context of this
song, the water dipper represented the Big Dipper constellation, which points
to Polaris and thus the northern parts of the globe. A guide to travelers for
generations, the North Star was a way to direct enslaved Africans to the
northern parts of the Americas, where they could be free from the Southern
system of chattel slavery. The North Star also took on metaphorical import
for enslaved Africans, as it signaled not only a literal destination but also a
vision of liberation, the reign of God, the kin-dom[3] come on earth as it is in
heaven. Similarly to when enslaved Africans made reference to heaven, when
they referenced the North Star, white folks thought they meant the afterlife
or the distant future. Both inside and outside hush harbors, enslaved Africans
used this coordinate and metaphor as a powerful tool to both resist the world
as it was and imagine the world as it should be.

Resistance took many forms. The most popular in the historical record
was running away or escaping slavery in Northern free territories. Organizing
alternative communities was another form of resistance. Temporary communities like hush harbors and permanent ones like maroon societies—hidden
communities of runaways—were organized by enslaved Africans in collective

---

3. This rendering of the biblical concept of kingdom was popularized by Dr. Ada María
Isasi-Díaz in her book *Mujerista Theology*. Taking out the g removes the gendered and hierarchical connotations of the word, as well as giving the idea a more familial and egalitarian
identity (*kin* as in kinfolk or kinship).

resistance to the plantation and in service to liberation. Given the terror and surveillance of the plantation and slaveholder economy, virtually any agency that enslaved Africans demonstrated was resistance. From using humor or being a "trickster" who teased and deceived white people to the double meaning used in Spirituals to veil revolutionary messages, enslaved Africans resisted in everyday actions. More risky actions of resistance included outright armed rebellion against the terroristic violence of the plantation and its slaveholding religion (such as rebellions led by Denmark Vesey, Nat Turner, and others). The North Star signified any collective, personal, mundane, and dramatic actions enslaved Africans took that resisted and built alternatives to the status quo, that demonstrated their agency, dignity, potential, and aliveness amid the death-dealing plantation culture.

Joy Unspeakable

Breaking an enslaved African was a common practice among slaveholders. Breaking plantations were used to tear down the body and will of an enslaved African to the point that disobedience to slavocracy was unconscionable. Or so the white master thought. What the white master assumed was that they controlled all the resources to which enslaved Africans had access. How did so many enslaved Africans endure this kind of torture and keep their dignity to pursue liberation? The psychological and bodily trauma of chattel slavery did not have control over the spirits of enslaved Africans. Grin-and-bear-it is the style of resistance most associated with contemporary justice movements. That kind of resistance works, for a while. Hush harbors taught another form of resistance: joy as resistance. Poet Barbara Holmes writes that for this kind of church,

> Joy Unspeakable is
> practicing freedom
> while chains still chafe. (Holmes 2004, x)

This was not the faux joy that the enslaved had to muster up to prevent the temper tantrums of the slaveholder. That was not joy or resistance but survival, which was also essential to the life of the enslaved. Joy as resistance came from a deeper place of abundance and mystery, a place that enslaved Africans accessed inside of the bounce back from tremendous pain. This bounce back had many names, but it was often called the Spirit. To "catch the Spirit" was to birth joy embodied through the ring shout (a circular, counterclockwise dance with African origins), singing, dancing, praying, prophesying, preaching, or simply the fellowship among nature and one another outside the gaze of whiteness.

All of these joy practices and more erupted from the Spirit's work in and through enslaved Africans in hush harbors. Florence Bailey, a formerly enslaved woman, spoke of her experience of joy: "Sometime a group of slaves would leave the house and go on the branches to talk and have pleasure among themselves and when they got ready for such meetings they would turn a pot down to keep the sound from going in the direction of their master's house" (Florence Bailey, formerly enslaved African).[4] In an environment where Black flesh was deemed impure, violable, and unholy, it was radical for enslaved Africans to practice joy on their own terms through the pleasure of their bodies.

Rituals like turning over drum-like pots and speaking into them were used to drown out the sound of their praise so they would not be caught and punished by white slaveholders. Such rituals were also reclamations of the belief that the sacred could incarnate the natural. The pot was a symbol of divine protection and a steward of their gifts of praise. Claiming dignity, love, and freedom for themselves was a means of connecting to the divine. This kind of joy was unspeakable. No words could contain its power and potential. Enslaved Africans would dance so hard in hush harbors that they would fall out on the ground. The collective singing of Spirituals buoyed the souls and unity of enslaved Africans as they fled the plantation for their freedom in the North. These joy practices "made a way out of no way" for enslaved Africans to be set free in their bodies and in the body politic.

Talking Book

Slaveholding Christianity rendered the Bible dead. The Bible was a tool of control in the hands of white masters and white slavery apologists. Not only did they whitewash the Bible's spiritual and theological power, but they also forbade enslaved Africans from gaining literacy. The Bible was one of the only books enslaved Africans had access to. Even on the rare occasions that enslaved preachers learned to read the Bible, white masters mangled their preaching and teaching. Repeatedly, enslaved Africans were force-fed the teachings of Paul about slaves obeying their masters as an act of Christian service (Eph. 6:5–9). Despite the control exerted by slaveholding Christianity, white masters and preachers did not know that the worldview of enslaved Africans was not captive to the literal interpretation of the Bible. Enslaved Africans did not always internalize this biblical literalism. Instead, they liberated biblical interpretation.

Many enslaved Africans demonstrated resilient spirits that gave them internal agency where they were denied material agency. Unlike their relationships

4. Interview with formerly enslaved Florence Bailey by John B. Cade found in the Cade Library Archives at Southern University in Baton Rouge, Louisiana.

with white people, enslaved Africans' relationship with the sacred text included making real and meaningful choices. A rugged literalism was no different than the chattel mentality in which the enslaved lived daily. Nancy Ambrose, the formerly enslaved grandmother of mystic and theologian Howard Thurman, articulated this unbound spirit of agency well: "At least three or four times a year [the master's minister] used as a text: 'Slaves, be obedient to them that are your masters . . . as unto Christ.' Then he would go on to show how it was God's will that we were slaves and how, if we were good and happy slaves, God would bless us. I promised my Maker that if I ever learned to read and if freedom ever came, I would not read that part of the Bible" (Thurman 1976, 30–35).

For enslaved Africans, literacy was not only or primarily about reading. Enslaved Africans used music and metaphor to understand and make meaning of the biblical stories and figures they heard about through sermons. Metaphor allowed enslaved Africans to consistently see themselves as the oppressed in biblical stories, as the ones whom God favored, loved, and was committed to liberating. Polly, an enslaved woman, said to her mistress, "We poor creatures have need to believe in God, for if God Almighty will not be good to us some day, why were we born? When I heard of his delivering his people from bondage, I know it means poor Africans" (Callahan 2008, 83).

By seeing themselves in biblical stories in this way, enslaved Africans engaged the Bible as a living text. They were in relationship with the Bible, talking back to its stories and its God. God was not seen as a distant, malevolent deity. The God of enslaved Africans was ever-present, would deliver them, and would punish their oppressors. The companionship of God was seen especially in how enslaved Africans interpreted Jesus, whom they saw as a friend on the journey with them to survive and be liberated from their oppression. The Spiritual "I Want Jesus to Walk with Me" depicts the deep friendship the enslaved had with Jesus:

> I want Jesus to walk with me
> I want Jesus to walk with me
> All along my pilgrim journey
> I want Jesus to walk with me. (American Spirituals Ensemble 2006)

Enslaved Africans demonstrated their resilience and innovation in crafting a folk theology from the Bible in the form of folk songs called Negro Spirituals. They sang the Spirituals in both the hush harbors in the wilderness and the mystical hush harbors of their souls while in the fields and on the plantation. The Spirituals allowed them to put biblical stories in a medium that made them alive, bodily, and thus their own. And it allowed enslaved Africans to offer creative new interpretations of biblical stories. The Spiritual "Oh Mary, Don't You Weep" is an example:

> Oh Mary, don't you weep, don't you mourn
> Oh Mary, don't you weep, don't you mourn
> Pharaoh's army got drowned
> Oh Mary, don't you weep. (Moses Hogan Singers 2011)

Enslaved Africans created a link between the resurrection story and the exodus story.[5] In the resurrection story, Mary of Bethany wept, believing she had lost Jesus and his movement to the oppressive Roman state. She discovered that Jesus had been raised from the dead, and she was one of the first people Jesus charged with delivering the good news that Jesus and his movement were not dead but would live on through his people. In the exodus story, Moses gained power from God to part a sea, allowing the Hebrew people he was leading to escape from their oppressors, Pharaoh and the Egyptians. The sea collapsed on and drowned Pharaoh and his army as they chased the Hebrew people. The Hebrew people were set free with God's help. In step with their radical interpretation of biblical stories, enslaved Africans would weave their own conditions into the biblical story through song. The subsequent verses of "Oh Mary, Don't You Weep" are illustrative:

> I don't know what my mother want to stay here for
> This old world ain't no friend to her
>
> One of these mornings, bright and fair
> Gonna take my wings and cleave the air
>
> When I get to heaven gonna put on my shoes
> Gonna run around glory and tell all the news
>
> When I get to heaven gonna sing and shout
> Ain't nobody there gonna turn me out. (Moses Hogan Singers 2011)

The message is clear: in the same way that God gave victory to the Hebrews over Egypt and to Jesus and the church over Rome, God will give victory to enslaved Africans over their bondage to white Christian American tyranny. And this victory, just like the victory God gave the Hebrews and Jesus and the disciples, will not be in "the sweet by and by" but in the present world. Enslaved Africans believed God would work through them to bring this deliverance.

5. They could have also been talking about Mary the sister of Lazarus or Miriam the sister of Moses. In either case, the point stands that God has victory over deathly circumstances.

It is no coincidence that antebellum revolutionary leaders like Nat Turner, Harriet Tubman, and Frederick Douglass used these same biblical stories as inspiration for their movements for liberation. These biblical stories so animated the freedom dreams and plans of enslaved Africans that they would give biblical names to the leaders of their abolitionist movements. Harriet Tubman was called Moses, for example. At the same time, enslaved Africans were clever to retain language in their songs that made it appear to their masters and the white establishment that they were only talking about the biblical past or the far-off future in heaven. Enslaved Africans were careful and witty in concealing from the white establishment that their songs and biblical interpretations were the source of their ethic of survival and their plots for resistance. Enslaved Africans' creative engagement with the Bible led to truthful theological interpretations that at the same time met their emotional, spiritual, and political needs. In the hands of slaveholding Christianity, the Bible was a dead and death-dealing book. In the hands of enslaved Africans, the Bible was the talking book, a powerful, revolutionary, and healing source of communication and relationship between the divine and the oppressed.

Sankofa

Enslaved Africans' memories were channels of the sacred, fluid sites of freedom that broke down the linear time line of white supremacy. The collective memory of Africa held by the enslaved was stronger than the psychology of American slavocracy. The lived memories may have faded after the first generation, but Africa continued to be a governing metaphor within the collective consciousness of the enslaved from generation to generation. African worldviews were passed down to each generation through embodiment, storytelling, singing, dancing, customs, and the like. Enslaved Africans truly practiced the African concept of *sankofa*—to go back and fetch it—as they carried forward the worldviews of their ancestors. The enslaved did not abide by a division between sacred and secular or sacred and profane.

> Talking among themselves brought them power to be themselves alone in the midst of God's created nature—"on the branches." They could only talk when they were isolated in the space of nature's surroundings. . . . But talking and walking in nature without the permission of the plantation authorities granted a true freedom and place for pleasure in the midst of their faith in a protective power greater than themselves. In this time and space, one sees and hears illegally created new creatures communing in holy greenery ("on the branches") and speaking in a liberated tongue unknown to the masters. (Hopkins 2000, 117)

In the plantation economy, the natural environment was considered property, like the enslaved. Inside the African belief of interconnectedness, the natural environment served as a co-congregant within hush harbors. Nature functioned to support the revolutionary spirituality of enslaved Africans. The trees and branches served as code and signal as well as a makeshift sanctuary. The ravines and swamps served as a place of safety and as cover to "wade in the water," especially if patrollers or masters were on the hunt for those in hush harbors or permanent runaways. The stars and moon communicated time and direction to keep the enslaved safe en route to the church off the plantation.

This reverence for the interconnectedness of all life also extended to the role of the ancestors. The enslaved saw a link between themselves and their ancestors, drawing on the wisdom and practices of ancestors passed down from generations. One formerly enslaved woman from Kentucky said, "Us ole heads use ter make 'em on de spurn of de moment, after we wrestle wid de Spirit and come thoo. But the tunes was brung from Africa by our grandadies. Dey was jis 'miliar song. . . . Dey call 'em spirituals, case de Holy Spirit done revealed 'em to 'em" (Murphy 1899, 660, 672).

The Spirituals animated dancing, such as the ring shout, and drumming as practices retained from the ancestors. Within African religious worldviews, these practices signified connection to the sacred and the spirits of the ancestors.

Ubuntu

American individualism was not the social contract of the enslaved. The African worldview of interconnectedness also shaped how enslaved Africans viewed one another. Hush harbors were guided by the South African philosophy of *ubuntu*—I am because we are, or as the Zulu phrase describes it, *Umuntu ngumuntu ngabantu*, which means "A person is a person (through other) persons." Not only was individualism not culturally relevant for hush harbors, but it was also not practical. Under the plantation system, the needs of enslaved Africans were not met. The needs of enslaved Africans were seen only through how they served white pleasures. Individualism only worked for wealthy white folks. Individualism depended on prioritizing the needs and desires of the white establishment at the expense of the true and full needs of enslaved Africans. The most important thing in the plantation system was the metric of productivity. Quantity was the driving value of the plantation economy and the plantation religion—the number of slaves, crops, and church members, and the size of the plantation, the church, and the staff. Inflating the significance of quantity and output meant elevating the value of only those at the top of that system—the preacher class, landowners, and slave owners.

To meet their needs, enslaved Africans had to operate by an entirely different way of thinking and acting. Ubuntu was the practice of mutual care in hush harbors, of attending to the emotional and bodily needs of one another. Describing hush harbors, enslaved preacher Peter Randolph said, "They first ask each other how they feel, the state of their minds. . . . The slave forgets all his sufferings, except to remind others of the trials during the past week, exclaiming, 'Thank God, I shall not live here always!' Then they pass from one to another, shaking hands, and bidding each other farewell, promising, should they meet no more on earth, to strive and meet in heaven, where all is joy, happiness, and liberty. As they separate, they sing a parting hymn of praise" (Sernett 1999, 67).

Hush harbors were small enough for people to truly belong and be known, to prioritize the quality of the shared experience.[6] Living by ubuntu meant first caring about another person as a person. No one had to check their feelings, mind, or body at the entrance to a hush harbor. Care and attention were given to the conditions of the souls, emotions, and minds of those gathered. The power of consensual touch and gesture cannot be underestimated. In an environment of terror where the utility of one's body was for another person's pleasure without consent, enslaved Africans engaged in bodily pleasure by consent through the shaking of hands and bidding each other farewell. Music served to meet the same communal bodily and emotional needs of enslaved Africans, to cultivate the joy and imagination necessary for them to continue to collectively believe and struggle toward freedom.

All God's Children Got Shoes

Rationing was the practice of the plantation church and economy. Only a few could benefit from the labor of the many. There was not enough to go around. God willed that some were natural leaders while the masses were followers. This is the scarcity theology of slavocracy. Enslaved Africans in hush harbors embodied a different way. The following Spiritual depicts this alternative:

> I got shoes, you got shoes,
> all God's children got shoes.
> When I get to heaven gonna put on my shoes,
> gonna walk all over God's heaven, heaven,
> gonna walk all over God's heaven.
> Everybody talking about heaven ain't goin' there,
> heaven, heaven, gonna walk all over God's heaven. (Jackson 1955)

6. One former slave recalled one occasion when a hush harbor had a larger number of the enslaved: "We assembled about fifty or seventy of us in number" (Smith et al. 1971, 165).

In hush harbors, and in the reign of God not yet fully realized, all God's children had a role. Shoes represented both everyone's material needs being met and, more starkly, everyone's ability to be a leader. One formerly enslaved man said, "The old folks used to slip out in the fields and thickets to have prayer meetings and my mother always took me along for fear something would happen to me if left behind. They would all get around a kettle on their hands and knees and sing and pray and shout and cry. My mother was a great prayer and shouter and she always asked God to take care of her son—meaning me" (Rawick 1979, 147–48).

Enslaved Africans had to put on the shoes of singing, preaching, praying, dancing, care, lookout, and the many roles played to sustain hush harbors and both the temporal and the permanent freedom actions they inspired. This is a theology of the priesthood of all believers, where everyone takes up a role in the work of liberation and survival. Hush harbors refused the divide-and-conquer theology of the plantation that reinforced patriarchy, racism, and any other tactic and mindset that separated and diminished. While white men and women and Black men were given leadership over the plantation church and economy, both Black women and children took prominent leadership roles in hush harbors. Hanna Lowery, a formerly enslaved women, said, "Everyone was so anxious to have a word to say that a preacher did not have a chance. All of them would sing and pray" (Johnson 1993, 76).

Toni Morrison speaks to the role of the Black woman preacher in her character Baby Suggs in the fictive hush harbor illustrated in *Beloved*. Suggs tells the all-Black audience of enslaved Africans that "the only grace they could have was the grace they could imagine. That if they could not see it, they would not have it" (Morrison 2004, 88–89). She tells them that in the hush harbor they can and should love on themselves because they will never be treated with love on the plantation: "In this here place, we flesh; flesh that weeps, laughs; flesh that dances on bare feet in grass. Love it. Love it hard. Yonder they do not love your flesh. They despise it" (103). There was no place for a Black woman preacher on the plantation and in its churches and certainly no place for Suggs's message of radical self-love and self-imagination. A children's book on hush harbors captures the role of children well, when the young Simmy is asked by his uncle Sol to be a scout or lookout during the hush harbor: "'Simmy, you scout tonight. . . . I been watchin' how quick and easy you pick up on thangs. You got sharp ears like a hound and fast legs like one, too.' Sho', he made me smile and I was glad to scout. . . . I was still kinda scared, 'cause things could go wrong. If we got caught, Cap'n Bill would beat us and sell some of us off, . . . but I knew the meetin' would help make us strong" (Evans 2008, 7).

The risk of being whipped, killed, or sold off did not displace the theology of "I am somebody" that was rooted in the hearts and spirits of those who gathered in hush harbors. It was this theology that inspired and equipped them to take up their role to serve and lead, not by formal education or by the violent theology of slaveholding Christianity but by the Spirit, the elders, and the ancestors.

Stay Woke

Between the Christianity of this land, and the Christianity of Christ, I recognize the widest possible difference—so wide, that to receive the one as good, pure, and holy, is of necessity to reject the other as bad, corrupt, and wicked. To be the friend of the one, is of necessity to be the enemy of the other. I love the pure, peaceable, and impartial Christianity of Christ: I therefore hate the corrupt, slaveholding, women-whipping, cradle-plundering, partial and hypocritical Christianity of this land. Indeed, I can see no reason, but the most deceitful one, for calling the religion of this land Christianity. I look upon it as the climax of all misnomers, the boldest of all frauds, and the grossest of all libels. (Douglass 1994, appendix 1)

What enabled the abolitionist Frederick Douglass, a former slave, to exercise this kind of bold judgment? Key to organizing and sustaining the physical and mystical hush harbor was developing the critical consciousness of the enslaved. This is the kind of critical consciousness on display in Douglass's indictment of colonized slaveholding Christianity. One site where Douglass developed this type of judgment was hush harbors. In her book *In the Wake: On Blackness and Being*, Christena Sharp introduces the frame "in the wake" to speak to what it meant for enslaved Africans to stay awake. Sharp says that being in the wake was "the keeping watch with the dead, the path of a [slave] ship, the consequence of something . . . awakening, and consciousness" (Sharp 2016, 17–18).[7] There is no evidence of any formal training or catechisms in the revolutionary religion of hush harbors. Being in the wake was not limited to the linear pedagogy of formalized education. The wisdom, analysis, and practices of hush harbors were passed down orally. The theology and ethics of hush harbors were refined and adapted through real-life experiences of trial and error.

Enslaved Africans had to become skilled in remembering and re-membering. The act of remembering was holy in that it gave enslaved Africans an internal power to claim their knowledge, experiences, and future even while the plantation had temporal power over their external lives. Re-membering was the act of putting back together the people, places, and perspectives that were stolen and ruptured from the expansive and emerging body politic of enslaved Africans. The memory of Africa and of their experiences of freedom, however

7. I owe the connection to Sharp's work to my friend and colleague Rev. Terrance Hawkins.

temporary at times, was crucial to keeping the faith in permanent liberation. Enslaved Africans used memories of the toil and terror of the plantation and plantation religion to identify and resist the internalization of their oppressors' ways. Resisting the plantation religion by holding on to what was true and just and beautiful about it was an act of re-membering. By claiming their own belovedness and welcoming accomplices of European descent into the ministry of the hush harbor,[8] enslaved Africans were re-membering through refusing the lie of the racial caste system (Raboteau 2004, 147–48). Staying awake meant exercising discernment, being freethinking and free-spirited enough to "call a spade a spade," to tell and live the truth, and not only when it was convenient or popular, even among Black folks. This type of discernment gave enslaved Africans the critical consciousness they needed to accept the risks of death or betrayal and yet still forge ahead in acts of freedom and liberation.

Conclusion

"Whatever those first gatherings of slaves for religious purposes outside the su-pervision of whites may have been like, it is inaccurate to think of the religious institutions that made their first appearance among Black people as 'churches' in the sense of the European or American model" (Wilmore 1998, 26). True to the spirit of their origin, hush harbors cannot be contained or domesticated. Hush harbors are not bound to organized religion or denominations. In the same way the church of Acts precedes the institutional church of today, hush harbors are the predecessor of the Black denominational churches that would later emerge.[9] In both cases, there is continuity and discontinuity between

8. One of the more notable examples is the abolitionist John Brown. A lesser-known example is that of a white preacher named George Boxley, "[a] proprietor of a county store, [who] was a regular participant in the religious meetings held by Negroes of Spottsylvania and Louisa counties" (Harding 1997, 113). Boxley helped organize enslaved Africans for an ultimately failed insurrection mission.

9. Gayraud Wilmore calls the emergence of Black denominational churches "the Black Church Freedom Movement" because "it was, in fact, a form of rebellion against the most ac-cessible and vulnerable expression of white oppression and institutional racism in the nation: the American churches" (Wilmore 1998, 103). The earliest independent Black congregations of which we have record were organized in 1758 (Baptist church constituted on the plantation of William Byrd in Mecklenburg, VA) and between 1773 (later known as First African Baptist Church, this church was organized by enslaved African George Liele in Savannah, GA). Henry Louis Gates writes, "The invisible institution . . . was the real Black Church" (Gates 2021, 39). Wilmore writes, "When a few independent black congregations began to appear in the South almost a hundred years before the Civil War, there was actually more rather than less control over the situation. Unlike clandestine meetings in the woods and slave cabins from sundown to sunup, these were religious institutions much like those of the whites. They were, after all, public places in full view of the whites and often erected with their blessing and financial as-sistance" (Wilmore 1998, 100).

the early grassroots expressions of church and the institutional forms that developed. The expressive, embodied, and evocative styles of praise, worship, and communication practiced in Black churches directly connect back to ring-shout dancing, the Spirituals, the call-and-response nature of prayer, teaching, and preaching exercised in hush harbors. Communal gathering that provided refuge, care, and encouragement that addressed the suffering and needs of Black people is a continuity between the institutional Black church and hush harbors. The belief in a God who delivers and cares for the downtrodden is another continuity. Many Black churches continue the prophetic tradition of protest from hush harbors seen especially through the marks North Star and Steal Away. Social justice activism is central to the life and ministry of these churches through activities such as marches, boycotts, strikes, political education, and community organizing.

Given these continuities, what is the relevance of hush harbors since the antebellum period? Is there still a need for a secret, grassroots expression of church?

I (Brandon) believe that hush harbors are urgently needed for our time. The differences between the hush harbors and the institutional Black church speak to this need. One divergence from hush harbors is that the majority of Black churches mimic the hierarchical and patriarchal leadership structure and organizational systems of white denominational churches. Womanist theologian Cheryl Townsend Gilkes speaks to this: "When describing, analyzing, and criticizing the black church, almost every eye tends to be turned toward the pulpits, pastors, and their convocations and conflicts" (Gilkes 2001, 7). The Black church's reliance on these institutional and white patriarchal religious structures is a departure from hush harbors as a network of intimate gatherings that were leader-full, egalitarian, outside, and on the edges of institutional church structures.

Another major difference is the role of protest. Protest is not widely proliferated in Black churches, whereas it was core to the identity of hush harbors (the very act of forming a hush harbor was an act of protest). Raphael Warnock, the current pastor of Ebenezer Baptist Church, speaks to this in his book *The Divided Mind of the Black Church*: "The black church has been both radical and unradical, the most prominent instrument of liberation within the African American community and the foremost conservative custodian of an uncritical evangelical piety that undermines the aims of liberation" (Warnock 2020, 29). Dr. Martin Luther King Jr. is the most notable figure of the civil rights movement, but because of his radical protests of war and capitalism and his vision to bring people together across race, class, and nation, he was grossly unpopular among the American masses, including among Black churches. King was not welcome in the overwhelming majority of Black church pulpits.

A remnant of Black Christians, clergy, and congregations during the civil rights movement, and ongoing social justice struggles, have embodied the prophetic tradition of protest. The majority of Black churches have been absent from past and recent social justice movements, such as the Movement for Black Lives (M4BL). Of course, M4BL's centering of women and queer leadership raises major challenges for the Black church's long history of heteronormativity, transphobia, and sexism. Black prosperity gospel churches and megachurches depart from hush harbors' commitment to being intimate in size and organizing against not only racism but also wealth and income inequality. In response to the widespread absence of protest among Black churches, some Black religious scholars, theologians, and prophetic leaders have claimed that the Black church is dead (Glaude 2012).

The embrace of traditional African religious beliefs and practices is another major difference. The vast majority of Black churches view many traditional African religious beliefs and practices, such as the veneration of ancestors and the mediation of the sacred through the natural world, as opposed to biblical teaching.[10] This is owed mostly to the influence of white evangelical purity culture, which conflates control and either/or thinking with truth. When Black churches limit the influence of Africa to the symbolic—wearing dashikis during Black History Month, for example—they fail to seriously reckon with so many of their accepted practices that originate from hush harbors' integration of a contextualized Christianity with African Traditional Religions. Some examples of modern practices that resonate with ancestor veneration that I have experienced as acceptable in most Black churches include everything from saving and treasuring obituaries of loved ones to the honor given to being visited by ancestors in dreams.[11]

There are no longer laws that forbid Black people from congregating. Yet, hush harbors are not only a reaction to Black repression. Hush harbors are characterized by fluidity and freedom. They have persisted over time inside, on the edge, and outside of religious institutions—in barbershops and beauty salons, on porches, on the block, in clubs, through social movements, in social enterprises, through nonprofits, in alternative faith start-ups. Rhetorician-philosopher Vorris Nunley, in his book *Keepin' It Hushed: The Barbershop and African American Hush Harbor Rhetoric*, calls hush harbors a sacred-secular church that can take various "vernacular cultural forms [that] permeate both sacred and secular spatialities" (Nunley 2011, 64). Nunley argues for barbershops and beauty salons as two of the primary contemporary hush

10. Pastor Jamal Harrison Bryant of New Birth Missionary Baptist Church, one of the largest Black churches in the country, made headlines in 2020 when he discouraged Christians from burning sage, calling it satanic and witchcraft (Bryant 2020).
11. I will discuss more contemporary examples in chap. 6.

harbor churches. Hush harbors are not religious institutions and cannot be reduced to so-called sacred spaces. And not every group whose composition is exclusively persons with a Black racial identity constitutes a hush harbor. Hush harbors take Black racialized bodies and the continuity of Black culture as their starting point. Yet the antebellum hush harbors attest that, even more than racial identity, what is most critical for participation in a hush harbor is *solidarity* with the aims of liberation, mutual care, and freedom for all Black people.[12] As the saying goes, all skinfolk ain't kinfolk, and some kinfolk ain't skinfolk. Nunley speaks to this radical democratization of hush harbors, defining them as "free zones of emancipatory possibility" that are "internally directed, working from the terministic screens of African American life and culture" (Nunley 2011, 34).

Hush harbors interrogate and agitate the institutional church. Building contemporary hush harbor communities provides a site of possibility and hope as I witness the declining influence of the institutional Black church as a spiritual home to many Black people, especially activists, artists, younger people, women, and queer folks.[13] Hush harbors persist where Black people's spirits and bodies are unbound, unbought, and unbossed! This prophetic legacy and lineage of hush harbors continues everywhere sacred-secular spaces are curated off the grid of oppressive structures where all Black people are fully seen and can pursue their full liberation. Seeking the proliferation of hush harbors within and without organized religious institutions is critical for exploring the future of alternative faith communities in our times and for moving into an increasingly globalized, intercultural, and decolonized future.

12. Under the heading "Steal Away," see that hush harbors were vetted for Black folks who were more accommodated to the plantation culture. In note 8 of this chapter, see examples of certain white folks participating in the work of hush harbors who betrayed the plantation culture, such as John Brown, George Boxley, and others.

13. The recent groundbreaking, large-scale Pew study on Black religious life corroborates my anecdotal experience. The study found that almost 50% of Black people say that Black churches are less influential than they were a generation ago. The number of religiously unaffiliated is increasing among Black Americans like the general public. Younger Black generations (millennials and Gen Z) are twice as likely to say that they seldom or never attend religious services compared to the older Black Americans in the silent generation. The study confirms the Black Protestants' more conservative views on homosexuality and same-sex marriage compared to the general American public. The study revealed that although Black Americans typically express egalitarian views on gender norms, Black women make up a small percentage of the religious leadership of Black congregations, and Black congregations emphasize the experiences and leadership of Black men more than Black women. Less than one out of ten Black Americans in the study say they organized or participated in a protest or rally. Black Americans surveyed participate in civic engagement (volunteering, attending community or civic meetings, contacting an elected official, organizing or participating in rallies or protests) at roughly the same level as general American public (Mohamed et al., 2021).

3

Kinship

Familia en Comunión

BEC Kinship

PANCHO: I'm just catching on to what this means here! They didn't have enough—right?—to feed the five thousand people. But then he says to them: It doesn't matter, share it. And there was more than enough! He made them understand that no matter how little they had they had to share it. And they shared it, and with his power he made it stretch out. The lesson is that no matter how little we have we always have to give.

FELIPE: The teaching is also that if we come together to hear the message, we're not going to be hungry, because with a united people, there are no problems. Maybe I won't have food, but my neighbor will. If we're together, something can happen to us like what happened to those people with Jesus Christ. If we're together, it doesn't hurt to share. And then we're practicing the message of God. (Cardenal 1976, 222)

BECs were known for the quality of their common life. They exhibited a sense of collective identity that often included a broader sense of connection beyond the local group, an inspiring degree of holistic mutual care, sacrificial sharing, and a commitment to reconciliation. While cultures of the Global South tend to be more collectively oriented, BECs became a familia en comunión, a family in communion, on a whole new level.

> Poor people depend very much on one another's support in order to survive adverse economic conditions; thus, they develop and value their neighborhood and kinship networks. . . . The existence and esteem of mutual help among kin and neighbors, however, does not necessarily indicate the existence of a community identity or an identity of the poor, such as CEBs attempt to create. Poor people help one another because they have needs, not because they identify with one another. What CEBs do is reinforce this value and attribute religious meaning to it. In their view, economic equality is one of God's goals for humanity, and helping each other and the poorest is an important part of their religious ethic. (Mariz 1994, 71)[1]

For us to learn from this achievement, we must understand what actually happened in BECs, the factors that made it possible, and the process used to reach that goal. This all fits under the first step of the conscientización methodology: "*Ver* (See) / What?" We will then examine the implications of what we have seen for our current time and context: "*Juzgar* (Judge) / So What?" Last, we will suggest potential actions that arise from these implications: "*Actuar* (Act) / Now What?"

Ver (See) / What?

Collective Identity

Ana, a leader of a BEC in El Salvador for over twenty years, talks about the process of learning to *pensar en el nosotros* (think about the "we"). Members of her BEC learned that they were called to serve and live collectively for the common good (Ortiz, October 10, 2020). We see in Ana's statement the image of a compelling, sacred collective identity. Pablo Galdámez describes it simply and eloquently: "Now we were a people. We were like a big family. We were friends. The community meetings bound us closer and closer together. The doors were open. We said hello to one another, we went to one another's houses. For the first time, this scattered people were united. Gone were fear and embarrassment. We shared everything, a cup of coffee, a glass of water—and the quest. We'd learned to search out the solution to our problems together" (Galdámez 1983, 21).[2]

This sense of identity as a people was larger than any individual BEC. Galdámez adds, "We were beginning to be one people. Everywhere little groups were forming, becoming communities. The Gospel was the book from which the

---

1. Part of this quotation appears in chap. 1, but as it pertains directly to the focus of this chapter, we are including a longer version here.
2. Part of this quotation appears in chap. 1, but as it pertains directly to the focus of this chapter, we are including a longer version here.

communities learned who they were, and from which they learned the reality of the situation in which they lived" (Galdámez 1983, 7). An early leader and chronicler of the movement, José Marins, describes the missionary quality of BECs: "The BECs that progress, sooner or later, feel the necessity of beginning other BECs. No longer is it a case of only some missionaries who go out in mission; in Bolivia, entire communities and groups go out to stimulate and encourage that birth of other BECs" (Marins 1981, 60). He links this missionary fervor to a sense that they were "a people on the march, making history" (57). The history that they saw themselves making went beyond the sociopolitical sphere. BEC literature relates multiple versions of a revealing story about the self-identity of BECs. A priestly visitor comes to a village and looks for the church but cannot locate the steeple. A local resident tells him, "The church tonight is meeting in the Sanchez home" (Hebblethwaite 1994, 29; O'Halloran 1990, 25). They were remaking not only society but also the definition of church.

BECs sent to communities in other countries greetings that were reminiscent of New Testament pastoral letters. One letter from a small BEC in Bolivia begins, "Dear Brothers and Sisters of the Church of Nicaragua: We belong to the peasant community of Taipillijellije in the av mara-quechua zone of the northern altiplano of La Paz, and we are gathering together in a meeting to pray, reflect and study. Despite the distance that separates us, we are very much united to the valiant people of Nicaragua and want to express our Christian solidarity in these moments of much trial and suffering" (Marins 1981, 59). Moises, a Salvadoran immigrant to the US who returned to experience the BEC movement during the civil war between the government and the revolutionary forces in El Salvador (1980–92), describes this ecclesial identity as transcending the boundaries of the Catholic Church. He shares a story about a Baptist pastor who was part of the BEC movement in a "liberated zone" (an area controlled by the revolutionary army). On the morning of the day that this pastor was killed by the military, the pastor told Moises, "Your life will never be the same." Being found with a Bible in public could be a death sentence, and Lutheran pastors in the Evangelical Lutheran Church of El Salvador were martyred side by side with Catholic catechists (Escalante, October 8, 2020).

Guillermo Cook, a Protestant Latin American missiologist, describes the collective identity of BECs as complex and varied, depending on how much they emphasized *comunidad* (community, or the social), ecclesial (the religious), or *de base* ("from the base," or the political/economic). However, Cook notes that regardless of their particular emphasis, they experienced themselves as part of something new and exciting (Cook 1985, 80, 98).

What was so exciting about this new collective creation? BECs were unique in the extent of their mutual care, sacrificial sharing, and commitment to reconciliation.

Mutual Care

Niall O'Brien describes the changes in a parish in the Philippines after BECs took hold:

> The whole shape of the parish had changed far more than I had anticipated. Within the parish, some sixty small Christian communities made up six or seven mini-parishes. Each community saw itself as a sharing community responsible for the sick, the oppressed, the lonely, the dying, the children in their community. When they prayed together on Sunday, they brought these concerns vividly into the prayer of the community. When they left the chapel, it was frequently straight to tackle some new problem that had been brought to their notice at the assembly: to help plow the field of a man who had T.B., to collect clothes for a family whose house had been burned, to investigate rumors of a child being maltreated. If there was another community with a problem, someone would be reporting and asking for volunteers to help in a rally or a long walk. And sometimes there was someone to be corrected—a youth who was being tempted to loiter around with half-time bandits, for example. (O'Brien 1987, 260)

The mutual care of a BEC could be carried out in more formal ways. Margaret Hebblethwaite tells a story of a community in São Paulo that had an employment crisis affecting the metalworkers. BECs in the parish started Project Five-Two, in which groups of five employed families adopted two unemployed families and shared with them basic food items such as beans, rice, and eggs. When a popular TV host heard about the project and showed up with cameras and a truck full of food donations from a wealthy area, they turned her down, saying that they were not engaged in charity but rather in being a community. Augusto Brito, a BEC youth leader, said, "Our plan is to become aware of the reasons for unemployment and at the same time show solidarity for our unemployed companions. No one here is giving alms. If we had accepted those donations, we would have been prostituting Project Five-Two" (Hebblethwaite 1994, 85).

The mutual care aspects of a BEC were interconnected with its mission as a whole. For example, Galdámez describes the "solidarity fund":

> We noted with a good deal of concern that practically only the youth, the unmarried could carry on this struggle with the world's sin and not falter. Responsibility for their children was hamstringing the efforts of married couples—however much they might have committed themselves to our mission. If you were seen at a protest rally you were out of a job, and if you were out of a job you were watching your children starve to death. Our communities set out to meet the challenge to create conditions in which married love would not conflict with social commitment. We started a kind of family co-op. We bought things in common, took care of the children in common, and had some savings in

common. The parish team put its money into the common fund, and every-body's income and expenses were administered in community fashion. We were all equals now since we all lived on equal resources. So, we each opened our purses and discovered that together we could make it possible for our married couples to love each other and risk their lives for others all at the same time. We say that to make this possible was a responsibility to be shared by everybody. This was a revelation to us and gave us a lot of courage. It warmed our hearts and made them strong. (Galdámez 1983, 60)[3]

The mission required not only social action but also gathering for mutual spiritual care. Galdámez reports on how the same kind of sharing made regular gathering possible: "Some watched kids during the meetings, others helped members finish their work so they could come on time, still others took chairs or glasses to the poorest hovels so there couldn't be any excuses. And when people were embarrassed to have the meeting in their shack because the roof leaked and the community would get wet, there was still a way to have a meeting. We fixed the neighbor's roof" (Galdámez 1983, 9). Mutual care in BECs was holistic. James O'Halloran reports, "The participants share all aspects of their lives: spiritual, intuitive, imaginative, intellectual, emotional, apostolic and material" (O'Halloran 1990, 14). Carolee Chanona, a Bolivian BEC trainer, articulates, "The community does not exist for meetings but for communion" (Hebblethwaite 1994, 16).

There were challenges to maintaining this level of mutual care and intimacy. Galdámez speaks about the "demon of individualism" that tempted some members of BECs to withdraw from or even betray the community. Trustees of common funds embezzled; people in co-op housing rented their units for twice the price. However, there were occasions when the "grace of exorcism" prevailed to bring people back into the fold (Galdámez 1983, 34). We will explore this process in depth in the section on reconciliation in chapter 6.

Sacrificial Sharing

"Poranga, in the Northeastern state of Ceara, is extremely poor. In order to raise money to restock their small communal medicine chest, they conducted a 'fraternal fundraiser' among the forty-five families in the community, the proceeds of which were used to buy the most urgently needed medicines. Their financial situation can be judged by the fact that thirty-five of them took out a loan of 200 cruzeiros (about $25 at the time) to be paid back over a two-year period" (Cook 1985, 76). A BEC's commitment to mutual care went beyond generosity into the realm of sacrifice. Sacrifice formed an ongoing

---

3. When I (Alexia) was part of the movement in the Philippines from 1984 to 1987, I saw members practicing this kind of mutual responsibility for each other's families.

part of the BEC experience and faith commitment. This quotation comes from a Bible study in Solentiname: "Another lady: 'To follow Jesus means to not think about yourself, the way Jesus does, to have the same mentality as Jesus. It also means to suffer for others and that is to take up the cross each day. Because to forget yourself means to sacrifice yourself and that is to suffer.' One of the boys: 'To get rid of selfishness, we have to practice that, we who follow him, right here in Solentiname, even though we are not rich. Because if we don't get rid of that old mentality, we're not his followers and we're not revolutionaries'" (Cardenal 1976, 276).

Stories of physical, financial, and personal sacrifice are ubiquitous in the BEC movement. Overcoming exhaustion, cold, and hunger is a regular theme, from the farmworkers who worked all day and walked for hours to arrive at a BEC meeting and then helped with the chores, to the older mine worker who gave his salary for the day to the youngest miner, saying, "This is so you can eat today. I am old. You are young, you have to help build a better society. You have to be strong and well-nourished" (Marins 1981, 62). Moises talks about the eggs from the communal chicken going first to the pregnant women although all were hungry (Escalante, October 8, 2020). A story that has circulated in several versions gives an account of a Guatemalan peasant who responded to the needs of BECs in Nicaragua by placing a small bag of beans on the altar and then, after starting to return to his seat, going back and leaving his only jacket as well, even though the night was cold (Hebblethwaite 1994, 52). When the new co-op of the Salvadoran market women began to be pressured by the moneylenders, the community fasted to take up a collection for them. One member, Salvador, gave ten centavos, even though his family regularly suffered from hunger, by skipping his breakfast of a hard biscuit and juice for all of Lent (Marins 1981, 62).

As government repression and retaliation intensified, sacrifice became martyrdom. O'Brien tells a story of two brothers who were tortured and killed as a result of their participation in BECs. One had recently played the part of Jesus in the Passion play on Good Friday and had taken the opportunity to make a simple statement of faith:

> My brothers: I, Alexander Garsales, of barrio Tan-Awan, do promise to be faithful, to continue teaching the people. I offer myself to defend the poor and oppressed, to stand for my brothers and sisters who are falsely condemned. I offer my life so that peace will prevail in this place of Tan-Awan. . . . And I will bear all sufferings so that you, leaders, will be not cowed by threats. I have experienced many sufferings, yet I was not shaken or discouraged. You made me Christ whom we are now celebrating, and all should stand for the truth, as Christ did in the past, so that everyone will have faith. (O'Brien 1987, 165)

Commitment to Reconciliation

We will focus on the reconciliation process in BECs in chapter 6. However, at this point, it is important to note the essential importance and role of reconciliation in the development of the kinship practice of BECs. Ana, a Salvadoran BEC leader, says that their BEC was characterized by an *acompañamiento permanente* (ongoing, lifelong accompaniment). She notes that as the struggle wore on, people were easily frustrated and often acted out in different ways, hurting others. She talks about rituals of public confession and forgiveness that included a wide range of offenses, from couples who needed to resolve their marital discord to women who publicly repented of *chismes* (gossip). In describing commonalities in BECs across the Global South, O'Halloran notes that they were "composed of sinners who in their brokenness often fall (c.f. Proverbs 24:16). Yet, they steadfastly refuse to stay down. They always rise again to be reconciled with God and their neighbor. Community is always being built through continual reconciliation" (1990, 13).

Underlying Contributing Factors

BECs were intentionally kept small enough so that members could know each other well. They generally numbered between 20 and 150 persons, including children, with more members per BEC in the countryside than in urban areas (Barbe 1987, 88). They were tied to a certain geographic location, for ease in gathering and the sharing of common problems and opportunities. BEC scholars and formal church documents describe a paradox at the core of BECs. To function well, they needed a certain level of homogeneity with regard to common beliefs and values as well as a critical mass of "base," a Latin American term for the majority of the people residing in a given area, which, because the majority of Latin Americans were poor, became identified with the poor.[4] Cook defines the "base" of the people in Latin America as describable by four characteristics: "social oppression, economic manipulation, political disenfranchisement and cultural alienation" (Cook 1985, 73). However, the founding ecclesial documents that describe BECs as well as their major theoretical proponents insist on heterogeneity rooted in catholicity. BECs represented a cell or a microcosm of the whole church and as such had to be radically inclusive. They were also intentionally intergenerational, even though there were often challenges in integrating youth and adults. While the Catholic Church continues to promote interconnected, small church communities around the world, there are clear differences between those communities

---

4. Mariz notes that the relative lack of BEC ownership by the poorest members of society in the context that she studied caused BECs to lose the allegiance of the poor to Pentecostal movements.

in the Global North, or in wealthier communities, and those in the poorer communities of the Global South. Whether or not it is necessary for a successful BEC movement to be primarily composed of and led by the base, the movements that fill the pages of the intimate accounts presented in this book fit that description.

The Formation of a BEC

There is always a first step to the formation of a BEC. The people must be gathered and must continue gathering. In *Faith of a People*, Galdámez likens the process of building a BEC to the steps of formation into the priesthood. (He sees a BEC as the incarnation of the priesthood of all believers.) He says that the first step was for the initial core of a BEC to become a porter, the first role of a candidate for the priesthood. A porter gathers the people for worship (Galdámez 1983, 3). The invitation was not to join a social movement but to become part of a spiritual movement with sociopolitical implications.

> In my parish, the first group was formed one Sunday at the homily. We were having a dialogue on the gospel and we were looking for a path to follow. We were looking for answers. We were even looking for questions. This collective homily annoyed some I remember. One gentleman stood up and said, "Please don't mix politics and Mass!" When Mass was over, some of the congregation stayed to talk. And that's when things got started. We had to train, we had to learn some answers. We had to learn to "give an account of our hope." Suddenly, there was the offer of a house to meet in, and I had my first base group. (Galdámez 1983, 7)

Marins says that a BEC sought to engage the poor and marginalized first and foremost around a personal and communitarian experience of Jesus as one "who identifies with and solidarizes with the poor" (Marins 1981, 53). Dominique Barbe talks about the need for an initial demonstration—having a pastoral agent live with the people until a certain level of trust is formed and then moving from prayer fellowships to the restoring of a voice to the people to restoring action to the people to the expansion of ministries (Barbe 1987, 94–106).[5] Not all BECs catch fire, and of those that do, not all persevere. For a BEC to catch fire, the leadership must shift from an initial pastoral agent or missionary team to the people themselves. To be sustained, a BEC must be formed and tested by collective action. We will explore both areas in the chapters that follow.

5. As the BEC movement grew, it appears that this demonstration role was taken on by an existing BEC that could show the new BEC how the hoped-for reality could unfold.

Juzgar (Judge) / So What?

> All the believers were together and had everything in common. They sold prop-
> erty and possessions to give to anyone who had need. Every day they continued
> to meet together in the temple courts. They broke bread in their homes and
> ate together with glad and sincere hearts, praising God and enjoying the favor
> of all the people. And the Lord added to their number daily those who were
> being saved. (Acts 2:44–47)

The explosive growth of the early church was connected to the quality
of communal life that they enjoyed and demonstrated. Similarly, the rapid
multiplication of BECs was rooted in the same attractional power of genuine
kinship. This is not new information for church leaders, but it is hard to take
in and act on, particularly in the highly individualistic dominant culture of
the Global North, which continues to spread contagiously around the world.

The kinship found in the BEC movement speaks a word of challenge and
inspiration into our lives. Why don't we . . . what would happen if we . . . how
could we . . . become a real family? In Genesis 4:9, God asks Cain if he knows
where his brother, Abel, is, and he responds, "Am I my brother's keeper?"
God does not answer, but the silence is eloquent. We are responsible for and
to each other; we are not called merely to be charitable to those in need. In a
BEC, the members live into and out of mutual responsibility. The experience
of BECs tells us that the example of the church in Acts is much more attain-
able than many of us recognize. It also tells us, in a way that strips us of our
rationalizations, what it takes to get there. BECs challenge us to call together
a critical mass of oppressed and marginalized people in the name and Spirit
of Jesus and to expect them to be able to share resources sacrificially as part
of a commitment to the way of Christ and the struggle for peace and justice.
This challenge has three core components: a critical mass of oppressed and
marginalized people,[6] a commitment to share resources, and a commitment
to the way of Jesus.

A Critical Mass of Oppressed and Marginalized People

> Brothers and sisters, think of what you were when you were called. Not many
> of you were wise by human standards; not many were influential; not many
> were of noble birth. But God chose the foolish things of the world to shame
> the wise; God chose the weak things of the world to shame the strong. God

---

6. This immediately raises myriad related concerns in people who are more privileged: What
is my role and place? What is the role and place of my primarily privileged church? Would it
be possible to attract a critical mass of marginalized and oppressed people to our church? How
could we possibly accomplish that goal? What would be required of us in the process? We will
respond to these questions at various points and in various ways in this book.

chose the lowly things of this world and the despised things—and the things
that are not—to nullify the things that are, so that no one may boast before
him. (1 Cor. 1:26–29)

The assertion that a church made up of a critical mass of oppressed and
marginalized people can share resources sacrificially as part of a larger mission
flies in the face of the assumptions not only of many conservatives but also of
many liberals. Many conservatives overtly measure worth in terms of financial
success and status, directly accusing the poor of a form of immorality—not
pulling their weight in society due to laziness and irresponsibility. While many
liberals would disavow those beliefs, they may carry a more subtle form of
the same perspective.

Humanistic psychologist Abraham Maslow's famous hierarchy of needs
claims that people cannot give energy and attention to love, personal growth,
and achievement unless their needs for food, water, and shelter are more or
less met. The obvious implication is that people who suffer deprivation and
injustice and who live in constant danger cannot be expected to practice
sacrificial love in service of a higher goal. The silent underlying assumption
is that people with more financial and material resources are likely to act in
ways that are morally superior to the actions of those with fewer material
resources. These toxic implications and assumptions serve to justify the power
of the privileged and weaken the faith of the oppressed in their own moral
and spiritual capacity. The example of BECs powerfully reveals the fallacy
of these assumptions, because BECs that were made up of a critical mass of
"base" were more successful in building an authentic, holistic, and dedicated
spiritual family than those that were not.

Dolores Huerta, the vice president of the United Farm Workers (UFW)
union and the main partner with César Chávez in the development of the
UFW union and movement, tells a story about her first months with the
UFW. Her assignment was to collect dues. (The UFW intentionally subsisted
only on the dues of farmworkers, and organizers earned the same wages and
experienced the same living conditions as the workers.) She went to collect
the $3 monthly payment from one single mother who lived in a chicken shack
behind a house. The woman was not at home, and her teenage daughter
came out raging, holding a small glass jar with $3 in it. She said to Dolores,
"How dare you ask us for this money? This is all that we have to use to eat
today." Dolores went back to César and told him that she could not keep
asking people this poor for the little that they had. César responded by asking Dolores whether she thought she would personally be able to carry the
cross. She told him that she hoped so if God required it of her. He then said
to her, "Dolores, why do you think that these people are less able than you to
carry the cross? They are more able. Go back and ask for that money or leave

the union." Dolores went back to the house, and the woman came out with the $3. As she handed it to Dolores, she said, "Please forgive my daughter. She doesn't understand." When the farmers won their labor battle and their wages increased significantly, the daughter came up to Dolores at the fiesta to celebrate and hugged her, crying. She said, "Thank you for believing in us" (Huerta, August 30, 2008). Dolores learned from that experience that we need three kinds of faith to win struggles for justice: faith that God lives in us, faith that God lives in our neighbor, and faith in the God of history. Members of BECs learned that God lived in each and every one of them—and most particularly in the poor, marginalized, and oppressed (for the sake of the conversion of us all). To accept the challenge of their testimony is to live as if the power of the living God is present in the oppressed as they struggle for abundant life and justice.

The presence of the power of the living God does not negate the need for training and formation. In subsequent chapters, we will explore the kind of training that equipped BEC members to carry out their calling.

A Commitment to Share Resources

The more resources we have, the greater the temptation to control them. After the rich young ruler walks away because Jesus asked him to sell all his possessions and give his money to the poor, Jesus turns to the disciples and says, "Truly I tell you, it is hard for someone who is rich to enter the kingdom of heaven" (Matt. 19:23). The just distribution of resources is a complex and knotty problem (around the world and throughout the ages). The question, however, is not only who receives the resources but also who decides their distribution. Wealth confers power on the person(s) who controls its distribution. Serious power-sharing requires attention to economic equity and financial decision-making power. Chris Lawrence is a pastor who moved from England to East Harlem in New York to plant a church. He had recently sold a house that had multiplied in value as the result of a sharp increase in housing prices. He initially put those funds into a bank account, believing that he and his family could use them to purchase a new home and fund their mission. He then heard the voice of God telling him to turn the control of that fund over to the core leadership group in his new church so that it would become the seed of the church's affordable housing fund. Lawrence did and then asked others to contribute to the fund (Lawrence, October 6, 2015).

This kind of creative sharing of power over resources is so countercultural in the Global North that it is difficult for most people to imagine, let alone implement. When a Christian community is led by a critical mass of marginalized people who share resources, the unimaginable becomes visible, inspiring and enabling others to move in that direction. There are many alternative structures and formats for economic power-sharing that balance the value of individual and communal contributions and dreams—but trying to incorporate any of them requires an inner shift and an interpersonal level of commitment that are rare and profoundly challenging to the status quo. This brings us to the final characteristic.

A Commitment to the Way of Jesus

Therefore, I urge you, brothers and sisters, in view of God's mercy, to offer your bodies as a living sacrifice, holy and pleasing to God—this is your true and proper worship. Do not conform to the pattern of this world, but be transformed by the renewing of your mind. Then you will be able to test and approve what God's will is—his good, pleasing and perfect will. (Rom. 12:1–2)

An additional challenge that the BEC movement throws at us is the extent to which we are fully committed to follow the way of Jesus. The famous community organizer Saul Alinsky said on several occasions that he did not attempt to move religious leaders on the basis of their faith because he found that it was much more reliable to persuade them to act on the basis of their self-interest (Alinsky 1971, 88). He was responding to the practical atheism that characterizes many of the decisions of most Christians. BEC members' courage and willingness to give their lives for their friends were not separable from their response to the call to carry the cross in the name of the love of Christ, putting their individual self-interest aside for the sake of the family of God. Alinsky was at least partially wrong though; most disciples of Jesus Christ have moments and practices of generous love. However, it is terribly easy to unconsciously accept the norms of the society around us, baptizing impulses that weaken our overall engagement in the transformation of the world and our investment in Christian community. BECs carried out an alternative formation through the depth and quality of the relationships they built with one another and with the living God. Their sacrificial love holds up a mirror; it merits our honest attention and reflection.[7]

---

7. The call to sacrificial love is controversial in the context of any situation of ongoing abuse, whether personal or societal. We must continually discern the difference between redemptive and nonredemptive suffering. Suffering that enables abuse is nonredemptive; suffering that comes from struggling for liberation is redemptive. The suffering of the cross leads to redemption for all parties because it is a necessary step in a larger process. We are often more sensitive in our context to the rights of the individual or particular oppressed group than we are to the ultimate goal of the well-being of the whole. This stance has its own legitimacy and merits. However, BECs challenge us to look beyond our natural perspective and examine whether their commitments and practices have relevance for us.

Actuar (Act) / Now What?

Amos

Many of us are taught that our communities are not capable of the level of unity and discipline evidenced by BECs. We may have had experiences of sabotage, violation, and betrayal that confirmed the negative messages we have received about who we are. Some of us have learned to see a failed action as the sign of a person who is a failure, a loss as the sign of a loser. (That is not how more privileged people see themselves. A businessman from a wealthy clan can have multiple bankruptcies and still expect banks to invest in his company—and they do.) We tend to judge ourselves and our neighbors harshly; we doubt ourselves easily. We may also be sick and tired of being required to sacrifice for others.

Hear the Word of God incarnated in the BEC movement. The living God, the God we encounter in Jesus, is in you and with you; God is in and with your family, your family in Christ, your neighbors. More is possible—more unity, more discipline, more profound solidarity, more mutual support in achieving common goals, more fierce and fearless love rooted in faith. Suffering can be redemptive or nonredemptive. It can be an experience of the cross that takes you to resurrection or just a waste of energy and resources. The examples we share in this book can help you discern between that which is redemptive and calls for courageous action and that which is nonredemptive and must be stopped as soon as possible. As we continue through this book, we will be sharing more details about the "how"—at least how it worked for fellow believers who went before us. For now, just hear the call and the promise. Allow yourself to imagine possibilities in your context, to dream God's dream of building a healthier spiritual family with a deeper common dedication to liberation.

Lydia

You may be in an area where most people are relatively privileged, or you may be in a mixed community with a variety of levels of power, status, and wealth. Our assumption is that you are reading this book because you would like to learn from the examples of BECs and hush harbors how to build a more vital and faithful Christian community with a more powerful, holistic mission. You may be intentionally engaged in outreach to marginalized people in your community, or you may merely want to broaden your perspective and spiritual resources. Either way, you may have been surprised at the extent to which these movements depended on a critical mass of marginalized people in leadership—forming a common identity, family, and mission team together.

Many of us have been taught that marginalized and oppressed people are not as capable or as competent as we are and that they need our help to succeed. We are often blind to the depth and breadth of our own weaknesses and failures. We do not get that when you are born on third base (in terms of external advantages and/or internal capacities), it is not a superior accomplishment to reach home. However, there is no question that some of us have more access to a variety of resources than others. Resources come with responsibility and are meant to be shared. Conversely, a lack of resources, opportunities, or training is not the same as a lack of wisdom or essential capacity. In BECs, the most effective pastoral agents with more privileged backgrounds or positions helped to light a spark and then took a step back and supported from the side, allowing others to determine how their resources were used. O'Brien shares that it took him multiple failed attempts to start BECs to figure out the key elements.

> The approach that worked was startlingly simple. At a marriage interview or at a funeral, I would meet a group from a certain hamlet. I would say: "Do you want to start a Christian community?" "Will you come and say Mass for us?" "No, not yet. Why don't you start your own worship service yourselves?" And I would give them a *panimbahon* book with all the steps for a worship service laid out simply. "Now you see the Gospel's here. . . . There are questions after them in which you can apply the Gospel to the problems of your own community. The next step is to list all the sick, the old and the lonely in your village and start to attend to them. . . . When everything is going, then call me." (O'Brien 1987, 128)

The critical element in building the leadership of marginalized people is trust in their capacity. Whether you are planning to plant a church in a marginalized area, change the composition of your church, increase the leadership of marginalized people, or partner with a church with a higher percentage of marginalized leaders, be intentional about sharing life with people who are marginalized and oppressed in a way that trusts their capacity and leadership. As the community grows and a critical mass of oppressed and marginalized people consolidates leadership, being part of that community will absolutely transform your life. You will be inspired, ashamed, converted, and nourished by the mutual care and heroism you encounter. Being part of that community will increase your willingness and capacity to carry the cross.

René Padilla is one of the leading voices in Latin America in the Misión Integral movement, the evangelical Protestant version of liberation theology. He shares a story about a middle-class church in Buenos Aires whose leadership had decided to intentionally pursue renewal, including an expanded mission to the community. However, they were barely beginning to lay the theological foundation when a young former drug dealer who had accepted

Christ while in the US wandered in the door and shared his plan to reach out to his former associates with the gospel. He asked if this church would be willing to be the host for the ministry, welcoming those who visited. The next Sunday, a large group of young drug addicts came to church. The pastor had misgivings: "What was our church to do with these dropouts—a church of 'nice people' for whom social advancement had unequivocal priority over involvement in God's mission? And then again, even if the members of the congregation were really positive toward the drug addicts, how could they avoid their very presence in the church projecting a bad image in the neighborhood as a whole? And how were they to handle the question of drug addiction spreading among the church families?" (Padilla 2004, 290–300). The church entered into a time of confusion and conflict as drug addicts and former drug addicts began to outnumber the other members. However, on the other end of the crisis, the ministry with drug addicts, which became a multileveled initiative, became one of the main channels of the church's mission. The identity and ultimately the leadership of the church changed. The renewed church that emerged continued to grow in numbers, vitality, and breadth and depth of mission.

Obviously, not every primarily middle-class church that begins down the road of holistic renewal ends up led and transformed by a critical mass of marginalized people. However, BECs challenge those of you from more privileged contexts to open yourselves to all that God may want to do.

Ruth

When my daughter was fourteen years old, she had a history teacher who was sophisticated about justice issues. She came home from class very excited one day. "Mommy," she said, "they have been compressing us for centuries!" We all laughed, but I realized that she had stumbled on an important insight. The expression of oppression is compression, of being made smaller than you were born to be.

Those of us who have found our way out of the box to some extent may tend to have deeply mixed feelings about going back into places where others are still trapped. On the one hand, we want nothing more than for everyone to experience liberation and abundant life—particularly loved ones who continue to suffer. On the other hand, we want to enjoy our hard-won liberty and not look back. We may carry survivor guilt, particularly around questions of mutual care and sacrifice. Survivor guilt can lead us to want to separate ourselves, in our own mind if not in our daily life, from those who were left behind when we stepped up and out.

The intricate balance between Philippians 2 and John 10:10, between the call to let go of power and share and the call to live into the promise of abundant life, is part of the art of the Christian life. Living this balance is not simple. It can be done only with integrity and in accountable relationship. How can your bridge status be a gift to you and to others? How can the example of BECs spark your prophetic imagination? How can you be in and out of the community at various times and in various ways? Answering these questions can lead to another kind and level of liberty—the liberty of a clearer consciousness and a deeper love.

Hush Harbor Kinship

Hush harbors were the *regular* fellowship of oppressed peoples. One formerly enslaved Black person said this about the rhythm and nature of their hush harbor gatherings: "My father would have church in dwelling houses. . . . Sometimes they would have church at his house. That would be when they would want a real meetin' with some real preachin'. . . . That was a prayer-meeting from house to house once or twice—once or twice a week" (Johnson 1993, 134–35).

For hush harbors, kinship was not defined by biology, Sunday morning, a building, or a particular order of worship. Kinship was about a lifestyle, about developing a life together with a spiritual family of oppressed peoples. Several patterns characterized kinship in hush harbor communities: the centrality of Black women and the influence of African worldviews, mutual aid and care, art and culture, and intimacy and safety.

Ver (See) / What?

Mother Africa

It is common to hear African Americans refer to Africa as "the motherland." Africa is the place of origin, the homeland, for African Americans, and for all of human life for that matter. Both Africa and Black women shaped kinship in hush harbors. The communal life of the enslaved, especially in the last thirty-five years of slavery, was characterized by a "remarkable lack of sexism" (Webber 1978, 149–50). Womanist theologian Cheryl Townsend Gilkes says that "Black [enslaved] women were the carriers of culture and tradition both within their families and the hush harbors of slave worship" (Gilkes 2001, 79). Slaveholders gave primacy to the mother-child relationship over all others. This was not because of sentimentality. Slaveholders used the wombs and child-rearing of Black women as a means of controlling the enslaved workforce. Slaveholders used the role of mothering among enslaved women for evil. Black women used the role of mothering for good, for the nuture of a whole community. They created an environment of community, survival, and care among enslaved Black people.

> In West Africa, women were recognized as competent religious leaders. They were priestesses and cult leaders, and they were responsible, as wives and mothers, for the socialization of their children. . . . African religions contained within them female deities and feminine imagery of the creator deity. . . . The importance of West African women to production and markets was reflected in religious life. . . . The emergence, then, of an independent network of slave women was a function . . . of African cultural foundations . . . , which enabled women to support one another in sickness, childrearing, childbearing, and work . . . [and] also conducted a religious life with one another. (Gilkes 2001, 95)

Black women played key roles, rooted in African lineage, in the development of family, education, religion, and in an independent women's network that was the basis for mutual aid and leadership in the larger community of enslaved Africans. Enslaved Black women, as the primary caretakers of the children on the plantation, cultivated the sense of connection to Africa among the younger generations. "Aunt" Adeline, a formerly enslaved woman, speaks to being shaped with this African cultural identity: "I had always been told from the time I was a small child that I was a Negro of African stock. That it was no disgrace to be a Negro and had it not been for the white folks who brought us over here from Africa as slaves, we would never have been here and would have been much better off" (Raboteau 2004, 43).

Black women's leadership also explicitly shaped hush harbors (Webber 1978; White 1999). Hush harbors were spaces where women regularly gathered with other women. Minskie Walker, another formerly enslaved woman, speaks about the "impromptu female religious services" that her mother would attend (White 1999, 124). Black women shaped the ethos and spiritual practices in and beyond hush harbors, marked especially by the power of prayer and ritual. Gilkes says that "men who left their autobiographies in the slave narratives attributed their early spirituality to the religious practices, especially prayer traditions, of their mothers and aunts, the women of their slave communities" (Gilkes 2001, 34).

My (Brandon's) experience leading a modern network of hush harbors attests to the power of ritual and prayer led by Black women. In one of our autonomous hush harbor communities for women and nonbinary people, one woman facilitated a ritual as the group relocated their gathering place from a Black-woman-owned coffee shop that was closing to a local grocery store co-op. I was invited to the gathering for this ritual, which involved pouring libations, incantations, and fire in a mini cast-iron pot. Each person wrote the name of something life-giving and challenging on a sheet of paper. When the person was ready, they were invited to place the paper in the fire as a symbol of honoring and releasing those memories. Hugs, tears, and singing accompanied the burning of memories. I remember apologizing for the uncontrollable tears that fell from my eyes. One of the Black women who leads this hush harbor said to me, "You don't have to apologize for crying here. Let them flow."

Mutual Aid and Care

Black women's spiritual and biological nurturing in hush harbors influenced the organizing of mutual aid and care among the enslaved community. In her book *Collective Courage*, Jessica Gordon Nembhard speaks to the origins and nature of mutual aid among the enslaved African community:

> Enslaved as well as the few free African Americans continued African practices during the antebellum period—cooperating economically to till small garden plots to provide more variety and a healthier diet for their families. . . . [They] formed mutual-aid, burial, and beneficial societies, pooling their dues to take care of their sick, look after widows and children, and bury their dead. These mutual-aid societies were often organized and led by women. . . . Religious camaraderie was the basis for African American economic cooperation. . . . *In terms of official organization, mutual-aid societies actually predate independent African American churches, but not Black religious activity.* (Nembhard 2014, 31–33, emphasis added)

During the first year of the coronavirus pandemic, I (Brandon) helped coordinate a mutual-aid drive across multiple Black and low-income communities. The drive included making wellness calls to neighbors, distributing a community resource list, offering direct cash assistance from a community-pooled fund, and inviting neighbors to pay it forward through their own talents and finances. I'd gotten one neighbor, a middle-aged Black man, involved with the drive, and he did not really understand the perspective and posture of mutual aid at first. He was eager to serve. He knew everyone on his street. All of his neighbors looked to him as a leader. So it was easy for him to reach out to the neighbors on his block to do wellness checks, to let them know about resources the community had pooled, to ask if they needed any of those resources, and to see if they had anything to offer the drive. One evening after a community meal at the homeless shelter, after we'd packed up all of the supplies and most of the neighbors had gone, this man came over to me. He didn't have the gregarious spirit that I was used to. With a downcast face, stuttering with timidity, he asked me if he could get some of the financial resources we'd offered to neighbors. When I first met this man and offered the cash assistance we'd pooled as a community, he said he didn't need the money but he did want to serve. That evening he opened up to me and said he originally refused the resources because he didn't want to take from others who needed them. That he was too proud to say that he was in need too. Even after engaging in political education about mutual aid with the community, he held on to an assumption that this was a charity drive. This man held deep-rooted beliefs about his worthiness compared to his neighbors. The lie of racialized capitalism is that anything the working-class lacks is because they have not earned it, that the poor are not made poor by an exploitative system but because they are lazy and can only be sustained by handouts from the rich.

Mutual aid and care are not charity. Mutuality is the key. Everybody has a right to have their needs met, and the community can pool their resources to meet those needs. Mutual aid and care are about the Black community controlling its own resources, not giving its entire existence over to the control of the white ruling class. Hush harbors were a base for organizing mutual aid and care before the formation of independent Black churches. The needs that mutual aid and care meet can vary from emotional to material to spiritual. Enslaved Africans organized a variety of forms of mutual aid, which demonstrated their attention to the diversity and holistic needs of Black people.

In addition to the forms Nembhard describes, mutual aid also included enslaved Africans forming their own intentional communities like the maroon societies (there were also racially integrated communities), mutual insurance organizations, fraternal organizations, secret societies, joint-stock-ownership organizations, and buying clubs. Nembhard also points out that more popular actions by enslaved Africans, such as the Underground Railroad, slave revolts, and buying their freedom, were also acts of social and economic cooperation (Nembhard 2014, 33).

Eating together was also a form of mutual aid and care. Former bondwoman Cornelia shares about her experience of food cooperation among the enslaved community:

> My father had a garden of his own around his little cabin, and he also had some chickens. . . . Sunday, Master Jennings would let Pa take the wagon to carry watermelons, cider, and ginger cookies to Spring Hill, where the Baptist Church was located. The Jennings were Baptists. The white folks would buy from him as well as the free Negroes of Trenton, Tennessee. Sometimes these free Negroes would steal to our cabin at a specified time to buy a chicken or barbecue dinner. . . . Pa was allowed to keep the money he made at Spring Hill, and of course Master Jennings didn't know about the little restaurant we had in our cabin. (Rawick 1972, 285–86)

Kinship in hush harbors was not just about explicitly religious activities. Even activities as mundane as eating good food, and doing it together, required enslaved Black people to steal away, and this act of meeting together outside the gaze of the slavocracy cultivated kinship. Black theologian Dwight Hopkins refers to this act as "stealin' the meetin'" (Hopkins 2000, 137): "Paths and trails . . . revealed the way to surreptitious multipurpose meetings—sometimes defined by explicit religious worship, other times fiddling and dancing, and, more than likely, other times by illegal gathering for slave resistance . . . [and] indicated the movement to a slave shack or hut that was a clandestine storehouse of reappropriated food" (128). Community control is more than private ownership of a building or land. At the core of stealin' the meetin' for mutual aid and care, or for worship, was that the meeting was independent and was controlled by the Black people it served. There was collective decision-making about the gathering. For kinship to develop, it was critical that life was lived together so that the community could meet the needs it found pressing at any moment. Everyone in the community was responsible for caring for the needs of the community.

Art and Culture

One crucial need of enslaved Africans was cultivating the power of art and culture. A hush harbor meeting often centered art and culture (Harrison 2009, 196–97). Those attending engaged in "fiddling and dancing," as attested by Minskie Walker when speaking about the women's gatherings her mother attended: "First thing I would know dey would be jumpin' up and dancin' around and pattin' their hands until all de grass was wore slick" (White 1999, 123). Still, no cultural act within hush harbors was as widespread as singing. Enslaved Africans created an endless number of songs. They created them extemporaneously or adapted old songs to meet new experiences and needs. The hush harbors didn't have songbooks. Art and culture were carried from generation to generation through the embodied memories of Black people. Some of the most powerful songs spoke to their collective vision of freedom.

> Walk together children
> Don' you get weary
> Walk together children
> Don't you get weary
> Oh, talk together children
> Don't you get weary
> There's a great camp meeting in the promised land
> Sing together children
> Don' you get weary
> Sing together children
> Don't you get weary
> Oh, shout together children

Don't you get weary
There's a great camp meeting in the promised land
Gwineter mourn and never tire
Mourn and never tire
Mourn and never tire
There's a great camp meeting in the promised land

Singing was not a solo act, nor was it about conspicuous consumption. Enslaved Africans' singing cultivated the feeling of family among hush harbor
members. Hopkins says, "Singing is an extended family chorus, . . . this ritual
of communal family feeling of comradery. . . . Thus walking, physical movement, united with the singing and buoyed the gathered throng. The more they
walked in the secret worship, the more they sang, the more they united as an
extended family of sisters and brothers in the presence of the holy. . . . As
bodies separated after secret meetings, the remembrance of the song served
as a spiritual glue to recall all who had gathered clandestinely" (Hopkins
2000, 142).

Singing served as a distinctive cultural marker of kinship, not only among
enslaved persons but also in their relationship with the divine Creator. Enslaved Africans believed that the ability to create impromptu songs and to
adapt old songs was a gift given by God. Hopkins speaks to this theological
dimension of singing as kinship: "The revelation of divine lyrics and holy
rhythm implanted in the aesthetic harmonizing of beautiful dark tongues
signified the co-laboring exertion of God and humanity in the reconfigura-
tion of the black self. African American servants knew about themselves and
how to take care of themselves" (Hopkins 2000, 124). This knowledge of self,
community, and God, learned through singing, was critical to building a collective identity as spiritual kin.

Intimacy and Safety

The kinship in hush harbors was not about building platforms or gathering
consumers. Hush harbors were about authentic community and substance.
They required intimacy and safety. Without them, oppressed people could
not develop a lifestyle of kinship. Several characteristics made hush harbors
feel like a safe haven. They were small, but not necessarily from a quantitative
perspective. Hush harbors were small enough for everyone to be known, a
personal and collective knowledge that was more intuitive than literal. Gilkes
speaks to the intimacy created by the size of hush harbors: "Whereas the
integrity of slave families was dependent upon having its members present in
an enduring household, the 'household of faith,' or one's 'church home,' was
dependent only upon the gathering of 'two or three who touch and agree'"

(Gilkes 2001, 102). Touching and agreeing were indicative of the unity of the people, of feeling like the gathering was home. Touching and agreeing meant that the gathered people could be themselves, could bring their hurt, could talk about anything with one another. It also meant they could physically touch and agree, greeting one another with hugs, handshakes, and warm embraces. The power of touch was a consistent indication of a hush harbor's intimacy and safety. Alice Sewell, a formerly enslaved woman, states, "When we all sung we would march around and shake each other's hands" (Albert 2012, 6). A popular song among hush harbors also speaks to the significance of touch and the unity engendered: "Our little meetin's about to break, chillen, and we must part. / We got to part in body, but hope not in mind / . . . We walk about and shake hands, fare ye well my sisters, / I am going home" (Albert 1988, 12).

Being able to talk freely among one another or to simply be together enjoying one another's company was radical in the context of constant white surveillance. Hopkins attests to this reality: "Another type of stealin' the meetin' or the Invisible Institution was . . . simply [having] 'a good time talking about their mistress and master'; others assembled around a big fire on the edge of the woods 'whar deir racket wouldn't 'sturb de white folks'" (Hopkins 2000, 137). The physical space of the hush harbor gathering was foundational for creating a safe place for the oppressed. Community spaces that were controlled by the oppressed were critical, even if control was only temporary, like when the enslaved gathered outdoors: "African Americans' construction of paths for walking marks . . . symbolic redefinition of landscaping as a vital indicator of the moment to reconstitute the black self. . . . These paths served a multileveled practicality known only to the black hearts . . . paths and trails into the countryside" (Hopkins 2000, 128). Even if these community spaces were not permanent, by constructing makeshift spaces in the wilderness, enslaved Africans were able to cultivate an environment of intimacy and safety, both necessary to create kinship.

Juzgar (Judge) / So What?

No Trespassing

Kinship was vital to the integrity of hush harbors. If we want to pattern our community building after hush harbors, we will have to be serious about a kind of inclusive exclusion. "In trying not to offend, you fail to protect the gathering itself and the people in it. . . . We fail to draw boundaries about who belongs and why. . . . If everyone is invited, no one is invited—in the sense of being truly held by the group. By closing the door, you create the room" (Parker 2018, 38). Enslaved Africans created kinship in hush harbors by gathering a purposeful group, not by merely amassing individuals or a random crowd. A purposeful group was made up of people doing with others what they could not have done by themselves. Many of these purposes have been laid out in this chapter—mutual aid and care, intimacy and safety—and more will be expressed in subsequent chapters. However, the first purpose was about the feeling of community or of kinship among the oppressed. To create the kind of kinship demonstrated in hush harbors, a certain kind of exclusion was necessary. Science-fiction social justice strategist adrienne maree brown puts it this way: "Your no makes the way for your yes. Boundaries create the container within which your yes is authentic. Being able to say no makes yes a choice" (brown 2019, 15). This will be one of the greatest challenges for embodying hush harbors in the contemporary moment. Values such as tolerance and inclusivity—which I (Brandon) deeply believe in—become idols when they unsuspectingly welcome oppression and injustice through the door.

The Challenge of the Public

The front doors and marquees of most churches display messages like "All are welcome." Worship is commonly understood as open to the public. Churches typically do not want to leave anyone out of their gatherings. Imagine how you would feel if you saw the words "Private Event" on the marquee in front of a church. Most people would be appalled. Yet the Gospels attest that Jesus spent the least amount of his time with the general public. Who can forget Jesus consistently telling his disciples and those he taught and served not to speak of his actions to the wider public?

Rhetorician-philosopher Vorris Nunley uses the term "public podium–auction block rhetoric" to describe the contested nature of the public sphere for Black communities. Nunley says that public podium–auction block rhetoric "requires the smoothing out of Black noise, dissonance, angularity, and improvisation tethered to African American memories, experiences, and knowledges smoothed and flattened into a more palatable brew of domesticated, tolerant, consumer-friendly Blackness" (Nunley 2011, 3). Nunley says that any space where Black people gather that requires public podium / auction block rhetoric violates the dissonance of hush harbor speech. And I would add that it does not maintain the honesty of hush harbors. The words of Christian abolitionist Frederick Douglass are relevant: "There are some things that ought to be said to colored people in the peculiar circumstances in which they are placed, that can be said more effectively among ourselves, without the presence of white persons. We are the oppressed, the Whites are the oppressors, and the language I would address to the one is not always suited to the other" (Howard-Pitney 2005, 21). The binary of public and private does not do justice to the nature of hush harbor gatherings.

Communications theorist Catherine Squires says that there are multiple publics: "The move away from the ideal of a single public sphere is important in that it allows recognition of the public struggles and political innovations of marginalized groups outside traditional or state-sanctioned public spaces and mainstream discourses dominated by white bourgeois males" (Squires 2002, 446). Having multiple publics is relevant not only for the relationship between marginalized groups and the white dominant society but also for the real differences of identity and ideology within marginalized groups, particularly for racial identity groups. To gather a hush harbor is to organize a critical mass of people who share a common oppression. This means that a hush harbor that gathers around the plight of Black women may not be a space where Black men are welcome. A hush harbor that gathers around the needs of Black people may not be a space that welcomes a multiracial composition. A hush harbor that gathers around the hopes of Black men may not be a brave space[8] if women are welcomed. Squires exposes the critical need for those who organize hush harbors to be clear about gathering a critical mass of people who share a common oppression or intersection of oppressions, what she calls social hierarchies. These include and go beyond racial identity. When people who share a common oppression gather, the leadership, needs, and cultures of those persons as a community take precedence in ways that would otherwise not be possible in the dominant public sphere.

Given the fluid and heterogenous nature of culture and oppressions within and without racial identities, Squires offers a threefold frame for different types of publics organized by marginalized groups: enclave, counterpublic, and satellite.

Enclave publics are spaces that hide "counterhegemonic ideas and strategies in order to survive or avoid sanctions, while internally producing lively debate and planning" (Squires 2002, 448). Within enclave publics, the oppressed maintain independence of thought, culture, and action away from the gaze and control of dominant publics or more generally from those who do not share a common oppression and commitment to dismantling that oppression. Enclave publics intersect with wider publics, both dominant and other marginal publics, where individuals and/or groups within the enclave "express previously enclaved ideas [in wider publics], or when surveillance by the state or dominant publics reveals these clandestine discourses" (458). Bringing enclaved actions into wider publics is a transition to engaging in counterpublic discourse.

Counterpublics are spaces that "engage in debate with wider publics to test ideas and perhaps utilize traditional social movement tactics (boycotts,

8. The language of "brave space" is inspired by Beth Strano's poem "An Invitation to Brave Space."

civil disobedience)" (Squires 2002, 448). Social movement tactics are not required of counterpublic action. Any action that brings the culture, needs, practices, ideas, and opinions of the enclave into wider publics constitutes counterpublic action. Counterpublics create opportunities for alliances to be made and solidarity to be formed with other marginal publics and with those from the dominant public who commit to the work of reparations and to decenter themselves and their culture. Real material, legal, and political changes can and have resulted from counterpublic action. We will share more about such action in chapter 7. Independent media often facilitates positive outcomes from counterpublic action. However, there is always great risk in counterpublic action because of the threat of co-optation, violence, dismissal, and disrespect. Squires gives the example of such threats in the "content of our character" saying from Martin Luther King Jr.'s speech, popularly known as the "I Have a Dream" speech. King's words have been co-opted to normalize colorblindness and post-racialism. This is domesticating and sanitizing King. When engaging in counterpublic action, the oppressed must beware of being co-opted in this way and also of playing into the consumer-friendly minority that serves the goals of the oppressor and the ruling class.

Satellite publics are spaces that seek "separation from other publics for reasons other than oppressive relations [and are] involved in wider public discourses from time to time" (Squires 2002, 448). Squires identifies the Nation of Islam as a satellite public. Satellite publics do not intend to integrate or build coalition with wider publics. Typically, only in times when they cause or are responding to a crisis or conflict do satellite publics intersect with wider publics. In this regard, any supremacist and separatist group can be a satellite public.

The fluidity and differentiation provided by Squires's approach give space for identifying the unique ways hush harbors are public bodies. Hush harbors operate inside both enclave publics and counterpublics. A critical mass of people who share a common oppression is the point of departure for hush harbors. A hush harbor can also welcome people from different social locations to form alliances, coalitions, and solidarity for greater collective identity and impact. Squires attests to the power of this vision of multiple publics: "Although still wedded to the idea that there is a Black social group, [it] does allow for heterogeneous Black publics to emerge, and also for people who do not identify as Black, but are concerned with similar issues, to be involved in a coalition with Black people" (Squires 2002, 454). Paying attention to the different types of publics that faith leaders and activists gather is critical. This challenges the entertainment-driven impulse that can make people uncritically believe that every gathering is more about size than substance.

The Challenge of Scale

"Small is good, small is all" (brown 2017, 41). This principle for social justice from adrienne maree brown is critical to understanding the issue of scale within hush harbors. Cultivating a sense of kinship within hush harbors depended on the small scale of the community. The commitment of racialized global capitalism to "go big or go home" flies in the face of the hush harbor commitment to go small. Neither did hush harbors operate by the captivity to the individual of the dominant Western culture. This was no worship of mediocrity or of valorizing small for its own sake. Brown helps identify why going small is powerful: "How we are at the small scale is how we are at the large scale. . . . What we practice at the small scale sets the patterns for the whole system" (52–53). Going small entails developing a strong analysis and practice of groups. The life and ministry of Jesus attest to the power and care unleashed through groups. Jesus spent the least amount of his time with the crowds and most of his time with the three in his inner circle (Peter, James, and John), the twelve disciples, and the seventy-two who constituted what Scripture calls the *oikos*, or the household of faith.

Remember, a hush harbor gathered for a purpose: to meet the needs and change the conditions of a critical mass of oppressed people. Right information, good policies, representative leaders, or a big crowd alone have not brought transformative change for Black or any oppressed people. It takes the people closest to the problem to identify the conditions and seek transformative change. And it takes a group, a powerful and unified group, whose members are actively building their collective knowledge and practices, to change its circumstances. Groups are not reduced to the individuals in them. As the popular saying goes, "The whole is different from the sum of its parts."

Groups take on a life of their own—which means it takes strong facilitation to birth and oversee the unique development of a group's purpose and maturity. We will say more about the type of leadership needed for hush harbors in chapter 4. For now, three characteristics of groups deserve more attention: their size, their stages of development, and where they gather.

Size Matters

Hush harbors were not megachurches. They were composed of a critical mass of oppressed people, but they were indeed small. It could not have been another way because enslaved Africans had to duck and dodge the law, which forbade them from congregating. The historical record suggests that hush harbors were never more than sixty or so people, and they were usually as small as three or four. The size of the group was not determined by numbers as much as it was by a kind of relational knowing—everyone gathered was known and seen and heard. Size was constituted more by shape and experience. Can those gathered sit in a circle and feel like a circle of community? Psychiatrist Scott Peck describes this type of gathering as a "group of all leaders" who embody the "community spirit" (Peck 1987, 50–51). This spirit can be described in many ways. Peck describes it as the spirit of love and peace that is not about the absence of conflict, or a warm fuzzy feeling, but about a space where "the people listen and can hear" and where there is "productive, not a destructive, struggle" (52). Dr. Martin Luther King Jr. describes the spirit of this type of group with the language of power and creativity: "We must not be tempted to confuse spiritual power and large numbers. Almost always, the creative dedicated minority has made the world better" (King 1998, 63). Merely having a small number of oppressed people together in a room does not guarantee authentic community. There was a dynamic relationship between the size and the spirit of hush harbors.

Hush harbors were made possible by being small in size, which was the container for the internal collective human spirit of the oppressed and the external gift of the spirit of fellowship (or koinōnia, as the Scriptures call it) to manifest. It really is a matter of being seen. I (Brandon) can remember many a circle meeting where members arrived heavy laden and departed with lightness and joy. Someone shares a testimony of a traumatic experience they are facing. Another member seeks to listen deeply. The defense mechanisms that we each enter with slowly come down as vulnerability is shared in the speaking and the listening. Tenderness guides each expression as we seek to do no harm, to invite connection rather than to assume it. We each walk away knowing that the healing we experienced was particular to the specific people gathered, people I can call by name and who know my name. This kind of kinship both is a gift and takes intentionality.

Stages of Development

The kinship of hush harbors was not developed passively. What were the group dynamics of hush harbors? What processes were needed to start and establish a hush harbor? No primary source evidence explains the group dynamics of hush harbors. Still, paying attention to stages of group development is critical for any leader seeking to build contemporary hush harbors. Peck offers a theory of group dynamics that centers the building of community and remains open to spirituality. He identifies four stages of what he calls "community-making": pseudocommunity, chaos, emptiness, and community. Pseudocommunity is a form of faking community. Members "attempt to be an instant community by being extremely pleasant with one another and avoiding all disagreement" (Peck 1987, 62). This form of false community is based on pretense, on minimizing the real differences and disagreements within a group and avoiding conflict—going along to get along. Peck says that this characterizes most groups and organizations that claim to be a community.

In my (Brandon's) experience, almost all newly formed groups begin in the pseudocommunity stage. It doesn't matter whether group members are familiar with one another. I was part of organizing a mass demonstration in response to wage theft in Chicago. Movement groups, who were pretty familiar with one another from working together for years throughout the city, came together to form a coalition to organize for a living wage. The energy was high among the coalition in the aftermath of a workers' strike at a local downtown business. The coalition was swift in its decisions and fierce in its public action. We were victorious in supporting the workers in negotiating a new contract with the employer. We celebrated big! Everyone was of one accord, until we had to deliberate about how we would move forward with our work. See, even though we got the contract with one employer, there was still no justice for the thousands of other workers in that industry with different employers. And we discovered in our research that other employers had similar or worse conditions and wages for workers. We didn't want to wait for the next strike before we did something. Our work was not done. But we could not agree on what the next course of action should be or how to go about reaching our goals. During a meeting there was an eruption of arguments, and insults were hurled between members. What was uncovered in that meeting was that even though members were excited about our victory, they had not truly been in agreement with the plan that led to the coalition's success. The argument that day included members exposing criticisms and hurt they'd suppressed early on in order to prioritize the urgency of the moment to organize the mass demonstration that won the policy change. The coalition imploded. It never recovered. We solved an immediate problem. But the coalition was not yet a community.

The stage of pseudocommunity can be a dangerous form of micro-fascism. Peck states, "It is not an evil, conscious pretense of deliberate . . . lies. Rather, it is an unconscious, gentle process whereby people who want to be loving attempt to be so by telling little white lies, by withholding some of the truth about themselves and their feelings in order to avoid conflict. . . . It is an inviting, but illegitimate shortcut to nowhere" (Peck 1987, 64). Once differences and disagreements and even conflict are encouraged and facilitated, a group typically moves into the chaos stage of community-making.

In the chaos stage, differences and disagreements come to light, but instead of trying to hide from them, as in the pseudocommunity stage, the group tries to destroy them. Order and control are the motivation employed by one or more people in the group to try to fix, heal, convert, or win over a particular norm. Peck says, "The struggle during chaos is chaotic. It is not merely noisy, it is uncreative, unconstructive. . . . The struggle is going no-where, accomplishing nothing" (Peck 1987, 67). Often, people in the group will eventually blame or seek to replace the designated leaders of the group. Or the group will seek to enforce some type of organization to fix the prob-lem. But the only way to effectively and creatively deal with the differences, disagreements, and conflict within the chaos stage (or at any point in the group development) is to go through them, to address them head-on at the root, with agreed-on facilitation. To go through the chaos, though, is to enter the stage of emptiness—which entails the emotional releasing of out-comes and a commitment to go through the chaos together as a group, not as individuals or factions.

Peck identifies several emotional barriers that the group must empty it-self of to move through the chaos to authentic community. The group must empty itself of expectations and preconceptions that try to fit the group and individuals within it into a mold of how they "ought to be" that prevents authentic listening and experiencing one another. The group must empty itself of prejudices that seek to put people into categories and thus prevent the emergence of complexity and possibility. Ideology, theology, and solutions become barriers when they function as hard lines of orthodoxy, of in versus out, as *the* path rather than as guides. Members of the group must empty themselves of the need to fix, heal, convert, or solve the issues of people and simply be present with each other to share in each other's suffering or pain.

Sometimes this may even mean letting some members of the group walk away. This reminds me (Brandon) of the work of Harriet Tubman, who is said to have argued with many an enslaved African to join her on the Under-ground Railroad. Yet many did not join her. Whether or not Harriet considered their reasons valid, she could not try to save people if they did not want to save themselves by joining the commitment to collective salvation through the ministry of the Underground Railroad. Harriet had to leave many Black people behind. She is said to have surmised that many of these Black people were so brainwashed by the slaveholder religion and racial caste system that they did not believe they needed to be saved. Because they did not believe that they were slaves in the first place.

In the emptiness stage, the ideas that emerge to try to address the prob-lems are not necessarily bad in theory, but these ideas serve to protect against the discomfort rather than to experience it together as a community. A final barrier, Peck says, is the need to control. This shows up as protecting an individual, the leader(s), or the group from failure or even harm. The logic can often be "If we don't let this get out of control, then we can prevent any harm from happening."

Would Harriet Tubman have freed anyone if she did not allow for any enslaved Africans to disagree with her mission? How would a kid learn to walk or ride a bike if their caretaker prevented them from trying because of the fear of falling or injury? How would a couple ever learn to be together through sickness, betrayal, death, and other loss if their families and loved ones forbid them from marrying because of the fear of them having a broken heart? This does not mean that a group does not seek to create agreements that try to prevent and heal any harm done. However, members of a group can never learn to apply those agreements if they never allow themselves to go through conflict or address disagreements and differences.

Ultimately, emptiness is about death, about sacrifices a person and the group must make of the barriers that get in the way of authentic community. Peck states, "On a certain but very real level we human beings are able to die for each other" (Peck 1987, 76). This death is not physical or forced but instead chosen as a way to live into authentic community, the final stage. Peck describes this stage with words like "soft easy quietness," "peace," "vulnerability," "eloquence," "gentleness," "laughter," and "joy" (76–77). When members are not trying to convert or heal or fix each other, healing and solutions emerge through a community that is born. Communities can have any number of tasks or purposes, but they must be a community for any kind of accomplishment or win to be collectively realized. Peck admonishes, "Community-building first, problem-solving second" (77).

The Importance of Place

Because problem solving so often prioritizes buildings and budgets, not people, money and edifices cannot be the center of how communities understand themselves and their sense of place. Contemporary notions regarding place and faith fail to acknowledge the role of colonialist logics. Modern missions and church planting too often operate with a settler ideology that controls and displaces the original inhabitants—both human and nonhuman—of a place. Theologian Willie Jennings exposes the risks of being agnostic about place: "I want Christians to recognize the grotesque nature of a social performance of Christianity that imagines Christian identity floating above land, landscape, animals, place, and space, leaving such realities to the machinations of capitalistic calculations and the commodity chains of private property. Such Christian identity can only inevitably lodge itself in the materiality of racial existence" (Jennings 2010, 293). This is not the orientation to place within hush harbors. The abundant testimonies of enslaved Africans attest to the value of the natural environment as co-congregant in hush harbors. This orientation is captured well by bell hooks: "Reclaiming the inspiration and intention of our ancestors who acknowledged the sacredness of the earth, its power to stand as witness is vital to our contemporary survival. Again and again in slave narratives we read about black folks taking to the hills in search of freedom, moving into deep wilderness to share their sorrow with the natural habitat. We read about ways they found solace in wild things" (hooks 2009, 48).

The turned-over pot held the passion of their cries and laughter. The logs invited their weary bodies and souls to rest on her lap. Wet, colorful quilts adorned the shoulders of the gathering and every so often whispered "shh" to keep the conversation at a hush. The thickets and branches wrapped their loving arms around those gathered to let them know they were embraced and protected. The river in the distance called to them to remind them that it could be their place of escape. Place was not a blank canvas. There was a mutuality, a reciprocity, between the natural environment of hush harbors and the enslaved Africans who gathered there. Hopkins describes this relationship:

> Talking among themselves brought them power to be themselves alone in the midst of God's created nature—"on the branches." They could only talk when they were isolated in the space of nature's surroundings. . . . But talking and walking in nature without the permission of the plantation authorities granted a true freedom and place for pleasure in the midst of their faith in a protective power greater than themselves. In this time and space, one sees and hears il- legally created new creatures communing in holy greenery ("on the branches") and speaking in a liberated tongue unknown to the masters. (Hopkins 2000, 117)

The mutuality of place will be a challenge for leaders who want to form contemporary hush harbors. An assumption that people gather in a specific place because "this is what we've always done" will fall flat. More creativity will be required to gather a critical mass of oppressed people into a hush har- bor. Theologian Whitney Wilkinson Arreche speaks to the creative exchange between place, purpose, and identity: "Place is not just where we are; place is who we are" (Wilkinson Arreche 2019, 1). Priya Parker, author of *The Art of Gathering*, echoes this rationale when she says that "you should . . . seek a setting that embodies the reason for your convening. When a place embodies an idea, it brings a person's body and whole being into the experience, not only their minds" (Parker 2018, 55). Brick-and-mortar houses of worship can often be a space where the bodies of the spiritually underserved feel most unseen, at risk, and unwelcomed. Leaders wanting to form contempo- rary hush harbors will need to be liberated from the boxes that traditionally determine what constitutes real church: stained glass, pulpits, front-facing pews, a male preacher, clergy, and so on. Cheryl Townsend Gilkes speaks to the dynamic nature of hush harbors: "Many slave churches existed without a black pastor (male preacher). . . . The tasks of worship were not dependent on 'his' presence. Shared notions of 'real' religion were not dependent upon a properly built edifice. . . . The various tasks necessary for adequate worship . . . were broken down and distributed among the members of a congregation according to their talents. *The essence of black religious tradition was completely portable*" (Gilkes 2001, 102, emphasis added).

The portable nature of hush harbors speaks to their transferability, that they are a church on the move. Hush harbors can take place in physical locations as well as online.[9] Group teletherapy in the midst of the COVID-19 pandemic attests to the sense of belonging and impact an online community of care can have. Licensed professional counselor Scott Gleeson was apprehensive about shifting his men's group counseling session online because of the pandemic. After beginning the virtual group therapy, Gleeson commented, "Despite my apprehension, our first quarantined men's group session was one of the best we have had in the nearly two years the group has been running. The reason? There was a true need to connect" (Gleeson 2020). A hush harbor can happen almost anywhere insofar as that place embodies the group's purpose for gathering a critical mass of oppressed people to see one another, care for one another, and seek one another's liberation.

Actuar (Act) / Now What?

Depending on whether you identify as Amos, Lydia, or Ruth, the size, scale, and place of your meeting may be challenging. What are the trade-offs by "going small" and keeping boundaries around social identity in service to cultivating kinship among a critical mass of oppressed folks? What are those boundaries for the oppressed community you gather with? What will it look like for you to attend to size so that everyone is seen, felt, and heard? These questions expose needs that your community will have related to place. What will it look like for your community to be portable and transferable? What will you do so that aspects of the community can be "broken down and distributed among the members"? What risk does this bring? What benefits? Additional questions to consider based on your social location are as follows:

Amos: What will it look like for you to acknowledge and make space for diverse gatherings within your community to meet the needs caused by multiple oppressions that you do not share in common?

Lydia: How will you take responsibility to stay in touch with your own kinfolk (biological and community of origin) as you enter into solidarity

9. For more on virtual hush harbors, see Sampson 2020.

with a (different) oppressed community? What will it look like for you to decenter yourself to be in solidarity with this oppressed community? How will you attend to your needs that cannot be met or centered by this oppressed community?

Ruth: What privileges and access will you have to negotiate and sacrifice to enter authentically into solidarity with the community with which you share a common oppression? How will you be impacted by this self-emptying? How will you guard against self-righteousness and setting up an unhealthy power dynamic with your community (e.g., "Look at all I've given up for you!")?

Our Common Kinship

Two are better than one, because they have a good return for their labor. If either of them falls down, one can help the other up. But pity anyone who falls and has no one to help them up. Also, if two lie down together, they will keep warm. But how can one keep warm alone? Though one may be overpowered, two can defend themselves. A cord of three strands is not quickly broken. (Eccles. 4:9–12)

In the stories of BECs and hush harbors, we have seen a kind of kinship that is not common either in our society or in our churches. Yet BECs and hush harbors were not the same. While they shared the anguish of oppression that results in dying before your time, their contexts and cultures were significantly, even wildly, different. What can we learn for this modern moment from their similarities and differences? We will first look at the markers of kinship and then at the processes of building and maintaining kinship.

What Does Kinship Look Like?

Pandemics cause terrible isolation. An African bishop shared that during an Ebola pandemic, his worst moments were watching a dying mother who, in order to avoid contagion, was unable to hug her child goodbye, and a mother who was unable to hold and comfort her dying child for the same reason (Yambasu, November 5, 2015). During the COVID-19 pandemic, hundreds of thousands of people died alone, separated from their loved ones. These are horrible images. Yet they echo a quieter horror. Many of us now live most of our lives without anyone we can depend on for help, particularly in situations of chronic need. Members of BECs and hush harbors were dirt poor, but their intentional commitment to mutual aid meant that no one associated with them ever had to suffer alone. They accompanied one another in joy and sorrow, in celebration and struggle, in sickness and danger. They went beyond the desperate acts of practical solidarity that occur in all poor communities to intentionally pool resources and share all aspects of life together.

Women leaders were at the center of these communities of holistic care. Black mothers, sisters, aunties, and grandmothers played a key role in hush harbors. BEC scholars and members alike note the preponderance of female leaders. This is not accidental; it is not surprising that if the community of faith becomes a true family, then women have historical capacities and commitments that are relevant and valuable.

We must also note that in both of these movements, the spiritual aspects of life were neither neglected nor separated from all other aspects of life. Family time was spiritual time; God was at the common dinner table. Sharing food when there may not be enough to go around is an act of faith.

What Makes Kinship Possible?

Core Conditions

Three common characteristics of successful BECs and hush harbors may or may not be necessary but are certainly consistent. First, these communities were small enough for everyone to be known personally by everyone else. Second, they were local, rooted in a particular place. Third, they were led by a critical mass of oppressed and marginalized people. This should not be surprising; these characteristics allowed for peer intimacy that organically deepened over time and was not burdened by gross inequalities.

The local aspect of BECs and hush harbors needs a little unpacking. The modern conversation about the value of place often assumes a level of control over where one lives that comes from privilege; it is often about the choice to be grounded in a certain place. BEC and hush harbor members did not have any assurance that they could choose to live in a particular place. In 1980, an oligarchy commonly referred to as "las catorce familias" (fourteen families) owned or controlled the vast majority of arable land in El Salvador (Haggerty 1990) as well as more than 70 percent of private banks, sugar mills, and coffee production in addition to television and newspapers (Hoeffel 1981). Most of their wealth dates back to Spanish land grants from the late sixteenth century, although a few broke into the oligarchy in the eighteenth century through the expropriation of coffee plantations. The basic agrarian economy throughout much of Latin America was a form of feudalism, sometimes modified to include a form of plantation capitalism through sweetheart contracts between elite leaders and international corporations. During the civil wars, members of BECs were disappeared by death squads or fled as refugees. Enslaved members of hush harbors were sold or ran away.

Local for BECs and hush harbors was not about choice or control; it was about being in close enough physical proximity to share life together. There were no commuter BECs or hush harbors. Members were close enough to experience one another's tears and laughter on an ongoing basis. When someone was taken away, the community held those lost family members in their hearts and memories, refusing to let their lack of control over where they lived stop them from maintaining this kind and depth of connection. In Central America, BECs had a ritual for those who disappeared. The members of the BEC spoke the names of the disappeared or assassinated, and the community responded, "Presente" (here). They believed that once people had shared life together, they were always connected. However, with the constant surveillance and risk of being hanged, whipped, or separated from one's family, physical proximity was not always guaranteed. There is no record of how often an enslaved person was able to attend a particular hush harbor. It is likely that each makeshift hush harbor had different participants each time. Thus, even though physical proximity was vital to hush harbors, emotional and spiritual proximity were even more foundational. Memories and names were sites of intimacy even when physical presence was not possible. The local was both physical and spiritual. It is fascinating to think about cyberspace and how the grounded and eternal quality of BECs' and hush harbors' local roots could apply in that context. In the context of the internet, it is possible to maintain intimate relationships with people who are not physically present, potentially allowing for the experience of sharing life together at a distance. However, in the context of the BECs and the hush harbors, the initial relationship was formed locally in sharing daily experiences of the struggle, which then gave birth to a sense of connection that could transcend distance.

Suffering into Liberation

BECs and hush harbors practiced the conversion of suffering into liberation in community. Samuel Solivan coined the term *orthopathos* to describe this alchemy (Solivan 1998). This was shaped somewhat differently in BECs than in hush harbors.

Traditional Spanish Catholicism, as it was practiced in Latin America and the Philippines, made suffering a goal in itself. Argentinian Nancy Bedford refers to this orientation as "dolorismo" (Bedford 1998, 385). Sacrifice was a way of earning God's favor. Psychologically, dolorismo provided a way for people who could not escape suffering to ennoble and transcend it. It provided a form of liberation and dignity to those without other options. BECs took this practice and turned it into a redemptive process of sacrificing for each other's well-being and for the future of the community, laying a foundation of trust that fueled ongoing, lifelong accompaniment. Hiding someone who was escaping government death squads (or even attending the funeral of someone who was killed by the death squads to support the grieving family) could lead to being imprisoned, tortured, or killed. Seeking justice for someone who was being persecuted meant placing oneself at risk. The depth of love involved in this kind of engagement created unbreakable connections. This practice bound people to one another in blood.

In hush harbors, members turned suffering into dancing. They mourned together and prayed together using spiritual songs and African rhythms, moving together until they were healed and had found hope again. Music was also important in BECs, particularly songs that integrated faith and justice, such as the famous *Misa Popular Salvadoreña* (Salvadoran Mass). However, BECs were not known for the passionate and ecstatic expression that characterized hush harbors.

Both BECs and hush harbors manifested the biblical principle proclaimed by Joseph in Genesis 50:20: God can bring good out of evil. Suffering can become liberation, creating powerful kinship in the process.

Holding the Paradox: Safe Havens and Active Reconciliation

Hush harbors were an enclave, a protected space for Black people. BECs were officially open to anyone as a microcosm of the Roman Catholic Church (which saw itself as universal). However, the omnipresence of poverty in Latin America and the Philippines as well as the economic segregation of neighborhoods resulted in the formation of natural enclaves of the poor. In certain parts of Brazil, where BECs had a higher percentage of people who represented the upper economic strata of their poor communities, they were not as committed to responding to the immediate spiritual and economic needs of their members. These BECs ended up losing significant numbers of members to the Pentecostal movement (Mariz 1994, 31–61).[10]

In both contexts, belonging to one of these enclaves could be dangerous if a member was discovered. Hush harbors were illegal. If discovered, participants could suffer retaliation. BEC members' commitment to justice made them targets of oppressive regimes. Carrying a Bible in the street in El Salvador during the civil war could lead to being targeted by death squads,

10. Mariz compares the impact of the Pentecostal movement and that of the BEC movement on poverty and the relative attraction for the poor. As Dr. Juan Martinez, a well-known Hispanic scholar in the US, has often been heard to say, "Liberation theology opted for the poor, and the poor opted for Pentecostalism" (Martinez, May 3, 2019).

with the assumption that the Bible carrier was a catechist with BECs. If there were members with more privilege, they might identify with societal leaders who were allied with the government and therefore could betray other members whose families were involved with the revolution. In a phrase often attributed to Woody Allen, "The lamb may lay down with the lion but the lamb won't sleep well." On a more subtle level, the kinship of BEC members was reinforced by members sharing similar levels of oppression. It can be challenging to create equal responsibility and authority in a community when there are significant power differences between members. Both kinds of communities had to set practical boundaries in order to function. This need for boundaries is an ongoing principle for communities shaped by resistance to the status quo and involving those who are vulnerable to retaliation for any resistance.

At the same time, both movements were shaped by the Christian principle of reconciliation, which requires risk taking. For hush harbors, this was manifested in their inclusion of any enslaved person in their activities with generous and open hearts, and those rare yet real occasions when white people joined the movement, even though any person welcomed into the hush harbors could potentially turn and betray the group. BECs, with more objective freedom to operate, created a highly developed set of practices of private and public reconciliation with traitors and enemies, using nonviolent strategies powerful enough to convert some of their opponents into allies. Mutual accountability practices, including interpersonal confession, forgiveness, and BEC intervention in family conflicts, were standard. Dramatic conversion stories passed around BECs regularly, including stories in which public predators were confronted and changed, or those who had formerly betrayed or violated BECs repented and were accepted back. At the same time, there are also stories of traitors, enemies, and persecutors who did not change. Martyrdom was common, particularly as civil wars or retaliation by oppressive governments intensified. Interestingly, BECs often included members who were actively involved with the revolutionary forces in the civil war in El Salvador alongside members who had a profound commitment to nonviolent change. BECs referred to retaliation against their members as "the cross," whether they were referring to people who were killed through their participation in the revolution or those who were murdered for simply participating in a BEC, carrying a Bible in public, or engaging in active nonviolence. These practices of active reconciliation also have ongoing importance for Christian communities of resistance and reformation. The paradox between creating a safe haven and the call to risky love and reconciliation is an important feature of both movements that provokes and inspires us today.

Conclusion

We are kin. We cannot escape from that truth. We can be a healthy family or a dysfunctional family, but as children of the same heavenly Creator, we cannot deny our familial connection. BECs and hush harbors give us a compelling picture of living into that kinship in ways that enable liberation. Use them as a mirror; use them as a portal; let them call you to a new and more faithful experience of relationships and community.

... 4 ...

Leader-full

Participación

BEC Leadership

"Come, follow me," Jesus said, "and I will send you out to fish for people." (Matt. 4:19)

DON JULIO GUEVARA, who was also a famous fisherman: He wanted to tell him in a word that he was going to be equal to him, right? Jesus was a fisher of men.

And one of the young people said: He looked for country people and fishermen to do his work, not aristocrats. And it's because the workers are the ones who really transform the world and are called to be the masters of the world. Even though a lot of them don't know it; but Jesus, he knew it.

One of the girls: Of course he wasn't going to look for bums, exploiters, parasites of society. He looked for workingmen, people with a job, like these fishers of fish that he made into fishers of men.

And one of the ladies: So they in turn could look for other humble people, that nobody paid any attention to before. People who didn't count for anything. Just like Jesus told Peter to cast the net where he thought there was nothing, and up came a terrific catch.

OLIVIA: Think of this: All us people gathered here used to be scattered, with our own selfishness and individualism, slipping away from each other, as slippery as fish. . . . We're the miraculous catch.

YOUNG JULIO: Well, they went away with him out of the faith they already had in him. And what they were taking away was a marvelous thing, confidence in this miracle worker who performed the miracle of the big catch for them and at the same time the feeling that somebody so miraculous had confidence in them. (Cardenal 1976, 74–75)

Father Dominique Barbe describes BECs in the communities he worked with in Brazil as "overwhelmingly made up of people who work with their hands: mothers of families, domestic servants, workers in industry, the unemployed, those who have retired from work (often at a young age because of sickness), peasants occupying the land without title for generations, agricultural laborers, small farmers, bricklayers, workers on big public projects or with urban contractors building the homes of the rich, migrant laborers and so forth" (Barbe 1987, 89). Father Gregorio Iriarte, in his guide for BEC leaders, describes the "base" of BECs as "la parte de la Sociedad que no tiene acceso al poder (político), al 'tener' (economic) y al 'saber' (scientifico)," which means the part of society that lacks access to power (political), to "have" (economic), and to "know" (scientific) (Iriarte 2006). Iriarte goes on to say that in the BEC movement, people from the base experienced co-responsibility, personal growth, and belonging to a group. This shift from deprivation and a sense of impotence and invisibility to capability and a sense of worth and authority was at the heart of the BEC process and goals.

BECs strived to give all members equal worth, shared decision-making power, training, and significant roles and responsibilities in the implementation of their common mission. In that cultural context and epoch, this proved to be particularly impactful for women (although it had class and racial implications and effects as well). In this chapter, we unpack the daily processes and structures through which these forms of empowerment occurred as well as the underlying beliefs and training/formation that supported them.

Ver (See) / What?

Equal Worth

Egalitarian processes and structures could not be instituted and supported without simultaneously changing the colonial beliefs that BEC members had been taught about themselves and each other. BEC members needed a voice with greater authority than their societal norms to tell them that they were worthy of the justice and peace of their dreams. Cecília Loreto Mariz notes that a foundational belief of BECs was the "egalitarian possibility of revelation" for all believers (Mariz 1994, 138).[1] In a BEC study, anyone has the right to interpret the Bible. Maya Angelou, the African American poet laureate, writes, "For what could stand against me with God, since one person, any person with God, constitutes the majority?" (Angelou 1994, 75). Traditional hierarches are trumped by direct communication with God. The BEC principle that God speaks to and through the marginalized and oppressed through the Bible was an immediate game changer for those from and of the base, blowing open the door to a new status and role in the community and society. Margaret Hebblethwaite shares an eloquent story about this: "An Indian group were examining what it meant that they were all made in the image of God. It suddenly struck them that this was news applicable to their present situation. 'It means that we are the equal of the landlord!' said the men. 'And that we are the equal of you' said the women" (Hebblethwaite 1994, 67). Joseph Healey and Jeanne Hinton add, "It was agreed by everyone that BECs have been a place where women can break the chains of machismo or male domination. One of the great achievements of women in Latin America has been their ability to say to the men, 'I'm off to the BEC meeting; your dinner is in the oven!'" (Healey and Hinton 2005, 35).[2]

Equal access to revelation formed the foundation for a broader concept of equal worth that informed multiple aspects of the daily life and function of BECs.

1. Throughout the history of the BEC movement, this understanding of biblical interpretation has been in tension with the Catholic doctrine of the magisterium. Even the priests who were most engaged in the movement often expressed concerns about whether the degree of freedom of interpretation offered by BECs could result in theological issues (Mesters 1981, 210). A priest in the Philippines said to me (Alexia) in 1984 that "the bishops tossed the football to the people at Vatican II and they ran away with it. Ever since, they have been chasing after them, robes flapping in the wind, trying to get it back."

2. This transition was not always smooth. At one BEC meeting I (Alexia) attended in the Philippines, we were planning late into the night, and one of the male leaders said that he was hungry. All the women immediately stood up and went into the kitchen to start to prepare food, while the men continued planning. Then, in the kitchen, we began to laugh, realizing what had just happened. The women resolved, then and there, to talk to the men over dinner about a more just allocation of domestic responsibilities. Mariz notes that women were always more numerous in the BEC movement. She attributes their relative empowerment to the lack of available men, noting that men often held the broader leadership roles. Ana, of a BEC in El Salvador, describes the situation somewhat differently. She says that the leadership of the women was a matter of principle but still often required a struggle to achieve. In Sierra Leone, male pastoral agents started by organizing men-only groups while female pastoral agents formed women-only groups, and then they switched so that the groups all ended up relatively gender balanced (O'Halloran 1990, 90).

An underlying assumption of the base communities is that there is a funda-mental equality of rich and poor, of powerful and powerless, in which roles can be readily reversed. And so true generosity means empowering people, enabling relationships to change so that the lowly can do things they never imagined would be possible, and so that the mighty divest themselves of the control they have been used to exercising. Then those who have played a pas-sive role, suffering poverty, and possibly receiving others' generosity, move to playing an active role, becoming agents of change, and subjects of history. (Hebblethwaite 1994, 93)

Shared Decision-Making Power

Belief in equal worth, if not supported by new processes and structures, could easily be eaten away by lifelong programming and continued social reinforcement of inequality. A common characteristic across the range of BECs was organization in the form of participatory democracy. Niall O'Brien describes the structures that evolved through BECs, which were unlike the typical form of organization in a Catholic parish of the time: "It was not a coterie of comfortably well-off people from the town making decisions to back their own financial interests. It was not a group of well-meaning lead-ers from the town, trying to guess what was good for the peasants. It was not a clique of ideologues manipulating people into what they, having seen the light, saw as the only solution. It was the elected leaders of the outlying Christian communities who were serving their own people and knew exactly what the hopes, fears, and aspirations of their communities were" (O'Brien 1987, 262).

BECs shared a commitment to review all their structures with an eye toward attaining greater simplicity and increasing the poor's participation and re-sponsibility in the life of the church and the task of evangelizing (Marins 1981, 72). The form of participatory democracy that emerged was not characterized by *Robert's Rules of Order* but rather by consensus. "What the leader of a community must do is to help it to run its affairs on the basis of dialogue and consensus—a process which requires great maturity in the members. They have to sit down in a prayerful atmosphere and calmly talk matters out together so that they come to an agreement as to what to do. The leaders normally make decisions in line with the consensus" (O'Halloran 1990, 99). BEC leaders were intentionally trained in this model through parish-wide or broader retreats led by a variety of groups in different contexts. The trainings were based on and drew from Paulo Freire's methods for critical/liberating pedagogy. His methodology was designed to enable and equip oppressed people to analyze their common experiences and become active agents in their learning process.

Training

In the Philippines, the barefoot doctor program initiated by Dr. Jimmy Tan was one source of training in this model of decision-making. O'Brien describes the results of the training:

> Now these leaders were coming back. The wives and husbands were waiting in the *convento*, and soon after the leaders arrived I could see the change. Until then I had been used to making out the agenda and presiding over the meetings, but now they no longer waited for me to start things. After supper, they divided up tasks among the group: prayer-leader, minute-taker, song-leader, discussion moderator. They made me an agenda and asked me whether I had anything to add. Then they set up a priority for the items to be discussed and allotted a cut-off time. Next came a reading from the Scriptures followed by a short sharing of reflections, and then into the first topic, which turned out to be nothing less than setting up a proper leadership course for our Christian community members. They were going to attempt the ambitious plan of echoing in the Christian communities of Tabugon the six-week course they had received in Ozamis City but they would do it in a ten-day seminar! I realized immediately the logistics this would involve—communicating with all the communities, organizing them to collect the food from each community to support those members who would be going, and so on. Until now, I would never have gone off before a meeting was over. I couldn't—the meeting was me. I would stay on, hurrying them up impatiently, saying that they were taking too long to get to the point, and coming in too often with the solution. But this time I went off to bed and left them still planning.
>
> When the actual leadership seminary began some weeks later, I was delayed and arrived back from the lowlands when it was already in session. The doors of our little seminar house were closed. I walked over to the open window and listened. Inside, two of the returnees, Exor and Junior, were standing. Exor was guiding a discussion. The participants, about twenty in number, had broken into small groups of four. Each group had come to some conclusions which their secretaries were now presenting. Junior wrote the conclusions of each on the board, while Exor asked them to say why they drew these conclusions, drawing out the members of other groups to say if they agreed or disagreed. The discussion was strong, and whenever the groups agreed, Junior wrote the agreed things on the blackboard. . . . I realized that the reason the returnees had progressed quite this fast was not just due to the course but because they had already been trying to give seminars before they went to the course; they had made all of the mistakes and those mistakes were valuable when they went to the course . . . Now they themselves were asking the participants to identify the problems in their communities and they were evoking solutions for the various problems from the participants' own experience, not shoving answers down their throats. (O'Brien 1987, 138–39)

From a parish in Sierra Leone, Africa, we have a report of a similar experience with a training entity known as the DELTA program (also known as the Development, Education, and Justice Awareness program), which was national and sponsored by the Roman Catholic Church. This program built in a reflection-action component, with evaluation and planning every six months (O'Halloran 1990, 89). Pablo Galdámez shares about courses offered specifically for BEC members at the Department of Theology at Central American University. Across BECs, this process used the Freirian concept of dinámicas, visual art, cartoons, or dramatic role-plays designed to awaken participants to key concepts.[3] Formation happened less formally as well, through conversations and dialogue at meetings.

In addition to initial and broader training sessions, BECs also had the option of selecting and organizing training sessions in any area that members felt would be helpful. There are various lists of training sessions from different BECs, but common components included Bible, basic theology, justice and peace, social teaching of the church, catechetics, liturgy, social analysis, integral development, leadership skills, group dynamics and counseling, and practical skills needed for common projects. The purpose of the trainings went beyond mere common participation in decision-making to ensuring that members had the capacity to carry out the tasks of mission.

Significant Roles and Responsibilities

Let us hope that all of us this morning will understand, in the light of the Lord's words, how much one of us can do, even the littlest among us, to respond hopefully and joyfully to the afflictions of this present time. In the midst of tragedies, bloodshed and violence, there is a word of faith and hope that tells us: There is a solution! There is hope! We can rebuild our country! We Christians wield a force that is unique. Let us make use of it. (Romero 1980, 4)

All are equal, but not all do everything. (Boff 2011, 27)

All the members of a BEC jointly took responsibility for accomplishing their mission, as part of their commitment to participación, the full engagement of every member of the community in all aspects of the mission, but they also had a process for wise allocation of tasks. BECs had coordinators or coordinating teams with the responsibility of allocating tasks. This could be an informal assumption of responsibility, or responsibility could be formally granted by the group through a consensus or voting process. Tasks were allocated on the basis of perceived charisms—gifts from the Spirit—which were revealed in the course of group meetings and joint actions. Barbe writes that these gifts were to be used for the common good:

3. We will go into detail on the pedagogy of BECs in chap. 5.

Gifts are revealed when one is put to the test during a struggle. Those gifts are charismata—gifts of the Holy Spirit, grace accorded, in view of service to brothers and sisters for the common good of the collective. In struggle, one person reveals gifts as head, as organizer; another is shown able to speak, to express things clearly; a third discovers qualities as a strategist. Also there appears the person to handle money and plan the budget. Certain men or women reveal awareness of the theological aspects of the struggle, others of the political aspects. Also required are wise ones who can keep in balance different aspects of the struggle of the people of God—family life, the life of activism. (Barbe 1987, 101)

These charisms could be traditionally religious but could also span the range of human capacities necessary for the implementation of a BEC's overall plan. As Barbe explains, "The same persons may take responsibility both for tasks called 'religious' and for tasks designated as human or political betterment; the same one who gives the Bible instruction or who preaches at the Mass may also be the chief union activist" (Barbe 1987, 89).

The lists of charisms and ministries (terms that were often used interchangeably) were reminiscent of the lists of spiritual gifts in the New Testament letters. Common themes arose, but the lists also differed according to context and season. Barbe talks about the phases of a community's plan as moving from a simple focus on learning the gospel and participating in religious activities to participating in broader community improvement to participating in larger political initiatives for justice and peace. Galdámez describes a similar process, with greater emphasis in the first stage on personal growth and deliverance as well as the healing of family and other relationships. In each stage, different gifts and tasks were needed, though some roles continued throughout all phases. *Animadores/as* were in charge of inspiring the community. This verb *animar* means "to encourage" but also has the connotation of animating or bringing to life. The title "animador/a" was coined in the BEC as a way of describing the person who was in charge of coordinating the inspirational aspects of BEC gatherings. Other common roles included ministers of the Word (Scripture teachers, preachers, or evangelists), celebrants (leaders of celebratory events and liturgical experiences and actions), prayer leaders, mutual care coordinators (who ministered to the sick and suffering who were not part of the BEC), ministers of human promotion (e.g., literacy program coordinators, community health workers, cultural workers, cooperative coordinators, or human rights advocates), financial managers, and political coordinators (who supported and guided engagement in the political sphere, integrating theology with action). Some sources mention meeting facilitators or commentators, although those functions were usually managed by the coordination team. Ana, a BEC leader from El Salvador, describes a rotating facilitator position. She also notes that individuals were gradually given greater leadership over time, in the under-standing that gifts emerge through empowerment. Individuals could also be sent for specialized training. O'Brien tells a story of a young man who was sent for drama training to help with role-plays inside BECs and prophetic theater (O'Brien 1987, 220).

Both Mariz and Ana refer to the tensions that could arise because of subtle but significant differences in members' economic and social standing. Ana speaks about having to regularly coax the poorest members of the commu-nity to continue taking on responsibility and participating fully despite their feelings of shame and inadequacy. Mariz states that most BEC members in the areas in Brazil that she studied were from the highest class of the poor-est sector, so they had more capacity to give. (This is not reflected in other reports or research, particularly in the Philippines or Central America.) At times, BECs also integrated professionals, which seemed to function well if a critical mass of the base was still in charge. The following story appears in different versions:

A lawyer came to a community to join with the poor, and to learn from them what it meant to belong to a truly Christian community. Over the years he came to love the people more and more. He began to identify with them to the point that he was bothered by his middle-class status. "I do not want there to go on being this division between us," he thought to himself, "that I am a well-paid lawyer while they are poor bricklayers. I must be brave enough to cross that boundary and accept the same humble position. Then I really will be able to say I am their brother." He went to the community and told them of his decision. "I am resolved," he explained, "to give up my job and my position, and to become truly one with you. I will learn bricklaying from you, and so become more fully a member of your community. I believe that is what God is calling me to do." But as he spoke he saw some hesitation on their faces. He had expected them to embrace him with joy, but instead they held back and were whispering among themselves. "One moment," they said. "We need to have time to talk about this. Please wait while we go away to discuss it." When they came back from their discussion, their faces were still grave. "If this call has truly come to you from God, we will not stand in the way. We must not oppose the will of God. But we have a problem. We need a lawyer. Who will give legal help to us poor people if you are no longer a lawyer? We have talked together and reached a decision. On the day that you leave the law to become a bricklayer, we will choose one of our number to study the law in your place." (Hebblethwaite 1994, 90–91)

Class differences were not the only challenge faced by BECs as they sought to create new processes and structures for power-sharing. Galdámez describes a variety of temptations and desertions. Ana describes the hit taken by the community every time a leader was killed or fled the country. New BECs arose and others disbanded regularly. Barbe notes that it could take up to ten years for a BEC to mature and become stable, pointing out that "it is at least as difficult to shape a Christian community as it is to train its members" (Barbe 1987, 105).

Juzgar (Judge) / So What?

First Corinthians 12 is well known for its description of the community of Christ followers as a body in which all members are essential. Few interpretations note, however, that the chapter goes beyond a call to equal treatment and respect. First Corinthians 12:24 tells the churches in Corinth that "God has put the body together, giving greater honor to the parts that lacked it." Paul then goes on to give the purpose for this special treatment: "So that there should be no division in the body, but that its parts should have equal concern for each other" (12:25). In order for all parts to have equal concern for each other, it is necessary to have an affirmative action policy, giving more honor to those who lacked it.

The early church carried this out in dramatic ways. In Acts 6, the Hellenistic Jews complain because their widows are being overlooked in the daily distribution of food. To understand this situation accurately, it is important to know that Hellenistic Jews by definition had been born outside of Israel and had migrated to the home of their ancestors. They were, therefore, immigrants, who had lesser social status than citizens. Instead of either denying their claim or adjusting the food allocation process, the all-citizen leadership council of the apostles formed a committee to oversee all food distribution. All the members of this committee had Greek (immigrant) names.[4] The shift in power to those parts of the body who lacked honor is dramatic.

Core to both Scripture passages is the understanding that the well-being of the whole depends on the flourishing and full contribution of all parts. Many of our churches are bodies with sleeping parts, people who are not seen (by themselves or others) as having anything in particular to contribute—and therefore contribute little to nothing. While we may give lip service to the importance of all members and permit almost anyone to volunteer, it is rare that marginalized people are chosen for leadership.

A more subtle set of actions that also reinforces privilege and discrimination is evident in the following story: A leader of color was chosen to head a well-known Christian institution in the US, the first leader from his background to have that role. When he was unable to raise sufficient funding for

4. For a clear and compelling presentation of this perspective on Acts 6, see González 1997.

the institution, he was fired. In his book on the roles of minorities in Christian mission, Leroy Barber writes, "In mission organizations funded and led by whites, minorities often have neither power nor influence, even when they hold titular positions of authority. Funders, missions partners, and accountability colleagues may silently, even subconsciously, withdraw their support from leaders of color. . . . Frequently, they are not given backing, confidence or latitude to make mistakes" (Barber 2014, 5). The privileged can be blind to the formation, opportunities, and connections that equipped them to succeed in a particular role, assuming that their capacity is inherent. Ironically, in the name of avoiding discrimination, they do not provide the necessary training or support for a marginalized leader to succeed. When they then fail, the original suspicion that they lacked the inherent capacity is reinforced. The person who fails may also carry that internalized societal perspective, and their sense of themselves as less inherently capable is also reinforced. For marginalized people to compete with privileged people, the playing field must be intentionally leveled, but this is so radically different from the way the world usually works.[5]

BECs assumed that anyone with the charism necessary for a role could learn to carry it out with training and support. They provided the training and support, unexpected people showed consistent competence in a wide variety of aspects of mission and ministry, and teams of marginalized people accomplished remarkable feats on a regular basis. BECs also provided training and support in nonhierarchical processes for group decision-making—a rare skill in most societies.

During the heyday of BECs, several faith communities in the US became destinations for BEC members fleeing intensifying conflicts in Central America. El Proyecto Pastoral at Dolores Mission (a Roman Catholic parish in East Los Angeles) and the Oakland Catholic Worker (OCW) both drew on BEC principles and governance practices brought by their new members. Implementing the power-sharing methodologies of BECs in the US context required developing new structures and processes. In a 2020 interview with Father Brendan Busse, associate pastor at Dolores Mission and the primary point person for Dolores Mission's organizing work, and Roberto Bustillo, Proyecto Pastoral's director of Communidad en Movimiento (Proyecto's community outreach), they described the birth and growth of their BEC network. Bustillo, who had been a secular activist, described how BECs were his first

5. The skewed evaluation of the capacities of marginalized people is also related to a system that requires skills prioritized by the colonizers or other dominant groups in order to succeed in the system they created and maintain. BEC members' capacity to throw off those assumptions and keep only the aspects of those skills that were in fact useful to them was developed through the process of concientización, discussed in chap. 5.

experience with a liberation-oriented church. He had been moved by the new energy for addressing problems in their community that came from the melding of Scripture study, mutual sharing, and community organizing. A wide network of BECs still exists at Dolores Mission; their greatest weakness has come from their success. A multitude of amazing initiatives were birthed out of BECs, including Comite por la Paz, in which *abuelos* and *abuelas* (grandparents) brought tamales and music to gang members on street corners, starting a dialogue that led to an enduring peace pact, and Home Boys Industries, one of the most effective gang intervention programs in the world. However, as Busse articulated, many of these initiatives have now become parish programs or independent NGOs—which also take volunteer energy that could have gone into the process of generating new responses to community issues (Busse, January 15, 2021). One structural difference between the Dolores Mission BEC network and BECs in Latin America and the Philippines is the size of each BEC. The average Dolores Mission BEC includes ten to twelve adults (plus children). The average BEC in Latin America and the Philippines contained 20 to 150 people, including children.

The OCW began to welcome the first wave of refugees from Central America—primarily radical college students who had participated in BECs—in the 1980s. By the end of the decade, they had begun to receive and host BEC members from the countryside. The OCW practiced a consensus model of governance that involved a bilingual leadership circle, which tended to move fluidly between languages. The college students fit right in. The migrants from the countryside, however, particularly the women, tended to say very little in circle meetings. To put into practice the BEC principle of shared decision-making, the OCW organized caucuses before the circle meetings—an initial caucus meeting for just the women from the countryside and then one for all the rural migrants. The translation methodology for the monolingual Spanish speakers also changed from someone translating in a corner to simultaneous translation by translators in the center of the circle. The circle meetings changed. Everyone participated actively, and the dialogue became more profound and the decisions more creative and effective.[6]

The lessons of the leader-full practices of the BEC are fourfold: (1) It is possible, valuable, and faithful for the marginalized to lead in every area of ministry and mission. (The gifts of privileged people are also needed and useful, in their appropriate place.) (2) There is an antidote in Scripture for inaccurate diminishing of the capacity of the marginalized. (3) The effective execution of the tasks of ministry and mission by teams with the necessary combination of charisms is an excellent goal, and it requires discernment and

6. I (Alexia) was a member of the OCW from 1991 to 1994.

intentional skills training. (4) Shared decision-making power also requires intentional formation and training. All these processes take significant time to achieve mastery, requiring a long-term perspective and commitment.

Actuar (Act) / Now What?

Amos

BECs teach oppressed people that in order for them to believe that they are worthy and capable, they must experience their worth and capacity in practical and ongoing structures. (At the same time, they must undergo an intentional process of decolonizing and reforming their consciousness so that they truly believe that the power of the Holy Spirit works through their leadership.) BECs worked to create simple and flexible structures to ensure equal decision-making and responsibility. What might that look like in your context?

They also made sure that everyone had the necessary training and support to perform their roles well. When we are all carrying multiple burdens, it is easy to assume that no one has time for the training necessary to take on all the tasks of personal, communal, and social change. BECs teach them to expect more from themselves, to assume that they can and should perform all the necessary roles if they receive sufficient support, time, and grace to grow, and if they receive integral formation. Discernment of charisms is also essential; not everyone can or should do everything. People who have been told that they are insufficient often have trouble identifying their gifts; in BECs, spiritual gifts and practical gifts were revealed and named in the context of collective action. Who names gifts in your context? Could that be more intentional and expansive, and could it be more closely related to collective action? What kind of training would specific individuals need to develop their unique gifts? How can you ensure that they are sent with the blessing of the community to receive it? In the next chapter, we explore some of the specific formation strategies used in BECs in order to strengthen the leadership of each and all.

Lydia

BECs call us to ruthless self-examination about whether our studies, processes, and structures incarnate the instructions laid out in 1 Corinthians 12 and the practices in Acts 6 for radical sharing of decision-making power and responsibility. Who makes decisions? Who ends up in leadership positions? Who decides who will make decisions and become leaders? We are speaking here not only about formal decision-making but also about the informal conversations in which the first level of decisions are made. Where and when are the decisions actually made? When I was a young mother, I unexpectedly became a single mother. The ministry team meetings of the network that I was involved with typically met for Bible study and reflection at 7:00 a.m. That was where the generative conversations occurred, where problems were hashed out and solutions floated. That was no longer possible for me. However, the majority had voted for the time that was most convenient for them. I was struck at that moment with the understanding that single mothers who might want to give their full gifts to the network were invisible to them. After some conversation, they agreed that they would help fund childcare for me. In BECs, the invisible people became as visible as they are to Jesus.

If you are from a church with primarily privileged members, it is important to ask the questions about decision-making with respect to areas beyond the local church. I remember a conversation years ago between a number of Christian speakers of color and the organizers of Christian conferences. The organizers said that they would be happy to book more speakers of color; they just didn't know any who would draw an audience. We then asked them who was on their committees reviewing potential speakers; we noted that any of us would know speakers of color who could draw an audience. If we were on the committees, we could have solved the problem. Here is another example of how an institutional decision-making process or structure can impede full participation: A major denomination was frustrated that the percentage of Hispanics in denominational leadership did not come close to matching the numbers in the pews, no matter how much outreach they did. They did not realize that their structure allowed a person to become a delegate only if they were representing a church that had reached a certain official status, which required a certain amount of financial contribution to the national church body. The vast majority of Hispanic churches retained the lesser status of missions, even though they were vital and growing in numbers. The policy did not allow these churches to send delegates into decision-making contexts where they could learn how to participate in denominational leadership or be promoted into other opportunities. The structure did not facilitate power-sharing. BECs expected marginalized people to grow into all the leadership positions necessary to run a church, a community organization, and a movement, and they implemented structures that were designed to meet that goal, including sufficient support and formation. The majority of people, as so often proves to be true, met expectations. What do you expect of the marginalized people in your context? What do you do to ensure that their full gifts can be developed and received—to honor those who have lacked honor?

In order to take the gifts and potential of the marginalized seriously, we have to change our image of a leader. The secular constructs of and standards for leadership are often swallowed unconsciously by our churches or organizations. The story of the selection of young David as king by the prophet Samuel in 1 Samuel 16 is instructive. David's father brings out all his older sons first because they are taller and stronger; they look like leaders in that cultural context. God tells Samuel not to pick any of them, saying, "The LORD does not look at the things people look at. People look at the outward experience but the LORD looks at the heart" (1 Sam. 16:7). God's understanding of power and leadership is different; most churches need to ask themselves harder questions about the assumptions they make about both. BECs showed the world what the poor can do. How will you fully build that truth into your ministry?

Ruth

I (Alexia) am on the board of a network of immigrant and nonimmigrant churches that come together to stand with and defend vulnerable immigrants facing detention and deportation. That network could not function without puentes (bilingual, bicultural, Latinx millennial and Generation Z leaders). When the nonimmigrant churches subtly begin to take over and assume that the immigrants are less able, and the immigrants begin to fall silent and pull back, it is the puentes who speak up and set the process straight again. Puentes know that marginalized and oppressed people have so much more to give than is usually recognized—even though the internalized colonial voices in their souls sometimes cause them shame and doubt. A Ruth is a puente. Ruths have the capacity to translate experiences so that the miracle of BECs—their equipping of the poor, marginalized, and oppressed to lead as a team in the church, the community, and the movement—can be seen, understood, and replicated.

Hush Harbor Leadership

Ask most people who a leader is and you're likely to mainly hear about politicians, business executives, entertainers, and clergy. What about the matriarch in the low-income neighborhood who organizes the annual community parade to raise funds for families that are victims of police brutality? The middle-aged man who assists elders on his block with all their home repair projects? The teenage boy who is always calming down conflicts between neighborhood kids by helping them see one another's point of view and actually communicate what they need? These folks are leaders! The hush harbors did not define leadership by the domineering or institutional qualities of the plantation economy. Leadership was much more about using one's talents and resources to wield influence with people—and to do this in ways that were liberative, compassionate, and collaborative. Everyone can be a leader. In the hush harbors this looked like everyone serving in some way, because everyone was somebody, no matter what the surrounding slaveholder culture said.

Ver (See) / What?

Everybody Serves

Leadership is about service. This was certainly the case in the antebellum hush harbors. Everyone was expected to serve. The size of a hush harbor required this principle. There were the material and emotional needs of members to address, as well as the tasks related to the gathering itself. Often, these were interrelated. On the plantation, trauma was like breathing. Where could an enslaved African turn that did not require them to cower and comply? Enslaved Africans carried the bags of trauma with them into every hush harbor gathering. How could the small size of a hush harbor carry those loads? There were no therapists. No social services. No food stamps. The members of hush harbors depended on one another. They carried one another's load, together.

Not only did the size of hush harbors influence the need for everyone to be a servant-leader, but the shape-shifting nature of hush harbors also required agility and adaptability that no one person could handle alone. Hush harbors appeared in diverse settings around and beyond the plantation. There was no telling when and where a gathering might be called. Would this gathering be like the others? Would it be about someone's plot to escape or perhaps about the decision of two young people to marry? Would it be about an elder of the community facing their final days? Or would they be gathering just to laugh and dance about a successful trick played on the slaveholder? Sure, there was a regular expectation that the hush harbor would gather. But there was no religious liberty for the enslaved that allowed them to take for granted *why* they were gathering, for them to just meet to be meeting! Who could accommodate the spontaneity and creativity required to gather the hush harbor under these conditions? Everyone had to put their hand to the plow of organizing and facilitating a hush harbor gathering.

Varied tasks and talents were needed to execute a hush harbor gathering (Harrison 2009, 147–48). Primary sources do not provide much information about logistics. However, much can be inferred based on the narratives of enslaved Africans: naming the convener(s) (the person or persons who called the hush harbor together), getting the word out, preaching, teaching, singing, drumming, humming, clapping, shouting and dancing, greeting, call and response, setup, cleanup, scouting (looking out for enslaved Africans that had run away and white surveillance), caretaking (of the young and the old), devising temporary escape and return plans, guiding people to and from the gathering, and much more. Many of these tasks do not look much different from what is required for most church gatherings. However, there were no hush harbor staff. The responsibilities were shared among those gathered in the hush harbor. These tasks were not carried out casually. Remember, a hush harbor was a site of risk. Most slaveholders and their ministers forbade enslaved Africans from congregating outside of their supervision. Enslaved Africans knew that if they were caught even plotting a hush harbor gathering, they risked being mutilated with the whip or worse. Carrying out these tasks required high risk, and thus the members had high expectations. An enslaved African carried out their role in the hush harbor with deep reverence that entailed the disciplines of both hope and sacrifice.

But a hush harbor's leadership was not focused on only the meeting. Everyone's service was also needed for the work of caring for the wider community of the enslaved when the hush harbor members were scattered back on the plantation in daily life. This speaks to the value of kinship. Members of the hush harbor were part of a wider family network that saw caring for the race as core to its identity as Black, as African. Because of this communitarian identity, the leadership of the hush harbor could not look away from the conditions that created needs among the enslaved community. The hush harbor's vision entailed mutual aid and often went beyond it with a commitment to abolition. In order for Black people's needs to be fully met, freedom was needed—freedom from enslavement and freedom for full political, economic, social, and spiritual agency in the Americas. The leadership for meeting the material, emotional, and spiritual needs of enslaved Africans in the gathering of the hush harbor and on the plantation was a starting point. Leadership for the abolition of slavery was the vision. Chapters 5 and 7 will speak more directly to what this entailed. For now, what is significant is acknowledging that the existential threats and possibilities that were part of hush harbor leadership were grounded in a bold vision, a vision that the way the world is now is not how it will always be—and that it is not the way God desires! Given the boldness of this vision, leadership entailed many things, but most fundamentally it required a movement. Hush harbor leadership meant that *everybody* was serving. It meant reaching the masses of Black people, not just those who were part of the hush harbor. The spirit and embodiment of hush harbors needed to go viral in order to create a movement to abolish the chattel slavery economy.

Everybody Is Somebody

Singular leaders do not build movements. Collectives build a movement. The pastors of hush harbors are unknown. If they had been widely known, what a target they would have had on their backs. Remove a single leader, and everything is undermined (Jones 1990, 163). Building the leader-full culture of hush harbors entailed a deep belief in the somebody-ness of everyone. To be leader-full does not mean being leaderless. Narratives of the enslaved often point to identifiable leaders of hush harbors based on their role of preaching or praying or singing. But the contemporary notion of identifying a church by its senior pastor would have been lost on hush harbors. The leaders of a hush harbor were catalysts, people who inspired and unleashed the leadership in others to care for the varied needs and for the long-term work of abolition (Harrison 2009, 150–51).

The belief that everybody could lead was also evidenced by the role of women and young people in hush harbors. The role of women was both symbolic and strategic. As discussed in chapter 3, Black women were core to the leadership and also represented Africa. Enslaved African women employed the warrior and nurture characteristics of the African feminine in their tasks of mutual aid, culture-making, and safety. Young people were right in the middle of the hush harbor experience as co-participants in the dynamic and expressive worship and spiritual practices as well as in providing care and safety for hush harbors.

Casting a wide net for leadership came with many risks. Many ideas from leaders of hush harbors were sometimes not popular. Leaders such as Harriet Tubman, Denmark Vesey, Nat Turner, and Frederick Douglass (and undoubt-edly countless unnamed others) promoted ideas that must have initially been met with suspicion. Whether using or dodging violence, these leaders' ideas for seeking abolition put them and the enslaved community in great danger. Still, given the pervasive violence of the chattel slavery economy, hush har-bors' leader-full commitment entailed experimenting with any and all ideas that would bring freedom for Black people. That leadership was not bound to membership, title, gender, age, or education.

Juzgar (Judge) / So What?

Leadership as Dialogue

What were the boundaries for hush harbor leadership? The testimonies of enslaved Africans point to conversation as a critical way to discern leadership (Hopkins 2000, 116–17, 120–24). Limitations on congregating and literacy meant that enslaved Africans used what was at their disposal to talk with one another on the planation: Spirituals, drumming and rhythm, storytell-ing, and more. Hush harbors provided a safer environment for talking freely among themselves. There were no governing bodies or institutions on which the enslaved could foist leadership responsibility. They had to decide and lead among themselves. Dialogue with one another functioned as leadership. So much was on the line that everyone had a stake in the ideas and plans for mutual aid and abolition. The following conceptual frameworks lay the foundation for fruitful dialogue.

Caucusing

Black people talk differently when white folks are around. That was true in the antebellum period, and it is true today. Even in a more inclusive and progressive America, where most people have relationships across racial lines, there are just some things Black people will not say or ways they will not say things around white folks. The history of white surveillance is not just history. White fragility derails Black truth-telling. Even when good, freedom-fighting white folks are around, Black cultural ways are not always up for explanation. Black people are rarely interested in giving impromptu history lessons to white folks. The work that Black people and white people must do to dismantle and create alternatives to oppression is often done together. From the abolitionist movement to the fusion populist movement[7] to the civil rights movement, when a multiracial coalition can come together led by Black people to work for the beloved community, it is indeed powerful! However, different work must also be done based on a person's or community's history with oppression. This work requires separate spaces.

Caucusing is a strategy in which people and communities work within their own social identity group to do the healing and justice work tied to their own lineages of oppression. A community can caucus by race, class, gender, sexuality, or another social identity shared by its members. It is always vital to bring the full body of persons back together after caucusing to discuss the themes and patterns within and across caucuses to see where coordination and coalition can happen in the work. Caucusing allows for more free conversation because there are shared cultural ways of being and knowing that do not have to be explained, defended, or discarded. Caucusing also allows people to get specific about history and shared conditions based on social identity and thus creates collective solutions.

In my (Brandon's) ministry and community organizing, people from all racial backgrounds—yes, including Black people—often respond to the call to caucus by saying something like, "How is separating by race helpful? Isn't separation the problem?" Such responses presume that segregation is the primary reason for oppression. They are not immediately able to see how systems they participate in create and reinforce oppression regardless of the racial diversity of a person's relationships. What is typically behind this response is fragility felt by white folks—they feel they are not in control, and that is uncomfortable. BIPOC people have been socialized to believe that white equals better or that proximity to whiteness is what will determine success, so being separated from white people signals deficiency. This is internalized inferiority.

7. This movement is not as well known, especially outside of North and South Carolina (see Chakraborty 2019).

Rather than shutting down the need for caucusing, fragility and internalized inferiority expose the urgent need for caucusing. Any leaders seeking to build hush harbor communities will need to champion both the role of caucusing for dynamic dialogue that generates collective ideas to address problems and the plural leadership needed to carry out those ideas.

Accompaniment

This kind of plural and caucused leadership requires risk taking. I (Brandon) can only imagine the fear and anxiety that enslaved Africans must have felt at being invited to a hush harbor, let alone the ensuing work should they accept the invitation. Taking a leader-full approach to leadership means inviting people into leadership who are not ready-made. They do not check every box of qualifications that institutions expect of leaders. They often lack formal education and specializations. They may not have done the work in the particular context in which they are being invited to lead. On top of the imposter syndrome that anyone would feel at not meeting these institutional marks, who would be excited to step into the kind of leadership that entails the threat of physical, social, and psychological violence? Hush harbor leadership is anxiety producing and trauma laden. Production is not the aim of a leader-full environment. Cultivating a leader-full atmosphere requires a culture of accompaniment that attends to emotional well-being and skill building through on-the-job training for hush harbor leadership.

Accompaniment can take many shapes. Care and coaching are two of them, though they are two sides of the same coin. Care is the emotional side of accompaniment, while coaching is the skill-building side. The distinction is more helpful in theory than in practice. A leader does not seek counsel only for their emotions to the exclusion of the particular leadership situation in which that emotion emerges. The contemporary field of healing justice is replete with a trove of wisdom for those who take on caring and coaching roles for leaders in hush harbor communities. A leading voice in the healing justice movement articulates it this way: "Healing justice . . . identifies how we can holistically respond to and intervene on generational trauma and violence, and to bring collective practices that can impact and transform the consequences of oppression on our bodies, hearts and minds" (Black Emotional and Mental Health Collective 2017). Healing and justice are not separate actions. The work of healing justice is to weave these two together. Healing is rooted in collective actions of justice making. And justice is rooted in the work of healing on personal and interpersonal levels.

Healing justice can look like one-on-one or group spiritual direction with leaders in hush harbors and movements, or it can look like care stations with everything from water to yoga mats to oils and candles set up in the center of protests. The work of healing justice as accompaniment can also look like restorative practice in holding people accountable for conflict, disagreement, or failure, rather than punitive approaches of termination, escalation, chains of command, probation and warnings, gaslighting, ghosting, and canceling. Healing justice looks like asking leaders of hush harbor communities some version of the trauma-informed question "What happened to you?" rather than the traumatizing approach of "What's wrong with you?" Accompaniment entails asking leaders what support they need to live fully into their leadership. That support can look like therapy, professional development, mentorship, or learning new spiritual practices. And it is a delight when the relationships between those providing care and those receiving it are intergenerational, when a young person holds the hand of an elder nervous about their place in the protest, or an elder reassures a young person that they are not their mistakes after an action the young person planned did not go as expected. Accompaniment honors and holds space for personal growth not as an option or an add-on but as critical to what it means to be leader-full in a hush harbor.

Participatory Democracy

Accompaniment is a natural companion to a community that has a rich culture of conversation. Participatory democracy is another conceptual frame that can inform why dialogue was critical to cultivating a leader-full atmosphere in hush harbors. Sure, charismatic figures from the antebellum period, such as Harriet Tubman and Nat Turner, have been seared into our memories. However, hush harbors did not depend on blind faith. I (Brandon) don't believe networks of enslaved people put their bodies and families on the line for freedom only or primarily for charismatic leaders. Enslaved Africans had to count the costs. Charismatic leadership was too expensive a risk. Enslaved Africans collectively decided on their actions to steal away to hush harbors and to plot for abolition. There were no board meetings. No *Robert's Rules of Order*. Their decisions happened through whispers out in the fields. The rhythm of the Spiritual carrying across the quarters signified an opportunity. Not bound by time or authority, the decision-making by members of hush harbors attests that "freedom is an endless meeting," like the title of Francesca Polletta's powerful book on the subject of participatory democracy says (Polleta 2002). Cultivating a leader-full approach to leadership means deliberative conversation is nonnegotiable.

Deliberative conversation is foundational to participatory democracy. What makes such conversation deliberative is that participants' ideas and views are intentionally and thoughtfully included. A deliberative conversation does not

look like a leader sharing an idea with the group as if the idea is up for con-
sideration when in reality the leader has already set up the idea to be acted on.
Getting the best ideas requires engaging in principled struggle over opinions,
over the strategy and tactics and worldview related to any idea. A deliberative
conversation takes time. It means sharing an idea with the group with the
expectation that members will give their actual reasons for supporting or not
supporting it or will offer an alternative to the idea. Every member seeks to
understand each other's reasoning. This is the savoring of an idea. Even if
the idea or the reasoning of a member is not your preference, you mull it over
out of respect for the intellectual and emotional labor of your fellow member.
The goal is not unanimity or uniformity but open and respectful discourse.
Members of the group develop skills of strategizing and building collective
leadership and collective ownership of decisions. This subverts practices of
authoritarianism, hierarchy, or loner activism. The frame I (Brandon) learned
to use for this type of consensus building is to ask member-leaders to choose
one of the following to reflect their orientation toward an idea or decision:
love it, like it, live with it, or loathe it—and then to back it up with reasoning. Typically a decision moves forward if no one among the decision-making
body loathes the decision.

Participatory democracy develops three key characteristics in groups: solidarity, innovation, and leadership development (Polleta 2002, 9–10). Participatory democracy theorist Michael Menser says that "participatory democracy
is not just about having a voice. . . . [It] is about sharing power . . . wielding it
not over others, but with them" (Kolokotronis 2018). Hush harbors could not
be sustained and do their subversive work if they functioned by replicating
the oppressive power dynamics of the plantation church and economy. This
is not to say that hush harbor members did not carry oppressive leadership
ideas with them. As the old saying goes, it is often harder to get Egypt out
of the people than to get the people out of Egypt. More will be said about
healing the consciousness of enslaved Africans in the next chapter. For now,
what is critical is that there can be no negotiating with the master's tools
if true liberation is the aim. Tolerating power over one another would have
undermined the very purpose for stealing away. Likewise, leaders who want
to cultivate contemporary hush harbors will need to challenge a culture of
powering over. Practicing participatory democracy through deliberative conversations will strengthen the muscles of the membership body to share power
as a team of leaders.

Leadership as Facilitation

CEOs did not build hush harbors. It takes a skilled facilitator to embody
and cultivate a leader-full culture. Facilitation is a lost art. Calling on people

to talk and keeping track of the time, though important tasks, are not facilitation. Brainstorming sessions are important, but they are not facilitation. Facilitation is not about being casual or chill. A chill facilitator is self-serving rather than serving the group. Priya Parker says that the chill facilitator "abdicate[s] leadership." They "don't eradicate power. [They] just hand the opportunity to take charge to someone else" (Parker 2018, 76). Facilitation is about making a group work more easily or making something happen more easily.

In their book *The Starfish and the Spider: The Unstoppable Power of Leaderless Organizations*, Ori Brafman and Rod Beckstrom call these facilitator types "catalysts" and "champions." The catalyst "gets a decentralized organization going and then cedes control to the members" (Brafman and Backstrom 2006, 92). The catalyst facilitates the creation of a hush harbor, connects the people, makes sure they have what they need, and then moves out of the way, giving the power, ownership, and responsibility to the members to move the group forward. The catalyst is still relevant as an inspirational figure and as someone who is connected to the animating ideas of the group, but they do not grab and hold on to the power. The champion is a person who takes the baton from the catalyst and makes the long-distance run. The champion "is relentless in promoting" and "inherently hyperactive" (99, 100). While catalyst facilitators create a hush harbor, then let it go, the champion facilitators sustain and develop the hush harbor. Champions are impacted by and believe so much in the vision that they can't help but talk about it, keep the people involved connected, and enlist new people. They too are facilitators because they do not keep only to themselves the power of knowledge about the hush harbor; they distribute it. These definitions barely touch the tip of the iceberg. Facilitation is better described than defined.

The world of nature is most illustrative of the art of facilitation. Ants stand out as a powerful metaphor for facilitation. In *Emergent Strategy*, brown writes, "Ant societies function through individual ants acting collectively in accord with simple, local information to carry on all of their survival activities. Every ant relies on the work of others in producing their own work" (brown 2017, 45). She adds that "ants tell each other where food is, not hoarding individually, but operating on a principle that the more of them that gather the food, the more food they will have as a community" (86). The operating system of ant societies is the magic of facilitation. The key question that ant societies raise for cultivating a leader-full environment is, How do you get individuals to act collectively?

Facilitation is interdependence and adaptation. A skilled facilitator operates on simple rules and high trust with a group to birth a community that can fight with grace, that can eat with everyone getting their share. A couple of key principles root skilled facilitation; we explore them next.

Generous Authority

A facilitator is someone who governs with generous authority. Parker explains, "A gathering run on generous authority is run with a strong, confident hand, but it is run selflessly, for the sake of others. Generous authority is imposing in a way that serves. . . . It is using power to achieve outcomes that are generous, that are for others. The authority is justified by the generosity" (Parker 2018, 81–82). I (Brandon) can imagine the leader of a hush harbor going around the slave quarters at night, checking in with everyone, with a whisper, to see how everyone was feeling about the meeting or to let them know that something special was going to be discussed, maybe a plot to run away, or that a ritual to bless the transition of an elder from life to death was going to take place. Maybe this leader asked each person if they had invited anyone else, and if it was someone new, why they had invited them. I can imagine many nonverbal signs of affirmation and encouragement—hugs, warm stares, clinching of hands. A facilitator's generous authority looks like going out of their way to cultivate connection and consensus among those being gathered, even before the gathering. It looks like checking in on how members are entering the gathering, sharing information and asking for input, getting a sense of why people are showing up, and asking people to bring this or that item or attitude based on what the facilitator hears is needed for the gathering to be whole. A facilitator may invite each person to check in on another person they know is planning to attend. Imagine the risk each time they gather. Having someone, in addition to the facilitator, check in with you was a welcome form of encouragement. The facilitator forms the space in the woods for intentional connection, putting the log seats in a close-knit circle, shaping the gathering to serve all that people are bringing with them and wanting to get out of their time together. After all, it is not the facilitator's gathering; it is the people's gathering, and the facilitator is part of the people. Efficiency is not the goal. Neither is urgency. Generous authority means taking the time before, during, and after the gathering to collect the fragments, to build deep unity, to collectivize the work.

Trust

Leading with this kind of generosity naturally builds trust among the group being gathered. And trust was the social contract of hush harbors. Imagine the facilitator of a hush harbor trying to gather people for this risky mission who do not trust the facilitator or one another. Just like an organized lie is pervasive, trust is contagious. "If you trust the people," writes adrienne maree brown, "they become trustworthy" (brown 2017, 214). Trust is built through facilitators creating safe spaces for those gathered to bravely be their authentic selves. Not having a single charismatic leader was a form of protection. Having one charismatic leader would have put a hush harbor at higher risk—there would have been more of a target on the hush harbor itself. Shared leadership provided a sense of safety inside of what was already the risk of stealing away to the hush harbor. Members of the hush harbor could truly be themselves because the violent hierarchies of the plantation did not govern the hush harbor. Hush harbor members said no to the scripts of plantation religion—the domineering religious leader, the theology that only some heard from God or could speak for God, those who were committed to respectability that concealed disloyalty and hubris. By saying no to these deadly ways, facilitators and members said yes to a space where everyone could speak or be silent, everyone could dance or moan, everyone had a role. Conditions were created that normalized bravery. Facilitators and members cocreated a space with the discipline of trust where reclining into the Spirit and into community and into freedom dreams was not otherworldly but instead strengthened their existing social bonds and helped them to see real possibilities on the horizon.

Actuar (Act) / Now What?

Leadership models in the West have been deeply influenced by corporations. The leadership models of hush harbors subvert this corporate orientation. How will congregations and organizations function apart from the singular leader model? What does a leader-full approach invite members and volunteers and constituents to do differently? What needs to shift to cultivate a culture of dialogue in organizations and congregations? Who are the natural facilitators, the catalysts, the champions in your congregation, organization, community? What impact do you believe cultivating their leadership would have on your congregation, organization, community? Additional questions to consider based on your social location are these:

> Amos: What would it look like for you not to settle for the homegrown hero mantle and instead build up the leadership of the multitude of your kinfolk?
>
> Lydia: What is at stake for you when you are not allowed to lead from the front line in hush harbor spaces? What leadership roles that are not out front can you envision for yourself?
>
> Ruth: What social capital and skills can you distribute to your kinfolk so that you are not a token minority because of your formalized and professionalized leadership background?

A Common Leadership

In military contexts, hierarchy is necessary. On a battlefield, when there is danger and lives are at risk, the group needs the unity that comes from command. People with no military experience can agree with this perspective as well. However, there are alternative ways to exercise effective leadership in a crisis. For example, when an earthquake hits, a tornado blows, the floodwaters rise, everyone pulls together. It's every person on deck, using all their energy and gifts to help in any way they can.

Immediately after the Indonesian tsunami in the Aseh region, a local organization of survivors turned the automatic and organic moment of mutual aid into an intentional and ongoing structure of participatory democracy. They built tent schools with volunteer teachers and pooled resources to revive microenterprises (Ismet, Hazan, and Kenny 2018). BECs and hush harbors embodied a similar response to the disaster of injustice. Members knew that they needed all the energy and gifts of every member. They also needed the creativity and wisdom of every member in the decision-making process, including every generation and gender. Decisions were made in dialogue and by consensus.

This does not mean that BECs and hush harbors were leaderless. They were leader-full. A postcard I (Alexia) once received from the Rockwood Leadership Institute read, "We don't need a leader to get us out of this mess; we need thousands of leaders." Leadership in BECs and hush harbors was responsive and fluid. Tasks were allocated as gifts were needed and revealed through the process of common action. There were always those who coordinated and those who catalyzed—but in a context in which sudden murder was a common risk of membership, it was necessary that no one owned those roles. The constant building up of new leaders required a spirit of generosity over judgment and the encouragement of experimentation. The common understanding of Christian faith as an adamant proclamation of the miraculous potential in every human being, particularly those who had been marginalized and despised, served to lift people up and weave them together.

BECs and hush harbors were also realistic about the need for training and mentoring. As part of the Catholic Church, BECs had access to spaces for formal training that were not available to hush harbors. However, this made BECs vulnerable to decisions made by the broader institution. For example, a pope who opposed BECs had significant power to damage the movement. Both BECs and hush harbors depended on informal mentoring that facilitated leadership development. In healing spaces of relative safety and intimacy, leaders had opportunities to stand up and take initiative.

··· 5 ···

Consciousness

Conscientización and el Mensaje de Liberación

BEC Consciousness

OLIVIA: It's on account of these gifts from the wise men that the rich have the custom of giving presents at Christmas. But they give them only to each other.

MARCELINO: The stores are full of Christmas presents in the cities, and they make lots of money. But it is not the festival of the birth of the child Jesus. It's the festival of the birth of the son of King Herod. (Cardenal 1976, 35)

Biblical exegetes, using their heads and their studies, can come fairly close to Abraham; but their feet are a long way from Abraham. The common people are very close to Abraham with their feet. . . . When they read his history in the Bible, it becomes a mirror for them. . . . In a real sense, they are reading their own history, and this becomes a source of much inspiration and encouragement. One time a farmworker said to me, "Now, I get it. We are Abraham, and if he got there then we will too!" (Mesters 1981, 203)

In this chapter, we are going down into the weeds. We plan to examine the details of the methods that BECs used to work their miracle of empowerment. These methods were built on the work of the great Brazilian educator and educational philosopher Paulo Freire, but the BECs' secret was the integration of his principles with a specific approach to Scripture. To understand the integration, we must first have some sense of the Freirian methodology.

Paulo Freire was born in 1921 in Recife, Brazil. Although he came from a middle-class background, through the Great Depression of the 1930s, he directly experienced the impact of hunger on a child's capacity to learn. Later, as a professor at the University of Recife, he became the coordinator of the adult education program of the popular culture movement. Its goal was to combat illiteracy. He realized that the traditional process of education, which he referred to as "banking" (limiting the scope of the student's action to receiving, filing, and storing deposits), was not going to be as effective as engaging the students in a more holistic way—as subjects of the learning process instead of objects of the educational system. He also believed that the banking process served to strengthen the psychological mindset that impeded effective opposition to oppressive systems. The meta-message of a passive education was that students had little to contribute to knowledge, causing them to devalue their own experience and perspective. Conversely, if students were encouraged to value their own and each other's knowledge and wisdom, they could throw off the disabling lies that kept them from challenging oppressive systems. The goal of education was praxis: "the action and reflection of people upon their world in order to transform it" (Freire 1992, 52). The following interchange between Freire and a group of peasant farmers provides a snapshot of the process:

> "Fine," I had told them. "I know. You don't. But *why* do I know and you don't?" . . . Suddenly their curiosity was kindled. "You know because you are a doctor, sir, and we're not." "Right, I am doctor, and you're not. But, *why* am I doctor and you're not?" "Because you have gone to school, you've read things, studied things, and we haven't." "And why have I been to school?" "Because your dad could send you to school. Ours couldn't." "And why couldn't your parents send you to school?" "Because they were peasants like us." "And what is 'being a peasant'?" "It's not having an education . . . not owning anything . . . working from sun to sun . . . having no rights . . . having no hope." "And why doesn't a peasant have any of this?" "The will of God." "And who is God?" "The Father of us all." "And who is a father here this evening?" Almost all raised their hands and said they were. I looked around the group without saying anything. Then I picked out one of them and asked him, "How many children do you have?" "Three." "Would you be willing to sacrifice two of them, and make them suffer so that the other one could go to school, and have a good life, in Recife? Could you love your children that way?" "No!" "Well, if you," I said, "a person of flesh and bones, could not commit an injustice like that—how could God commit it? Could God really be the cause of these things?" A different kind of silence. Completely different from the first. A silence in which something began to be shared. Then: "No. God isn't the cause of all this. It's the boss!" (Freire 1992, 39–40)

Freire's other contributions included the following:

- analysis of the nature and consequences of the psychological internalization of the voice of the oppressor[1]

- the refinement of the concepts of concientización (an analysis of reality in terms of the nature, impact, and root causes of injustice in a specific context), the reflection-action cycle, and praxis[2]

- dinámicas—the use of images, arts, games, and role-play to provoke awareness, enable the articulation of experience, and surface and combat the internalized voice of oppression

Members of BECs used these principles to practice concientización, to become more aware or conscious of the social, economic, and political structures and systems that impacted their lives. They did this through an activity referred to as naming "reality." They then analyzed what they discerned in light of Scripture, a practice that can be described as el mensaje de liberación, the message of liberation. Because many members of BECs were functionally illiterate, dinámicas were particularly useful in the study of Scripture. Here we explore the practices of concientización, el mensaje de liberación, and integration and application to see how members sought to become creative agents—subjects, not objects—in the world.

Ver (See) / What?

Concientización

To better understand their place in the world, members of a BEC gathering, after song and prayer, engaged in an activity often referred to as naming

1. Internalized oppression is the phenomena in which a person's self-understanding and framework for understanding the world are formed through the experience of oppression. It is a form of programming, intensified by the objective dependence on the dominant sectors of society for survival. If uncorrected, it keeps oppressed people from standing up to their oppressors or fully valuing each other.

2. The concept of concientización existed before Freire's work, but he explored and deepened the understanding of the process of learning to pay attention to all the aspects of reality that affect the life of an individual and a community, including the truths that are often obscured by internalized oppression. Freire also taught that awareness comes through action, not only through reflection. It is the rhythm of the cycle of reflection and action, planning-implementation-evaluation, that deepens the knowledge of reality. Praxis can be defined as action with reflection; as a person carries out an action, they hold in mind the strategic intention of the action and seek to learn from the experience while in the midst of it.

"reality." Reality was the common experience of the base in a given place and usually focused on their common problems and challenges. The group's awareness and analysis of reality were evoked by dialogical facilitation—not taught by an expert or an ideologue. The goal of this process was not only to understand the realities and roots of the injustice they were experiencing but also to grasp the potential for change. "*Communidade* members have begun to understand that their reality is not a divine 'given.' They are seeking to understand it, not so that they can accommodate to it more efficiently or functionally in order to attract new followers, but in order to change reality as an integral part of their Christian witness" (Cook 1985, 90).

The process of naming reality began with the sharing of daily life experiences and was followed by the news. The news may have been merely local or may have included a broader, even global, dimension as reports were shared from other BEC communities or larger BEC assemblies. In the early phase of the formation of a BEC, the participants also created a diagram of relations, presenting a map of their families, friends, colleagues, neighbors, and regular contacts. In the process, they discovered common connections. Through sharing daily experiences and their map of relationships, they began to elevate the importance and value of their lives by making them visible in the context of a group. A common exercise was called "Who am I?" In the exercise, each person first answered the question independently, and then the question "Who are we?" was posed to the group so that their commonalities were lifted up and underlined.[3]

Here are two examples of the insights gained through the activity of reality:

Carlitos [a 5 year old son of a BEC member] taught us that sickness wasn't the result of irresponsibility. Sickness came from unsanitary conditions. And unsanitary conditions were the result of poverty. We also discovered that children's sicknesses were almost always due to malnutrition. And we learned that children weren't malnourished because their mothers were irresponsible. They were malnourished because their mothers were poor. (Galdámez 1983, 22)

Felix was in his teens, the second of nine children. Nobody in the family had a job, and we couldn't understand how they managed to survive. Then Rodolfo got Felix a job as a bricklayer's helper. Felix showed up for work and then came to us for advice. "What shall I do? The boss says I start next week. He took me on because Rodolfo asked him. But to make room for me, he has to fire another guy. I don't know what to do. I need the job to help my family. But so does the other guy! What should I do?" No one in the community could answer him.

3. The details of the BEC process are included in multiple sources, including documents written by Dominique Barbe, Gregorio Iriarte, José Marins, Carlos Mesters, Niall O'Brien, and Guillermo Cook.

The only answer was a cruel one: One person's bread is another person's death. I remember that this was when we started reflecting more deeply on personal sin and what the structures of sin are. (Galdámez 1983, 47)

The process of analyzing a given reality was not accomplished in one session. It could take the form of reflection-action, beginning with an initial analysis of the problem, which resulted in a plan, implementing the initial plan, and then reflecting further on how to improve the response. Included in the evaluation was any additional information that had emerged about root causes and other aspects of the problem. This would then result in a new plan, starting the cycle over again.

The reflection-action process could also be organized systematically; the BEC could create a pastoral plan (to be evaluated every six months) after taking an extended period of time to complete a community analysis (O'Halloran 1990, 76). The reflection-action cycle typically started with small and simple actions but ended up carrying the group into engagement in broader movement struggles. Cecília Loreto Mariz notes, "The first step in CEB [BEC] grassroots mobilization is a description of everyday needs and hardships. But deprivation without a political orientation does not create political motivation. Alice, a teacher, and Margarida, a housewife, are both widows and CEB leaders. Both women became concerned with the need to organize poor people in order to obtain their rights as well as social improvements. Both had seen injustices before coming to the group, but only after reflecting on those injustices in the CEBs did they perceive them as a political problem" (Mariz 1994, 114).[4]

BEC's dialogues arrived at broader goals through a process of constant evaluation (Marins 1981, 41). In the Philippines during the movement for democracy against the Marcos regime, BECs carried out a process called CSE (Critical Self-Evaluation). After every activity, the members evaluated not only the overall success or failure of the activity but also their own participation. Each person would name what they had done well and what they could have done better, and then the group would confirm, nuance, or challenge what they said. The commitment to humility and constant learning was a basic requirement for participation and influenced overall leadership practices.[5]

4. BEC trainings provided through different Catholic structures incorporated social science tools for analysis. These could include a dialectical analysis of socioeconomic reality adapted from Marxism and/or tools taken from the sociology of knowledge and frameworks—such as the see, judge, act model—drawn from the Catholic Action methodology. A central tool was the breaking of the plausibility structures that explain and justify the status quo through ideological suspicion, rooted in praxis. For a comprehensive analysis of the BEC use of social science methods, see Cook 1985, 91–94.

5. This is based on my (Alexia's) personal experience as a BEC member in Manila, Philippines, from 1986 to 1987.

El Mensaje de Liberación

After coming to grips with a particular reality, members analyzed that reality in light of Scripture, viewed from the perspective of its core mensaje de liberación (message of liberation).

> We knew we had to proclaim the kingdom of God, and we had to learn to read the signs of God's coming into people's lives. . . . A few gains, a few "miracles" and some people's euphoria knew no bounds. It was just as when Jesus had multiplied the loaves: for some, Jesus was the one to follow all right—but only because he ran a cut-rate bakery. The same thing happened to some of us. The day when our little school, smack in the middle of the slum, was finished, some people could only see all those bricks that had been laid. . . . But this shouldn't have been enough. The little school, the co-op—these things ought to have created community for a further purpose, for greater commitments. So this was a challenge. The community readers had the mission of reading these signs out loud for everybody to hear. Their job was to drag us out of our illiteracy. (Galdámez 1983, 35)

This activity often began on a personal and intimate level. Dominique Barbe talks about sessions in which the next activity after sharing daily lives was "telling the past," going over their personal autobiographies in relationship with historical events and asking where God was manifest in both, discerning "signs of grace" (Barbe 1987, 98). Groups that used this exercise then moved to evoking the future, naming their hopes and dreams (for themselves and for their community), and then articulating the obstacles, the potential solutions, and the promises of God in Scripture. These groups were strengthened in their faith by this process, making it possible for them to move toward solutions. Barbe describes this process as a "gentle and gradual pedagogy" (97) showing the people their intrinsic worth and their potential for abundant life.

In order for people to discern signs of grace, they had to know the Scriptures. Bible study was the core of every BEC meeting. However, Bible study was done with the goal of interpreting not the Bible but rather life with the help of the Bible (Mesters 1981, 205). BEC members were allowed to free associate, drawing natural connections between the lives of the biblical characters and their own lives. Both the agrarian backdrop of the Bible and the experience of overt injustice practiced by economic and political leaders were familiar to them. "The Bible is in some sense the ideal mediation: it allows all those who live in oppressive situations to find themselves in a character of the Bible who lives the same reality, and thereupon to see how grace operates in salvation in them and in us—a true liberation of the whole being, individual and social. (Zacchaeus, that's me! I am Magdalen!)" (Barbe 1987, 99). Here are three poignant examples:

Once in Goias, we read the passage in the New Testament (Acts 17:19) where an angel of the Lord came and freed the apostles from jail. The pastoral worker asked the people "Who was the angel?" One of the women present gave him the answer: "Oh, I know. When Bishop Dom Pedro Casaldaliga was attacked in his house and the police surrounded it with machine guns, no one could get in or out and no one knew what was going on exactly. So this little girl sneaked in and without being seen, got a little message from Pedro, ran to the airport, and hitched a ride to Goiana where the bishops were meeting. They got the message, set up a big fuss, and Dom Pedro was set free. So that little girl was the angel of the Lord. And it's really the same sort of thing." (Mesters 1981, 207)

The catechist from Managua was showing them a slide of a conventional, Spanish-style crucifix—a very bloody portrayal—and she was asking simple questions about what they were seeing. At first, the answers came slowly. Then, one woman began to speak more fluently. "It shows Jesus shedding his blood for us," she was saying, and then she suddenly became very agitated and burst into tears: "And that is what my son did—he shed his blood for us. He fought to free us from the Contras, and they killed him. He shed his blood like Jesus and he is dead, and I don't know how to go on living. I pray that God may help me to forgive his assassins, but I find it so hard. . . ." Another woman went to fetch her a glass of water, and the catechist from Managua—who had also lost a son in the war—gently spoke. "On the cross, Jesus said 'Father, forgive them, for they know not what they do.' That is our example. We have to say with Jesus, about the death of our sons, 'Father, forgive them, for they know not what they do.'" (Hebblethwaite 1994, 69)

Why did Jesus *choose* to be born poor and humble? "Maybe," said one woman, a mother of ten of whom three had died and only two were working, "maybe it was to show those rich people that we are important too." A ripple of excitement ran through the room. Was God really making such a clear statement about *their* humanity? About their *rights* as people? The discussion progressed, but with an electric charge in the air. Half an hour later, a young woman said, "I think that God chose his son to be born like us so that *we* can realize that we are important." (Cook 1985, 121)

While the entire Bible was studied in BECs, the Gospels were seen as critically important,[6] and Jesus himself was central. Guillermo Cook quotes José Comblin, a pastoral agent, as claiming that "the content, import, and underlying norm of mission is Jesus himself" and goes on to note that in BECs, the "proclamation of the gospel, in word and action, is both the *announcement* of salvation and liberation in Jesus Christ and the *denunciation* of the structures

6. *The Gospel in Solentiname* by Ernesto Cardenal consists of 634 pages of transcripts of Bible studies in a BEC, all focused on texts from the Gospels.

that oppress and alienate humanity. It is both re-evangelization of the masses of nominal Christians and prophetic confrontation with repressive powers" (Cook 1985, 106). Two stories eloquently demonstrate the meaning of faith in Christ on the ground for BEC members:

> A CEB member, a migrant worker in the booming construction industry in Brazil, answered my question, "What does Christ mean to you?" In his thick peasant accent he replied: "Christ means everything to me because he accompanies me in all my problems. . . . He helps me to bear my problems." He raised his hands in an eloquent gesture as if to say, "What more is there to say?"

> After an entire *communidade* in a small town was arrested and brought before the local police chief on charges of subversion, he demanded to be told who was behind them, guiding and manipulating them. They at first replied, "Nobody. It is all of us you see here." The police, unconvinced, insisted, "Take me to your leader." They answered, "The one who encourages us and guides us is our Chief. It is our Lord Jesus Christ!" (Cook 1985, 81)

As BECs studied the Bible, they found in the Word of God, in the words of Carlos Mesters, "a reinforcement, a stimulus for hope and courage. . . . Bit by bit, it helps people overcome their fears" (Mesters 1981, 200).

Many of the members of BECs were functionally illiterate. The Scriptures were read and studied aloud. However, BECs also realized that even people who were literate needed both right-brain and left-brain input in order to fully comprehend complex realities. Freire created a system of pictographs that related to the daily life of his students to teach literacy. BECs used art, song, drama, and role-plays both to open up dialogue about the meaning of Scripture and to confront the full import of their reality. Dinámicas included participatory exercises that engaged multiple senses and encouraged creativity. (We will talk more about this process in chap. 6.)

The freedom given to BECs to arrive at their own interpretation of the Bible was risky from a theological perspective. Niall O'Brien describes the danger well: "Did we not risk their falling into a combative fundamentalism on the one hand or being co-opted by a narrow, dogmatic Marxism on the other, well capable of using the Scriptures for its own purposes?" (O'Brien 1987, 132). BEC leaders sought to lessen these risks through constant evaluation in the context of reflection-action. The communal test of their interpretations in daily experiences helped them question both biblical and political literalism. In doing so, they found the core message of Scripture to be relatively clear and simple. In the words of one community, "What is difficult about the Bible are not the passages that one doesn't understand because those are not binding. What is most difficult are those passages we do understand and because we understand, we are committed to translating them into action and into our lives" (Marins 1981, 61). Individual BECs were also part of a broader network and an overarching church structure that tended to hold them within a foundational set of orthodox Christian beliefs. Of course, as Cook reminds us in his comparison of historical Protestant movements and BECs, the tension between the freedom to discover new spiritual insights and the continuity with the history of orthodox interpretation is endemic to all renewal movements in the church (Cook 1985, 235).

Integration and Application

Members of BECs did not merely analyze their reality and reflect on Scripture. They intentionally integrated these processes, beginning with the reality, moving to Scripture, and then exploring the whole picture with regard to their potential and ongoing actions, individually and as a group. Mariz and O'Brien both speak about the psychological impact of this process. Mariz notes that BEC members she studied were better able to cope with the psychological effects of poverty, even before they achieved any objective results, because of the process of organizing together to improve their lives (Mariz 1994, 116). O'Brien talks about a BEC meeting that trained people about their legal rights.

> We trained the people to know their rights, and if they had to meet a judge, a landowner, a barrio captain, a lawyer, to discuss the whole thing carefully beforehand. They would even act out the possible reactions of their adversary and in this way get used to absorbing anger. We asked them to sign nothing unless it was in Ilongo and until they had first taken it home to show the community. By doing this, we were undermining the feudal mentality which kept so much of the system in place. Victory was the process more than in the product. In fact, in one sense the process itself was the real product. (O'Brien 1987, 200)

It is important to understand that even though each BEC meeting incorporated the three phases of conscientización (analysis of reality), el mensaje de liberación (reflection on the Bible), and integration and application, members did not always spend the same amount of time on each. James O'Halloran describes BEC meetings as being responsive to the real needs of the people at that time—one meeting could focus more on analysis, one on planning. Freedom and flexibility were key (O'Halloran 1990, 114).

Juzgar (Judge) / So What?

Liberation theologians, proponents of Misión Integral (transformational development), postcolonial missiologists, and a wide variety of progressive church leaders proclaim the importance of the voice from the margins for theology and ecclesiology. However, in practice, that often means that professors and other highly educated authors and thought leaders (who may have less privilege than others in their context because of their race, gender, or origins but who certainly have more privilege than the poor) speak on behalf of those on the margins. Marginalized individuals may also have limited opportunities to speak at specific church gatherings or courses, or perhaps even to be interviewed by the media (although being interviewed does not necessarily imply being taken seriously). I (Alexia) once heard famous liberation theologian Gustavo Gutiérrez lecture in the early 1980s at a prominent seminary. He was introduced by the moderator as the "voice of the poor." He began his presentation by saying that he was not the voice of the poor. He went on to say that when he was eleven years old, growing up in a poor barrio in Peru, he was the voice of the poor because no one listened to him. He concluded his opening remarks by saying that the essence of the experience of poverty was invisibility to the larger world, and now that moderators were introducing him as the voice of the poor, he was clearly no longer a representative of the poor.

BECs enabled the poor, oppressed, and marginalized to create their own collective, living theology and to put it into practice. If BECs inspire us, we should ask whether following their example would be worth pursuing and prioritizing in our time and place. Does God have a gift for the church in the twenty-first century that we can receive only if we take seriously the words of Jesus in the Beatitudes: "Blessed are you who are poor, for yours is the kingdom of God" (Luke 6:20)? The critical components of the BEC example of consciousness include the following:

- A critical mass of marginalized people in leadership: The communal reflection on Scripture and society was led by a critical mass of people who were poor, marginalized, and oppressed.
- A collective voice on common life: When poor people study Scripture in most contexts, they relate it to their individual lives and experiences. Any solutions that they come up with to their problems are individual solutions. BECs intentionally facilitated the process of people relating Scripture to their common life so that the implementation of solutions to their problems would also have the weight and power of collective action. BECs allowed for wide differences of opinion but worked toward synergy with respect to a level of agreement in vision sufficient for joint action.
- Action: Communal reflection in the BEC context was also always linked to collective action in a cycle of reflection and action that included regular time set aside for planning and evaluation. The goal was always to ensure that collective analysis and voice resulted in real-world change.

- Educational opportunities: BECs provided the opportunity to learn theology as well as practical tools, such as models for consensus decision-making, power-sharing, and liberating pedagogy—with the expectation that BEC members would discern their educational needs and that different models and tools would be freely adapted as needed.
- Reading for healing and liberation: BECs intentionally used the Word of God to heal and liberate. Often, either we act as if all scriptural messages are the same at all times for all people, or we recognize that sometimes people in a specific context have greater need for a certain message—but we apply the wrong message to the wrong people. For example, I have heard preaching that tells the poor to be content with their lot and the rich to be ambitious for abundant life—when perhaps it is the opposite message that each group needs to hear to move toward the common goal of becoming "mature, attaining to the whole measure of the fullness of Christ" (Eph. 4:13). In BECs, Scripture was recognized as having the power to heal and liberate, to address the internal damage caused by oppression, which perpetuates it. While BEC leaders created the space for multiple perspectives on a particular scriptural passage, leaders and members practiced the discipline of seeking the liberating word in the passage.
- Right-brain techniques: BECs used dinámicas—right-brain exercises, rituals, and tactics—to deepen understanding and promote healing.

In the complex socioeconomic context of the US, in which different forms of privilege and oppression blend, it can be difficult to identify how to create a group in which a critical mass of leadership is marginalized. The US Catholic Campaign for Human Development uses economic indicators, requiring that all their grantees ensure that 51 percent of the people in their decision-making body live below the poverty line. (They intentionally exclude from this measurement individuals who are voluntarily poor, as they do not experience the limitations of oppression in the same way because they have the choice of whether to stay or leave.)

Other organizations differentiate between BIPOC and white people. In a workshop a few years ago, we (Brandon and Alexia) encountered reluctance and resistance among participants to identify themselves as having privilege. We then asked the participants to enter into honest self-reflection about their partnership experiences with people whom they regarded as significantly different from themselves. We asked them to notice whether they spent more time worrying about the capacity of the others to carry their share of the load competently and responsibly or whether they spent more time worrying about others seeing them as incapable and irresponsible. We then asked them to group themselves according to which worry was more prevalent. We ended up with white people on one side of the room and people of color on the other side. Perhaps this same set of questions in another group could have ended up with a division by economic class, gender, or sexual orientation. In BECs, there were also more subtle distinctions of class and race, although there was often sufficient similarity to minimize the impact of those differences. Regardless of the precise definition of marginalized, replicating the full experience of BECs requires intentionally creating a group led by a critical mass of the marginalized.

Actuar (Act) / Now What?

Amos

BECs experienced the miracle of empowerment. When we are part of a marginalized and oppressed community, we experience the tragedy of disempowerment on a regular basis. It is not only the external barriers that stand in our way but also the internal barriers, the power of hopelessness to immobilize and how we internalize the perceptions of the broader society in our perceptions and treatment of one another. In the Philippines, Latin America, and Africa, I (Alexia) heard the same parable shared by the people I was training—each group thought that the parable belonged to them. The parable described an actual occurrence. When fishermen are hunting crabs, they put them in a large basket without a lid. You don't need to put a lid on the basket because if one crab tries to climb out, the others will jump on its back, pulling all of them back down into the basket. When those who are most affected either freeze in despair or sabotage each other, the struggle for a better life for all stops dead in its tracks.

Empowering the marginalized and oppressed requires moving from object to subject. The person who has been acted on becomes the creative agent, the one who lives the birthright of shared dominion given in Genesis. In the process, however, you must avoid the trap of internalizing the values and mindset of the privileged; you must intentionally hold on to the "we" instead of focusing on the "I." Freire provides a process for enabling those internal and interpersonal movements that remains valid and valuable today.

The inner voices arising from programmed societal messages can be incredibly strong. In Revelation 12:10, the devil is referred to as the "accuser"; these voices are certainly voices of accusation. It may take a voice with greater authority than our human ones to overcome the power of those voices. The liberating messages of Scripture in a BEC have that role and impact. We recommend using *The Gospel in Solentiname*, which consists of transcripts from

BEC Bible studies with Nicaraguan peasants during the regime of the dictator Somoza. It can be useful to read a passage and then allow the members of your group to reflect on it. Then read the reflections of BEC members and ask your group to compare their reflections to those of the BEC members. This process challenges the typical distortion of the biblical messages that comes from the dominant interpretations by privileged experts whose questions and perspectives are different.

Collective action and evaluation are also essential. In the process of collective action for peace, justice, and the improvement of common life, group members experience their power of transformation. This experience can have enormous impact in countering the dark inner voices telling you that change is not possible. An immigrant pastor taking one of my courses once reacted with horror to the possibility that we might interpret the Magnificat as promising justice in our communities. He said, "But that would lead to despair! My people would stop believing in the promises of God." He was so sure that justice was not possible that any interpretation that linked a vision of justice to the real lives of his members would be immeasurably painful and discouraging. The only way to combat that reaction is for you and the other members of your marginalized community to experience the hope of change through your collective action and to see that the Spirit of God dances with you in that process. My personal experience is that little miracles of synchronicity happen all the time in a faith-full organizing process. When prayer is woven into all the steps of collective action, the participants often see the hand of God guiding and supporting them.

It is not enough to have individual members make progress in their own lives or become engaged with larger projects; that can mean that other members of the group just begin to see those who move forward as "other." The group must have a common experience of victory, even if those victories are initially small in scope. In the field of community organizing, we talk about the "streetlight" strategy. In low-income communities, the public authorities often do not invest in streetlights, causing a situation in which children and elderly people are more likely to be hit by cars when crossing the road. The first victory that community organizing in these communities achieves is to get the municipal authorities to place a streetlight at a dangerous intersection. This process can be a Magnificat experience that empowers and encourages.

Embodied experience is critically important in other ways as well. The use of dinámicas in education and training speaks to the trauma embedded in people's bodies in a way that words alone cannot. Music and art are important tools in that process. In designing dinámicas, the Freirian criteria is always whether they increase awareness as well as open up creativity and participation, not whether they communicate a specific concept. In *Pedagogy of Hope* (Freire's follow-up to his groundbreaking *Pedagogy of the Oppressed*), he warns about a rigid dogmatism of "liberation" that ends up suppressing the leadership development of marginalized people.

Lydia

What kind of formation is needed, particularly for the privileged, in order for more oppressed and privileged people to enter into just partnership and intimate communion? This is one of the core questions in the development of consciousness for the Lydias in our midst. "Reality" does not look the same from the perspectives of the CEO and the worker. If you are privileged, one approach to awakening you to the view from below is exemplified by the Crossroads anti-racism program, one of the original twentieth-century models for anti-racism work in the church. The Crossroads program assumes that knowledge is the missing ingredient. It focuses on a systemic analysis of racism and other forms of oppression, enabling participants in their workshops to understand the history of and current facts about racism. Unfortunately, this approach may result in guilt, despair, and fear without a clear vision, understanding, or hope about how to move forward into liberation together.

Another approach focuses on spiritual awakening. Using *The Gospel in Solentiname* to give Bible study members a peek into a different way of seeing and interpreting Scripture can be as useful with privileged people as it is with oppressed people who have internalized majority perspectives. Yet another approach is relational. In a relational model, privileged individuals take the perspective of a learner and intentionally enter relationships with more oppressed people who are actively leading liberation struggles.

In the fall of 2018, caravans of asylum seekers from Central America began to arrive at the US border in significant numbers. A number of border ministries, refugee organizations, and denominations stepped up to organize border-immersion experiences for concerned and confused church leaders. The most effective of these tours visited Mexican church leaders who were actively responding to the refugee crisis. Matthew 25/Mateo 25 used this approach but created a unique variation on these experiences. Instead of the North American leadership of these tours being chosen from a pool of primarily white experts, Matthew 25/Mateo 25's tours were led by puentes (bridges)—bilingual, bicultural, Latinx millennials who made the connections between the experiences of immigrants in the US and their struggles for justice and the broader picture across and on the border. When we were standing in the long line waiting to return across the border at the end of the day, a young white woman from the Midwest US turned to us and said, "You changed my life today. You changed the hero." The young puente who had been her guide, the youngest of the team at twenty years old, responded, "I never thought of myself as a hero before."

Short-term experiences are typically not enough to create long-term change. Another approach is for more privileged individuals to join ministries or organizations led by more marginalized people or to seek out mentors of color. Through these ongoing "reversed" relationships, the "other species" dynamic breaks down. The "other species" dynamic is a shorthand way of referring to the implicit assumption that people who are across the power lines are fundamentally different as a group (more capable or less capable, with greater or less moral integrity). Those assumptions are part of the matrix that justifies inequality and allows privileged people to feel that they deserve their privilege. When such beliefs exists, one side can appreciate or resent the other, but they have limited capacity to learn from each other. In the context of reversed power relationships in which people share life and work together, a much deeper level of consciousness occurs.

A key juncture in this conscientización process is the moment when the more privileged person suddenly experiences privileged people or systems treating them how the marginalized are normally treated. A Catholic priest who was the senior pastor of a large parish and a leader in the archdiocese was approached by a group of low-wage workers to advocate with the local Catholic hospital chain to support their call for better treatment and compensation. He was sure that he could talk to the nuns and all would be well. Instead, when he went to speak with them, he was thrown off the premises. He described that as a moment of awakening; through his association with the workers, he had a taste of the injustice that they had experienced.

Ruth

Standing between two worlds can be a disorienting experience. We see through the eyes of oppression; we see through the lens of privilege. The battlefield is inside our souls; the inner violence of the *choque* (clashing) of the two selves can manifest in a variety of ways—from shame to frustration to withdrawal from arenas that spark the conflict. The experience of conscientización with a group can be painful at first but ultimately healing, as the process evokes and then integrates our multiple perspectives—elevating and respecting the voice that is often less valued by the world around us. We can be a critically important participant in the dialogue that happens in a base community that includes people along the complex and intersecting lines of privilege and oppression, helping people understand themselves and each other. We just need to commit to getting past the initial tension and discomfort in order to fulfill our vocation.

Hush Harbor Consciousness

Oppression is not only physical violence. All forms of oppression begin as the internalization of lies. One lie of plantation religion was that it was all-knowing. Many enslaved Africans internalized and assimilated into plantation Christianity. One former enslaved woman responds to the question of whether slavery was God's will for African people:

> No Ma'am, dem heathen didn't have no religion. . . . The Lord made three nations, the white, the red and the black, and put dem in different places in de earth. . . . Dose black ignoramuses in Africa forgot God, and didn't have no religion and God blessed and prospered the white people dat did remember him and sent dem to teach de black people even if dey have to grab dem and bring dem into bondage till dey learned some sense. . . . You got to believe on Him if it tek bondage to bring you to your knees. (Harrison 2009, 127)

To internalize the religion of the master was to accept a supremacist interpretation of Christianity whose god operated by scarcity and retribution. The god of plantation Christianity was a childish bully. The church of plantation Christianity was a house of cards. To maintain the white lies was to take the bribe for a feeling of superiority, of self-righteousness, of security. Theology functioned to disguise this false religion as orthodox, holy, and good. This kind of fundamentalist indoctrination was widely proliferated among enslaved Africans. And the internalization of plantation Christianity by enslaved Africans was aided by each subsequent generation of Africans moving further and further away from the direct memories of diasporic ways as well as the physical and psychological trauma of chattel slavery.

What the purveyors of plantation Christianity failed to see and subvert were those enslaved Africans who cultivated an alternative consciousness, away from both Black and white plantation churches. This alternative consciousness developed contextually. Enslaved Africans in the Caribbean shaped a theology that incorporated Africanisms such as the veneration of ancestors and the tradition of conjure.[7] This was more palatable to Catholicism, the prominent Christian tradition in the Caribbean, with its emphasis on mystery, symbolism, and sacramentalism. In North America, the veneration of ancestors and other features of African Traditional Religions persisted but in more clandestine ways. Protestantism, the dominant religious tradition in North America, with its emphasis on rationality and a literal interpretation of Scripture, was not as amenable to the folk religion of enslaved Africans. Enslaved Africans were more covert with integrating their love-and-justice-infused interpretation

---

7. Conjure will be discussed more in chap. 6. The terms *hoodoo*, *voodoo*, *vodun*, and *conjure* are often used interchangeably.

of Christianity with their folk religious ways. This alternative consciousness in North America took shape orally and aurally through covert independent spaces like hush harbors. Hush harbor consciousness can be understood by exploring two principles: make it plain and body knowledge.

Ver (See) / What?

Make It Plain

You don't have to spend much time in a Black community to learn that high value is placed on "keeping it real." From sanctuaries to barbershops to the corner to the playground, cultural currency is placed on telling the truth and making that truth plain for people, without fluff and fanfare, without dancing around what really needs to be said. But living under the tyranny of the plantation economy and slaveholder Christianity, enslaved Africans used deception and trickery to survive. To tell the truth and to tell it plainly, in the presence of the white master and preacher or the Black surrogates they'd brainwashed, was to risk your very life, to be under a constant state of threat to be hanged, whipped, sold off from your family and friends. Black people became good at doublespeak on the plantation and in the plantation churches, of speaking respectably but harboring their real feelings and views. When slaveholders thought Black people enjoyed being enslaved, those same Black people wanted to burn the whole plantation institution to the ground.

Through hush harbors, enslaved Africans developed an entire underground language and belief system that Christianity both reinforced and functioned as a cover for. Cultural theorist Vorris Nunley describes this system as "Black lifeworlds where a distinctive political rationality has been and continues to be privileged; where the unsaid in the public sphere gets said; where the unhearable gets heard; and where the filtering of American and African American culture and life occurs through African American hermeneutics" (Nunley 2011, 18–19). Because this underground world was oral-aural and largely covert in hush harbors (and other unmediated and unsurveilled spaces), there are no creeds, constitutions, or councils for us to analyze. The Spirituals reveal enslaved Africans' creative and subversive interpretation of the Bible. The narratives of the enslaved reveal fragments of their worldview. The bold and revolutionary campaigns and actions of the enslaved are also revelatory. Enslaved Africans drew from at least a few key sources that they syncretized to meet their needs and vision for what was possible.

In Spirituals, enslaved Africans used biblical stories and imagery to code their beliefs in their own dignity and in God's hatred of the institution of slavery. For example, consider the chorus of the Spiritual "Everybody Talkin' 'bout Heav'n":

> Everybody talkin' 'bout heav'n that ain't goin' there
> Everybody talkin' 'bout heav'n that ain't goin'
> Everybody talkin' 'bout heav'n that ain't goin' there
> Oh my Lord. (Acappella 1993)

According to a traditionalist interpretation, this song is talking about people who profess to be Christians, who talk about heaven but whose lives break the personal morality code of conservative evangelicals, such as using profanity, having sex outside of marriage, breaking the law, and so forth. The narratives of enslaved Africans attest that this song was really an indictment of the system of chattel slavery and of the white Christians who used the Bible to support slavery. That white Christians were in fact the ones who talked an awful lot about heaven but were not heaven bound because of how they lied about slavery being holy when it was really a sin in God's eyes. In this one song, enslaved Africans effectively reinterpreted traditional Christian beliefs on holiness, sin, anthropology, and God's sovereignty to serve their own well-being and vision of freedom.

Enslaved Africans did not accept the Bible wholesale the way plantation Christianity delivered it (Callahan 2008; Dunkley 2019, 116–17; Levine 2007, 57; Wilmore 1998, 30). For hush harbor Christians, white preaching was an occasion to develop a critical consciousness and ask tough questions about God and the Bible. Stories about the exodus, the book of Revelation, and more informed the prophecies, dreams, and oracles of enslaved African leaders such as Nat Turner, Denmark Vesey, and Harriet Tubman, to name a few. Countless sermons in the plantation churches interpreted these stories as meaning that Black people should wait for heaven for their freedom, that they were meant for subjugation, that white folks were more spiritually and morally deserving. Hush harbor leaders retooled these stories to mean that God was on the side of the oppressed, that liberation was for this earthly life and not only for the afterlife. The Bible informed abolitionist actions to escape, rebel, and revolt.

Enslaved Africans also retained aspects of Islam, folk theology, and African Traditional Religions. As Renee Harrison relates, "One former enslaved man previously asserted, 'Our religion and superstition was all mixed up.' Old Lady Gray, a former enslaved Muslim woman, affirmed the above sentiment when she stated that: 'Christ built the first church in Mecca and he grave was da'" (Harrison 2009, 206).

Enslaved Africans sang hymns and publicly accepted Christian ideas while existentially and in clandestine ways worshiped Allah and followed the practices of the Islamic religion many of them inherited from their African past. Or they combined belief in a supreme God with many smaller deities, the veneration of ancestors, and other folk and African traditional theologies.

Body Knowledge

The epistemology and learning of enslaved Africans were not limited to the mind. How did enslaved Africans know how to interpret the trees and ground to know where to enter hush harbors? How did they know to wade into the water as a survival tactic when they were escaping the plantation? A certain knowledge came from enslaved Africans being in touch with their bodies and the earth's body, the natural environment. This knowledge was deeply influenced by the intersection of the Christian experience of the Holy Spirit through conversion and Africanisms such as the belief in the sacred and healing power of the drum, rhythm, and the natural environment.

> Momentary body autonomy allowed them to see their bodies as more than one-dimensional tools of labor and subjugation. . . . The rhythm within each of them was transformed into a collective rhythm that transcended them. This collective rhythm connected them to deities, spirit(s), and one another. . . . The drum, its rhythms, and the spirit world unified them; each transcended language and ethnic barriers and helped them to forge a new collective identity rooted in struggle and a desire for freedom. . . . The drum and drumming functioned as an act of conjuring; it invoked the spirit world and stirred women and men to gather to pray, sing, dance, revolt, and escape. What slavers once saw as a form of mindless entertainment, soon posed a threat on many slave-owning properties; they eventually banned "talking drums" and other "talking instruments" that fostered self-respect and pride and awakened the consciousness of black peoples. (Harrison 2009, 199)

The liberating experience of drumming, dancing, and singing in hush harbors functioned inside the experience of Christian conversion. Whether responding to an evocative and roaring sermon, singing a Spiritual, or praying meditatively, enslaved Africans could catch the Spirit and be taken through powerful feelings of contrition, humility, and deep personal regard. Ultimately, conversion was one of the most profound identifications of their personhood. Through conversion they were called by God. Through conversion they experienced radical self-love, raised self-esteem, and intimacy with the divine. Gayraud Wilmore writes that "the secular and the sacred met and embraced each other in the bodily celebration of the homologous unity of all things—the holy and profane, good and evil, the beautiful and dreadful. To give oneself up with shouts of joy and 'singing feet' to this wholeness of being, to the ecstatic celebration of one's creaturehood taken up and possessed by God in a new state of consciousness, was to imbibe the most restorative medicine available to the slave" (Wilmore 1985, 34).

Through conversion, the enslaved also felt empowered with a sense of mission, but not the kind of messiah complex and religious indoctrination associated with slaveholder Christianity. Rather, this was a profound mission that provided a sacred existential basis for a critique of slaveholding Christianity.

> Slaves believed that God had transformed them into new beings with a radically different mission in the world—a mission that required them to live counter to plantation values. First, converted slaves believed that their status of new being in Jesus interiorly distanced them from the psychological abuse of slavery. It gave them the needed transcendent means of getting a critical perspective of both their masters and themselves. Second, slaves believed that their definition of conversion gave them a radical sense of God having disengaged them from the world for the purpose of calling them to radically engage it. (Earl 2003, 46)

As was often the case, when several enslaved Africans experienced conversion simultaneously, this only increased the feeling that God was indeed with them. "Corporate conversion must be interpreted to mean God's empowerment of the individual authentic self to become a member of the new social body of salvation. Slaves who experienced this divine miracle knew that they had been delivered from the false theological and ethical separation that masters made between their bodies and souls" (Earl 2003, 7).

What this alternative, subversive knowledge shows is that enslaved Africans developed a consciousness of their own about Christianity, about society, and about themselves that was not bound to the rules and limits of the Eurocentric, white supremacist worldview of the slave economy. Enslaved Africans worshiping and learning in hush harbors felt free to draw from any source that would reveal their inherited goodness and beauty and the truth that they were meant to be free. "The overarching question was one of survival—mental and physical—and whatever slaves could appropriate from the conjurers, or later from the charismatic Christian preacher, to deal with the aleatory quality of their situation and to ward off the evil influences around them was seized upon as a gift from 'de Lawd'" (Wilmore 1985, 33).

Enslaved Africans had a truly Pentecostal consciousness, a belief that the Spirit was providing them with all the knowledge they needed no matter the educational and learning restrictions the surrounding slavocracy system placed on them.

> It was reported that in Georgia some slaves had a religion of their own based on their own experiences, the experience of God with them, and various revelations

and visions. Even though "churched Negroes" respected the Bible and learned to read it before they could read much of anything else, there was a contempt among many slaves for "book religion." They rejected it not merely because they had to depend upon oral instruction, but because they had considerable self-esteem and confidence in their own manner of believing in worshipping God. "The Spirit within" was considered superior to the Bible as a guide for their religious knowledge. (Wilmore 1985, 30)

Juzgar (Judge) / So What?

A Hermeneutic of Searching

I (Brandon) remember those Sundays, rare as they were, when the preacher would say something about a controversial subject—homosexuality or poverty, for example—and, as much as I respected the preacher as God's instrument, my inner thought-life would never take what the preacher said for granted. As a kid, I always asked that most simple yet thorny question: "Why?" For enslaved Africans who held on to their inner lives, their memories, their African cultural inheritance, there must have been a war always taking place between the world and words of the plantation and the plantation church, and the world and words as they knew them in their inner lives. At the site of that war, that tension, that contradiction, I can imagine my ancestors asking, "Why?" The question was never uttered in the company of the slaveholders or assimilated slaves. On the inside, the dialogue was riveting. In hush harbors the grappling was plain and found companionship with other enslaved Africans who also questioned the theology and politics of the imperial order of things. Liberation theologians call this practice a hermeneutic of suspicion. I am not sure that the practice of hush harbors can be reduced to suspicion alone. Neither was this true for my own moral and theological questioning as a child. Critique alone remains at the site of deconstruction. Only knowing what is wrong is no place for the soul to rest.

Suspicion was present in the consciousness of hush harbors, but there was much more at work. A hermeneutic of searching is a more fitting description. The challenge and interrogation one hears in Spirituals such as "Oh Freedom" reveal a more constructive tone, not bound exclusively to a response to white supremacy but also including an imagining, a possibility. They asked not only "Why does slavery exist?" but also "What if God intended for me to be free?" They answered that question by singing, "Before I'd be a slave, I'd be buried in my grave, and go home to my Lord and be free" (Golden Gospel Singers 2007). Sure, this freedom was about the afterlife, but this did not mean that the enslaved were willing to accept slavery for heaven. Their conviction was that they would risk death before accepting the identity of being a slave.

Death to their body meant freedom with their Lord. Either way, freedom was their only choice. Their freedom wasn't limited by anything, including white supremacy. This kind of consciousness-raising began with the basic yet bold commitment to question the order of things. To search for the truth, for joy, for love, for freedom, which required having to unmask the lies being told and embodied, no matter the cost.

As enslaved Africans sang this Spiritual, their external experiences of the terror of the plantation economy and church did not change. Just singing the words for others to hear did nothing to change their external environment. Many who overheard songs such as these, both white slaveholders and other enslaved Africans, dismissed the songs as making Black people desensitized to their own subjugation and suffering, or as purely entertainment and performance and emotionalism, or simply as songs to help the "workday" go by. The power of this hermeneutic of searching was not limited to the material world or to words. True liberation happens internally and externally. The oppressed can recognize and feel and despise the suffering they face at the hands of unjust systems. But this does not mean that the oppressed believe that the suffering they face is not deserved, not due them, not tied to their being less than. The oppressed must believe in their own self-worth and dignity, must believe that they are not less than, believe that they deserve life, love, and wholeness. In hush harbors, enslaved Africans practiced raising their consciousness by plainly singing and speaking the truth about their own personhood and inherent value, by plainly singing and speaking the truth about the injustice around them, and by truly believing what they sang and spoke.

The Wisdom Is in the Room

This searching—this speaking and believing the plain truth—was not an individual act. It also wasn't primarily an intellectual matter. Gathering in hush harbors was a practice in desire, the desire for belonging. Political education as a mode of consciousness-raising is commonly fixated on ensuring that the oppressed have the right information to assess their conditions and wage a struggle for change. Bold campaigns and actions like the Underground Railroad that emerged from hush harbors required political strategizing and analysis, to be sure. Still, information and strategy alone were not enough to ensure the kind of trust required to struggle against the pervasive and organized lies of the colonialist order. There needed to be high trust. The risks were lethal—being hanged, being separated from family and loved ones, being raped. Further, the conditioning of the colonialist order had already made several classes of Black folks: the field Negro and the house Negro, the respectable Negroes and the rebellious ones. The internalized oppression was already running deep within the Black community, with a pecking order of those who were willing to reinforce the chattel system: at the top were often the slave preachers or the slave field hands who participated in whippings; then came those enslaved Africans who stayed silent; finally, those at the bottom and most despised were enslaved Africans who sought to escape and upend the prevailing social order. Trust was costly.

For those who gathered in hush harbors, trust was spent through the mutual desire for connection, care, and courage. When a person entered a hush harbor, they genuinely wanted to be with those gathered. They wanted to know how others felt, what they were facing, what questions they had, what ideas they had for addressing issues in the community and getting free from chattel slavery, what they could join others to solve. The standard pedagogy tells us that we need a scholar who is the authority, who has the most knowledge, while everyone else is a student who learns from the scholar. The scholar or teacher is always in the seat of instruction, a seat of security and service. Hush harbors turned this dynamic inside out. The pedagogy of hush harbors was communal wisdom, where every person in the community was both teacher and student. The belonging was the learning, and the learning was belonging. From this basis—of the wisdom in belonging—consciousness is ever expansive, going beyond only the intellect, the individual, and the verbal.

If the wisdom is not controlled or contained but shared and emergent based on the questions and ideas and needs of those gathered, then any and every part of what constitutes reality is within the scope of knowledge and learning and growing. For hush harbors, this included learning from the natural environment how to set traps to interrupt a slaveholder plotting a whipping, or growing one's perception of urgency and ease from the tone of the drums, or unknowing the fear instilled by the plantation through new forms of touch and embrace and dance. This somatic knowing of the gathered body learning and acting collectively to grow their sense of peoplehood, of identity, of vision, of character was essential for the kind of risks that they then took to unravel and upend the plantation economy when they were dispersed.

Actuar (Act) / Now What?

Education and training in churches, the academy, and social justice spaces have overemphasized the rational, logical, and individual dimension of learning. Personal achievement is the desired outcome. The learning is a means to an end. In a global, predatory, capitalist economy that divides and conquers by debt and production, the student is often overwhelmingly concerned about learning as a means to get creditors off their backs. The marketizing of education and training has made learning just another commodity in the rat race of conspicuous consumption. Ancient radical pedagogues such as Paulo Freire, Myles Horton, Septima Clark, and others are turning in their graves. The wisdom they taught us, which falls in the lineage of the wisdom of hush harbors, is that learning and formation are always first acts of humility and belonging and creativity. Education is not a means to extract or seize or control or achieve. There is a poverty of imagination in the West about the transformative possibilities and impact of learning and formation as belonging and radical praxis. Theologian Willie Jennings says it this way: "The cultivation of belonging should be the goal of all education. Not just any kind of belonging, but a profoundly creaturely belonging that performs the returning of the creature to the creator and a returning to an intimate and erotic energy that drives life together with God" (Jennings 2020, 15).

The major shift needed to cultivate hush harbor consciousness-raising is from transaction to transformation. To shift the core question of the learning environment from "What can I accomplish?" to "Why am I here?" To ask "Why?" is to interrogate the origin or root of a problem. To seek identification is to call forth your lineage and shaping, or in the words of Southern folks, it is not the question "Who are you?" but "Who are your people?" To investigate place is to question the history and basis of the learning and the teacher and to what end this learning is in service. Teachers, trainers, coaches, facilitators, and any others who carry the holy responsibility of shaping, instructing, developing, and forming leaders will need to contend with the critical pedagogical questions here and throughout this chapter. And depending on your social location, this will, of course, look very different. A few questions to consider based on your social location include these:

Amos: What knowledge, wisdom, and tools for connection with the sacred, with community, and with pursuing justice are native to your people and place? What has been hidden and needs to be reclaimed? Which elders and sages in your community can reveal these to you?

Lydia: How have hegemonic ways of knowing and learning hurt you and disconnected you from your ethnic heritages? How have you benefited from these? What step can you take to raise awareness among your family members and those from your racial/ethnic background? How can you interrupt hegemonic curriculum and teaching practices in your local school and/or religious education spaces?

Ruth: What formal learning and ways of being have you internalized that have misshaped and miseducated you? How can you raise awareness about this in your community, especially among the young? Who can apprentice you in reconnecting with the ways of knowing and being that are indigenous to your people and community?

Consciousness: Seeing with the Heart

Jesus said, "For judgment I have come into this world, so that the blind will see and those who see will become blind." Some Pharisees who were with him heard him say this and asked, "What? Are we blind too?" Jesus said, "If you were blind, you would not be guilty of sin; but now that you claim you can see, your guilt remains." (John 9:39–41)

And now here is my secret, a very simple secret: It is only with the heart that one can see rightly; what is essential is invisible to the eye. (Antoine de Saint-Exupéry 1943, 65)

What is essential is not always merely invisible; it is often intentionally hidden. Gandhian nonviolence starts with the understanding that leaders' capacity to govern depends on the consent of the governed. The oppressed must be convinced to collaborate in their oppression in order for it to continue over time. Both the privileged and the oppressed must maintain the illusion that the way things are is the way they should be, which requires that the raw reality of injustice be hidden. The process of becoming conscious in both BECs and hush harbors required the claiming and reclaiming of the validity of the members' own experiences and perceptions. These experiences and perceptions integrated the material and the spiritual, the body and both sides of the brain. Members encouraged each other to see with their hearts and to trust that they saw God's truth more clearly than the dominant consensus.

The process of consciousness in both contexts was not simple. It required intentional, strategic work and creative resistance. It also necessitated leaning into the Holy Spirit and the liberating Word to continually confirm and shape their understanding. This confirmation and shaping happened in the process of reflection and action. Doing the work of liberation together helped to clarify and refine their common vision.

Members of BECs and hush harbors understood that seeing the truth from their perspective within the frame of faith enabled them to both bear the truth and change it. The eyes of faith make possible the transcending of the pain and the vision that sustains the struggle. When the church supports this process in the marginalized, amazing results can occur.

The story of the birth of the order of deacons in Acts 6 is an excellent example of how the early church prioritized the perceptions of those with less social power.[8] The Hellenistic Jews (immigrants) perceived that their widows were receiving less in the daily distribution of food. Instead of arguing with them, the apostles (all citizens) respected their perceptions and created a

8. We are indebted for the articulation of this analysis to González 1997.

special committee consisting solely of immigrants to govern all food distribution for the community. This act on the part of the apostles was a tangible recognition of the principles of respecting and prioritizing the perspective from the margins as part of the conscientización of the whole. The result was a level of power-sharing and power shift that amazed the world and drew numbers of people to believe and belong.

The dominant consensus is often subtle. We read in Romans 12:2, "Do not conform to the pattern of the world, but be transformed by the renewing of your mind." The patterns of this world are pervasive. We need all our best tools to overcome them. BECs and hush harbors developed an array of useful instruments and practices, forged in the fire of struggle.

We conclude by offering these suggestions:

- Use and adapt the tools developed by BECs and hush harbors.
- Refine them in the struggle for liberation in your context.
- Trust that it is possible to overcome the lies of the devil embedded in the systems of this world.
- Encourage those who suffer the daily reality of injustice to see with their hearts, and establish the foundation of your church's common life on that vision.

6

Spirit-uality

Sanidad and la Teología de las Abuelas

BEC Spirit-uality

JOSE ALANIZ, Olguita's husband [In response to the story of the wedding at Cana]: I think we should ask for wine for everybody, like Christ taught us to ask for bread in the Our Father. Bread and wine are equally important. Bread is the food and wine is the joy, and that's why he made one miracle with bread and another with wine. Because there are so many poor people, who don't have any parties, drunken brawls maybe, but not joy. The joy of the kingdom will come when everybody loves each other and everybody is friends.

FELIPE: There will be no lonely people, no frustrated ones, then, will there? This love is going to be for everyone, for every single one. No one will be excluded from that wedding. That will be true social justice.

OLIVIA: Everybody, men, women, old people, children, even nursing babies, we all form a single body: humanity, the bride loved by God. (Cardenal 1976, 80)

The most common criticism of BECs is that they were a social movement masquerading as a spiritual movement. This was clearly not the position of the BEC leaders themselves: "We must say it again very clearly; what has traditionally been called spirituality has been and continues to be one of the most characteristic marks of Christians committed to the process of liberation and the theological reflection that arises from it" (Torres and Eagleson 1981, 7). Spirit-uality in BECs was unique in many ways, evident in the peace and joy present in individual lives and community gatherings even in the midst of danger, the tangible sense of God's presence, the lived experience of Jesus, the role of prayer and liturgy, the healed lives and relationships, the commitment to reconciliation and martyrdom, and the ability to prioritize risky nonviolence. We use the term *spirit-uality* to describe this kind of incarnational spirituality because it is a way of living faith that is infused and permeated by the living Christ and the Holy Spirit.

Ver (See) / What?

Peace and Joy

Ana, a BEC leader from El Salvador, tells the story of her initial encounter with a BEC as a college student. "What drew you to come back?" I (Alexia) asked. "The joy," she answered. "People were so full of joy, so excited. You could feel the Holy Spirit in the room, moving us, everyone hoping for a great change." BECs were as effective as they were in sustaining the movement for justice in the midst of violent repression because they were places where people experienced the Spirit of God, often as a sustaining joy that came even in the midst of sorrow. Moises, speaking about his experience in El Salvador, adds that there was a calm, a peacefulness, to BEC members and leaders. He relates his experience of sitting in a Bible study on the book of Acts, everyone studying and reflecting calmly while waiting for a bombardment—bombs imprinted with "USA." He tells another story about a priest who was traveling to an area where the government death squads had been active to attend the funeral of a BEC leader. A commander in the revolutionary forces offered him a gun, but he refused, unafraid. The commander smiled, "I knew you would say that."

I (Alexia) remember similar experiences in the Philippines. The broad coalition Bayan Ko had organized a large demonstration just a few months before the Marcos regime fell. The clergy and other Christian leaders were in the front. We were close to crossing the bridge to the palace when the troops came out to block our passage. When we saw them positioning the water cannons, we were not surprised. We had seen them before. Then we looked again, and there were also soldiers pointing their rifles at us. I was terrified. A young priest who was a pastoral agent in a BEC turned to us and asked us to join him in the celebration of the Lord's Supper. He had a small piece of bread and a small flask of Communion wine. In the middle of the ritual, I looked at his face, and his expression was so peaceful that he shone. The soldiers waited for the impromptu Communion service to end before they started shooting. I don't know what happened to that young priest, but I have never forgotten him. I knew another young BEC leader who could never stay in the same house for two nights in a row because he needed to stay one step ahead of his persecutors, but he too exuded peace and joy.

The Tangible Sense of God's Presence

The scholars and leaders who tell the story of the spirit-uality of BECs often struggle to articulate it clearly. It could manifest differently from traditional Catholic or Protestant spiritualities. In *The Gospel in Solentiname*, the majority of the conversations about Scripture focus on building community, living love, and creating justice. They tend to emphasize the horizontal aspects of the kingdom instead of the vertical. However, the sense of God's presence is tangible. "Other churches may be richer in institutions or talk more about the gospel. But the CEBs are more evangelical because of the evangelical notes of joy, hope, enthusiasm, joviality, largeness of heart, good news despite oppression and certainty of victory despite evident obstacles" (Libanio, quoted in Cooke 1985, 85). Niall O'Brien describes these communities as subverting a culture of fear (O'Brien 1987, 218).

The Lived Experience of Jesus

In BECs, Jesus was a constant topic of conversation as a model and source of strength. As José Marins states in his manual for becoming a BEC, "The person of the Lord Jesus Christ, crucified and resurrected, occupies the center of life of the BEC. . . . The life of Jesus is seen as an eloquent experience of fidelity to the Father and of commitment to humanity in a concrete, historical context. Jesus is the friend who invites us to follow him in the experience of a new communion and community, in a more prophetic lifestyle, committed to the service of others" (Marins 1981, 29). Guillermo Cook shares two telling vignettes:

A CEB member, a migrant worker in the booming construction industry in Brazil, answered my question, "What does Christ mean to you?" In his thick peasant accent he replied: "Christ means everything to me because he accompanies me in all my problems. . . . He helps me to bear my problems." He raised his hands in an eloquent gesture as if to say, "What more is there to say?"

After an entire *communidade* in a small town was arrested and brought before the local police chief on charges of subversion, he demanded to be told who was behind them, guiding and manipulating them. They at first replied "Nobody. It is all of us you see here." The police, unconvinced, insisted, "Take me to your leader." They answered, "The one who encourages us and guides us is our Chief. It is our Lord Jesus Christ!" (Cook 1985, 81)[1]

Prayer

Two leaders of twentieth-century church renewal efforts, Mark Lau Branson and Alan Roxburgh, define Christian spirituality as "the real, daily, communal connections between God, the world and the church" (Branson and Roxburgh 2021, 30). By that definition, BECs are exemplars of Christian spirituality.

That being said, BECs definitely represented a shift away from traditional forms of spirituality. O'Brien talks about his initial concerns about the BEC movement's relative lack of emphasis on the classic rituals of prayer. He then began to realize that the new context required a different kind of prayer: "We needed a spirituality suited to our hectic situation, and so through the years we began to build it up. . . . Our prayers had to be triggered not by the clock or the church bells, but by events. If a group came to the convent to discuss some problem in our community, we would frequently finish by praying together for help or in thanksgiving" (O'Brien 1987, 253). Marins also notes that in Brazil the focus of prayer increasingly became the daily lives of the people and that prayer became a regular and spontaneous event. The definition and use of prayer expanded: "We had to learn to read the signs of God's coming into people's lives. We learned to do this by staying faithful to our prayer. Prayer is listening to God's word in our conscience, in Holy Scripture, in the community, and in the poor. Praying was the most important thing the community leaders did. They had to pray faithfully so as to be able gradually to learn to 'read'" (Galdámez 1983, 35).[2]

A New Liturgy—La Teología de las Abuelas

Catholicism in Latin America and the Philippines has historically been infused with symbols and practices rooted in indigenous cultures, such as *danzas* (dances), pilgrimages, dramatic enactments with masks and elaborate costumes, saints as spiritual presences, and rituals for specific needs and life events.[3] However, by the middle of the twentieth century, many of these rituals

---

1. These quotations also appear in chap. 5 but are repeated here to support the point.
2. The practical theology field and missional church movements in the US emphasize a similar form of discernment with less focus on power dynamics and typically coming from a more privileged perspective. See the works of Mark Lau Branson and Alan J. Roxburgh, for example.
3. *Curanderismo* (traditional healing practice) in Latin America and folk healing traditions in the Philippines use everyday substances like salt, candles, and oils, combined with prayers, to help people deal with the sufferings and struggles of daily life. However, these are about individual or family healing, not the common life of the people.

had become rigidly superstitious, disconnected in many ways from the communal life experiences or profound hopes of the people. In BECs, the liturgy began to shift toward a fuller sense of incarnation, and members brought the symbols of their livelihoods and cultures into their worship celebrations—shells and nets for fishermen, bowls of earth for farmers, traditional weavings and dishes for women.

The symbols honored the sacramental quality of the daily lives of the marginalized, including women. Older women had traditionally sustained the daily activities of the church in Latin America and were often primarily responsible for passing on the faith to their children and grandchildren. However, they had no formal role in the liturgy or visible responsibility. The symbolic inclusion of the daily lives of women in the liturgy and the actual distribution of responsibilities to women, including traditionally sacred responsibilities, made visible their value and contribution. The lives of the grandmothers who had sustained the church were now publicly recognized as full of sacred content.

Any event could be an occasion for a spontaneous worship service—the birth of a child, the time for planting, the time for reaping, victories and defeats in the struggle for justice. The worship centered on the Word of God, song, shared reflection, and creative expression. Hymns were pulled from a variety of sources, but new songs were also written that expressed the desires, suffering, and hopes of the people. "For CEB participants, singing has become an instrument of conscientization that helps them understand their reality, gives them strength to endure it and the determination to do something about it" (Cook 1985, 119). The famous liturgical celebration *Misa Popular Salvadoreña* (Cuellar 1980) traveled through the BECs. A particularly moving element of the *Misa* was the *presente* ritual in which the names of those who had died as a result of injustice or the struggle for justice were read one by one, and after each name, the people all said, "Presente!" (meaning "present" or "here with us").[4] O'Brien talks about the BECs' decision to change the age of confirmation to eighteen, because the promises contained in the ritual had been expanded to cover the sacrifices that following Jesus might lead to in that time and place, sacrifices that it would not be appropriate to expect a child to make (O'Brien 1987, 167).

This shift in liturgy had its negative side. In the transition from traditional to new forms of liturgy, sometimes people lost their way, and the ritual actions lost their mystery and power. Some members became materialists, sure they could accomplish the change they desired without God. When the spiritual aspect weakened, BECs did not survive. In certain areas of Brazil, BECs

---

4. For the exact text of the *presente* ritual in the *Misa Popular Salvadoreña*, see Torres and Eagleson 1981, 217.

"attempted to arrive at a new model of the church without a personal, communal and structural conversion," and the result was "a complete failure" (Marins, quoted in Cooke 1985, 68).[5] The negative impact of moving toward materialism was partially a result of the spiritual worldview of most Latin Americans. Even if they were not Christians in any internal or active sense, the poor of Brazil, according to Dominique Barbe, lived in a world in which magic and miracles were trusted and needed (Barbe 1987, 96).[6]

Healed Lives and Relationships—Sanidad (Healing)

Evidence that spirit-uality in BECs was a real connection with the divine was found in the changed lives of members who were healed from self-destructive patterns.

Pablo Galdámez talks honestly about the self-destructive habits and violence that characterized the lives of many of the poorest members of his pueblo (people) before they organized BECs. He also tells stories of many profound conversions that led to changed lives. The story of Chico is one of many:

> He would spend all day drinking. Every weekend he could be found either in a bar or outside one throwing a fit. He would talk to himself and shout, completely possessed by the spirit of rum, an evil spirit that had destroyed him. He and his wife Maria had seven children. They lived in a pasteboard shack. Chico belonged to the paramilitary group ORDEN, "Order." His papers saved him from jail. Loan sharks chased him in one door and out the other trying to get back their cash. But he'd already spent it on booze. And he'd already sold the best things in his house to pay them something. He was at the end of his rope. And so, in the middle of a binge one night, he decided to kill himself.
>
> He went off and got some rope to hang himself. The evil spirit had overcome him. When he started getting the noose ready to put around his neck, neither his wife nor his children were frightened yet. They were used to his crazy actions. But when Maria saw him actually hanging, she went for the neighbors. They all came running with machetes and cut the rope. Chico fell to the floor, still alive shouting "Lemme alone, I want to die! Mind your own business, I wanta die!" And he went for his own machete then to go after his neighbors. But they didn't give up, they took his machete away and tied him up. They kept him prisoner for several days. Then they opened the community doors to him, and the doors of Alcoholics Anonymous. Only those neighbors of his, members of

---

5. Cecília Mariz notes that in her research on Brazil, the poorest of the poor often preferred a Pentecostal or animist alternative because BECs did not offer immediate practical and spiritual solutions to their daily problems. That was apparently not the case in El Salvador.

6. Paul Hiebert's works discuss this kind of spiritual awareness and belief system in the Global South.

a base community, would ever know how many fits the evil spirit, the spirit of booze, had given Chico before finally going out of him and leaving him free. (Galdámez 1983, 5)

This experience of personal liberation from addiction was not achieved solely by an internal miracle. The support of a courageous and dedicated community (which also drew on "secular" resources such as Alcoholics Anonymous) and the personal experience of conversion to active faith defined the powerful mix that led to a new life. His new life was then reinforced by his new identity as someone who served and was valued by the community. Chico became a leader in helping other young men overcome addiction and in a wide spectrum of other BEC activities.

Healing in the lives of BEC members included healing in their family life. BECs regularly offered couples a chance to be married, a ritual too expensive and inconvenient for many of the poor. BEC communities would perform group ceremonies in which multiple couples were married sacramentally at the same time, often with the children present and cheering. In line with their perspective on alcoholism, BECs adapted the Marriage Encounter program to help couples reform their relationships to match their new identities and intentional values.

Reconciliation

Of course, people were not always able to maintain their new lifestyles and habits, particularly in the face of peer pressure and reprisals. However, BECs were extraordinarily "grace-full" communities, ready to welcome people in or back who were known for violence and betrayals. This included people who "sold out" BECs, selling their share of a collective enterprise or a home in a land trust, as well as people who returned to former lifestyles. They called for a ritual of confession and forgiveness in front of the community, which was also used to reconcile couples who were estranged. This ritual built on the practice of communal self-evaluation after common activities that accustomed members to the confession of their mistakes without condemnation for the sake of common learning.

Perhaps the most powerful testimonies in the BEC reconciliation literature concern dangerous individuals who were lovingly confronted by the BEC community at personal risk and were transformed in the process from enemies to allies. The story of Angel is a prime example.[7] He was a thug for the landowners and the government security forces in the Philippines, a position that supported his personal hobbies of sadism and murder. He

---

7. For the full story, see O'Brien 1987, 209–18. It is more powerful than the summary offered here.

was said to eat the ears of his victims. As his violence escalated, BECs held a debate. Should they all buy guns? Should they give the problem to the "boys" (the guerrilla forces in the mountains)? After deep reflection and dialogue, they called in the leaders of BECs from another area well-known for reconciliation encounters. They then decided that all BECs in the area would walk together to Angel's home, deep in the jungle, and hold a Mass at his house. They carefully planned all the details. The twelve members of the community who would take the lead were called the apostles (partially to combat Angel's claims of satanic spiritual power; he constantly wore amulets and claimed to be invincible). The people wore their BEC T-shirts bearing a logo with an open Bible at the center from which rays of light came down smashing a machine gun, and a sword with the inscription "The Word of God is mightier than a two-edged sword." When they arrived, Angel was outside with his machete. They began a worship service and a conversation that lasted most of the night and resulted in Angel and his followers giving up all their weapons. A turning point was when the group went to the local church and continued the conversation under a painting of Christ being scourged, which also portrayed all the evils that were happening in the community (land-grabbing, army atrocities, robbery, rape, religious hypocrisy, and so on). Angel pointed at a Roman with a whip in the painting and said, "That's me." He then talked about how the army had paid him for his crimes. The encounter with Angel was the first of a series of similar experiences that strengthened the faith of the people.

The reconciliation process was not over after the initial encounter and repentance. There was a series of steps to full integration or reintegration into the community. Angel was required to go into exile at his grandmother's home in a nearby town and demonstrate a changed life before he could return. The reconciliation process was seen as a way to overcome evil, which included both demonic forces and government death squads.

BECs also used a process for reconciliation that I (Alexia) learned to identify and articulate in a different Latin American context. In 1992, I had the privilege of witnessing a series of behind-the-scenes roundtable discussions led by Óscar Arias Sánchez, president of Costa Rica, who was working to build peace in Central America by resolving the long-standing civil wars in El Salvador and Guatemala. I worked for an international Lutheran organization that had helped raise funds for the project. The United Nations peace process had stalled, and Arias Sánchez intended to build the necessary foundation for success.

Instead of framing the process as a negotiation between the warring armies of the state and the rebel forces, Arias Sánchez invited all the top leaders of all sectors of society—the corporate CEOs, the union leaders, the leaders of civil society, the political leaders—to attend. When I first entered the room, the mutual hatred and distrust were palpable. Arias Sánchez began the process by asking each of them to write down their dreams for their country in twenty years. They then had to create a dream wall, putting up their dreams on the wall and describing them to the assembly. As they realized that they had common dreams, the atmosphere in the room tangibly changed; the potential for the future became more powerful than the pain of the past. Over the next four days, they came up with solutions that were reflected in the formal peace pacts, which were signed just a few weeks after the discussions ended.

The Spanish word participants used for the process that they had experienced was concertación, literally "coming into concert or harmony." Instead of being based on negotiation—intellectually figuring out a meeting point between two positions—the conflict resolution was a meeting of hearts, mutual empathy regarding the achievement of a common hope. I saw that process play out in BECs, even though the word was not used in BEC communities (neither in my experience nor in the literature).

I also used the process successfully in family counseling as the pastor of a Hispanic immigrant congregation. Instead of trying to get couples to negotiate, I focused on trying to build empathy and the awareness of a common dream. It worked.

Martyrdom

Love did not always overcome hate. BECs produced thousands of martyrs. However, the civil wars in both Central America and the Philippines formed the context for the BEC movement; the government and the local thugs it hired tortured and killed thousands of people who did not belong to BECs as well. People also died in the crossfire between the revolutionary army and the government. The choice was not simply safety or risk; the choice was how and why to risk, and the interpretive frame given to the process of risking death for the sake of justice. Galdámez talks about becoming acolytes, accompanying the people in their suffering. He includes in this accompaniment support for refugees driven off their land by military campaigns, medical care for revolutionaries, and public condemnation of atrocities. "Being an acolyte meant risking your life. There was the day when a youth was shot fifty yards from the parish center. One of our 'acolytes' ran up to help him. Suddenly he felt the barrel of a rifle in his shoulder. 'Are you a relative?' 'No' came the quick reply, 'But he is a human being, and he needs treatment.' 'Get lost, unless you are looking to get the same.' Up rolled an army truck. They gave the boy the coup de grace and dragged his body towards the truck, hauling it by the hair, leaving a bloody trail across the street" (Galdámez 1983, 78).

BEC leaders often felt deep sorrow and survivor guilt: "I'm just in agony. Sometimes I think it would have been better not to preach the gospel. If people's consciousness had not been raised at least they wouldn't have died. I feel sad. I feel deathly sad" (Galdámez 1983, 79). Their consolation came from spiritually reframing their losses: "We came to understand that, in that historic hour, El Salvador was the Suffering Servant of Yahweh for all the nations. We were a challenge to the hope of all peoples: a small, poor country was standing up to the most powerful empire on earth. We understood that in our struggle all the poor of the earth were struggling too" (79).[8]

It would be logical to assume that the threat of martyrdom would deter people from joining or staying with BECs. The opposite occurred. As church father Tertullian famously said, "The blood of the martyrs is the seed of the church." A common saying in the BECs was "They tried to bury us; they did not know we were seeds" (Christianopoulis 1978, n.p.). In *Wind and Fire*, Ian Fraser calls the growth of BECs in this era the "spontaneous combustion of the Spirit" (Healey and Hinton 2005, 4) as a way of describing the explosive growth of the movement in spite of persecution and loss.

The Question of Armed Struggle

In BECs, young people who identified with the guerrilla movements (and who might actually have been rebel soldiers) sat side by side with older people whose commitment to nonviolence was core to their faith. Laureano is a member of the BEC in *The Gospel in Solentiname* who can always be counted on to mention the revolution and to interpret Scripture in light of revolutionary struggle. Here is a typical dialogue in response to the following Scripture: "I am sending you out like sheep among wolves. Therefore be shrewd as snakes and as innocent as doves" (Matt. 10:16).

LAUREANO: [Jesus is] telling us that we must be aggressive and peaceful. I understand it this way: When you have to use violence, use it, and when you can do things peacefully, do them peacefully. It's only a matter of tactics.

ALEJANDRO: There's a difference between being good and being a sap. Just because you're good doesn't mean you have to be an idiot, and Jesus is telling us here to be good without being idiotic—not letting anybody get ahead of you. Be sharp, sure! Watch out for the people's interests, and don't let anyone exploit them—that's to be as sharp as a serpent. And you can combine this with the methods of non-violence.

8. Samuel Solivan, a Pentecostal Puerto Rican, uses the word *orthopathos* to describe the Latin American liberation theology process of turning suffering into liberation, using suffering to awaken, motivate, and energize change, deepening faith in the Christ of the cross and resurrection (Solivan 1998).

WILLIAM: We must have the sharpness of the serpent without its evil, without its poison. That is, we must have the cunning of the enemy without his evil. In that way, we must distinguish ourselves from him. Our goodness must be like the goodness of the doves. (Cardenal 1976, 125)

Different perspectives on violence did not separate the members of BECs. Those who were committed to nonviolence often understood the commitment to armed struggle as a holy commitment even if they disagreed with the means.

Juzgar (Judge) / So What?

The dominant culture of the Global North in the twenty-first century combines casual materialism with diffuse spiritual sensibility. This combination does not provide the spiritual spine for a sustained struggle for justice. The spirit-uality of BECs, on the contrary, fueled the movements for peace and justice in their place and time. What is the lesson for us?

Most churches' practice reflects a belief in either the divinity of Christ or the humanity of Christ. Watching a church's daily activities, it's easy to see where its priorities lie—in activities that focus on the seen or activities that focus on the unseen. The spirit-uality of BECs was incarnational, the seamless union of the divine and the human, the unbroken line from earth to sky. Members believed in the love of God for the earth with such conviction that they constantly fought for the promise of abundant life to be concretely available to all.

At the same time, they believed in the divine presence of God with them with such faith that they were able to give themselves to this battle even when it threatened the loss of their possessions, relationships, or lives. They could overcome the urge toward self-preservation because they trusted that their lives were hidden with Christ and that those who lost their lives for the sake of the kingdom would find them anew.

Some of the practices that fueled their spirit-uality were fundamentally incarnational. They met God in *lo cotidiano* (daily life), which was reflected in these ways:

- spontaneous use of prayer and worship for celebration, support, and guidance
- integration of the symbols of their daily lives and cultural practices into their worship and their acts of struggle
- interpretation of their common life through a biblical frame (up to and including martyrdom)
- practices of radical reconciliation

Let's imagine our twenty-first-century churches in North America living out this kind of spirit-uality.

- An organizing campaign is focused on an industrial plant that has refused to upgrade to minimize air pollution in a low-income area with high rates of asthma among children. Members of local churches engage in a street protest. Some of them are risking their jobs to do so. In preparation, the churches hold a worship service in the street in which the megaphones, the yellow jackets for security, and the banners and signs are all taken to the front as an offering to be blessed. They receive Communion, knowing that their identification and property will be taken from them if they are arrested but that no one will be able to take the bread and wine out of them, with all the real power they bring. Those with more social power take a position in the protest that ensures that they will experience the brunt of any negative police reaction. Church members have agreed that if anyone goes to jail for an extended period of time or loses their job, they will care for their families.

- When church members meet with the County Board of Supervisors to push for the development of affordable housing, they are dressed as angels, reminding the civic leaders that people who need shelter can be angels in disguise (Heb. 13:2). When the affordable housing development finally goes up, the development is called "The Promised Land." The residents understand it as God's love and justice made tangible in their midst.

- A group of immigrant workers stands up to a big company as part of a union campaign. As they are waiting to meet with the boss along with other members of the churches who are there in solidarity, they begin to spontaneously sing praise songs in anticipation of their coming victory. They then join in prayer, asking God to give them the words to speak. In the meeting, a young sister begins to speak and others give her the floor, even though she was not the planned speaker, because the Spirit is so clearly on her.

- Warring factions in a church or coalition have stopped speaking to each other, and it's affecting the work. Instead of ignoring the split and gossiping, the entire community comes together for a time of confrontation, seeking mutual confession from the feuding parties and calling for peace. The wisest members of the community are called on for a fair mediation, but the factions are first expected to open their hearts and feel empathy for the others.

- A slumlord is unwilling to fix the health hazards in his building. He is a Christian. The members of his own church and the members of the churches of his residents come to him to call him to be a true brother to those who live in his development. They use creative strategies to reach a critical mass of pressure, but they also intentionally work to understand his spirituality, to engage his own pastor, and to awaken his sense of justice, believing that he can experience a conversion.

Successful struggles for justice are not simple; they require a broad coalition, short- and long-range strategies, and a comprehensive campaign. However, faith communities have unique gifts to bring to the struggle. These gifts arise from and are rooted in the kind of incarnational spirit-uality BECs practiced. The next chapter will focus on faith-full strategies for social transformation.

Actuar (Act) / Now What?

Amos

Churches made up primarily of oppressed and marginalized people can be the most disconnected from broader movements for change, partially because they lack resources and partially because their traditional function in the lives of the poor is as a refuge from the pain of an unjust world. They provide shields but not swords—tools for transcendence but not for incarnation. However, when their members awaken to the real potential for change in their daily lives and their common life, when they know that the pursuit of this kind of change is meant to be seamlessly integrated with faith, rooted in the power of the Spirit, there is often a deep joy, marked by tears and laughter. You can be the spark that sets the fire.

Lydia

We all long for the living power of God to transform our lives, for the fulfillment of Isaiah 65:17–25, a vision of a community in which all have access to abundant life. "The danger of privilege is modernity's wager,"[9] the belief that God is irrelevant to the fulfillment of our dreams. We can get the good life for ourselves and our family without an incarnational faith. However, we know in our souls that this pursuit is hollow. We cannot dance with a dismembered body[10]—a body with parts that have been cut off and thrown into the corner. Be the voice in your church seeking to partner with those who are most directly affected, not as a political commitment but as the core of an incarnational spirit-uality.

9. We are indebted to Branson and Roxburgh (2021) for this apt phrase.
10. The image of a dismembered body comes from a wonderful sermon on Gal. 2:10 preached by Tim Dearborn, senior World Vision leader (September 2012). Galatians 2:10 calls on the early church to remember the poor. To re-member the poor is to take the members of the body politic that have been discarded and reconnect them to the rest of the body.

Ruth

You know that God wants more for the family and neighborhood you come from—more abundant life, more shalom. It's easy to feel powerless in the face of the isolation of the church in the barrio and the indifference of the church outside. You are not powerless; you are part of a chain that goes around the world and throughout the ages. The living Christ wants this goal more than you do and can work through you to help achieve it. Dare to enter into a more incarnational spirit-uality and invite others to join you.

Hush Harbor Spirit-uality

It was at night, when the antebellum world was asleep and the spirit world was stirred, that they could affirm and feel within them the power of their rivers. Such power was best reflected and energized in them when they sang, danced, ring shouted, drummed, conjured, root-worked, educated themselves, affirmed one another, and contemplated and strategized their way to freedom. Through these mediums they reclaimed and reconnected with the spirit world of their African past. (Harrison 2009, 147–48)

Only a dark spirituality, catalyzed when the empire is asleep, can fortify true liberation. Enslaved Africans, during the day, listened to the white supremacist Christianity of the slaveholder. At night, they spit out the bones of white violence and white greed, kept the meat of love and liberation from Christianity, and mixed it with their African spiritual beliefs and practices. This dark spirit-uality anchored them so they could make a way through the terrifying white Christian light that dominated the day. What exactly were those African spiritualities? What were the beliefs and practices they retained from Christianity? How were they related? What conceptual frameworks can help the contemporary practitioner make sense of this dark, creative spirit-uality and theology of hush harbors? Enter, however briefly, the syncretistic spirit world of those who stole away to the brush. "African Traditional Religionists regard God, natural phenomena, and the ancestors as intrinsically related to each other, and the traditionalist's primary interest in them is not philosophical, but practical, that is, how they together affect the lives of human beings" (Wilmore 1985, 4).

Hush harbor religion was not primarily about "the sweet by and by." Metaphysics was not the point. The interest was about how religion informed daily life. When a monarch butterfly glides past your nose, you recall the way your great-grandmother's words of affirmation settled so softly on your spirit. The monarch is not there to be analyzed. Your great-grandmother is visiting you; experience the butterfly's message to you. This is the syncretistic Afro-

Christianity of hush harbors rather than the philosophizing of Euro-American Christianity. This spiritual creativity was especially powerful in rhythmic movement, conjure and healing, and word power of enslaved Africans.

Ver (See) / What?

Rhythmic Movement

In [the brush harbor], they tapped into their inner rhythms and used the very same artistic expressions that master and some slaves saw as mindless entertainment, as subversive devices to invoke the spirit world and resist bondage and violence. Artistic expression—drumming, singing, and dancing—served a political and religio-cultural purpose; it was a means of resistance, subversion, invocation, inspiration, and retention. (Harrison 2009, 196)

The voice carried over the air like the blown seeds of a dandelion: "Oh freedom." The words hovered over you as an invitation to respond: "Over me, over me." And collectively, voices sang together, "Before I'd be a slave, I'd be buried in my grave, and go home to my Lord and be free!" (Golden Gospel Singers 2007). The words themselves were powerful, but the power was also in the rhythm and harmonies, the ringing in your chest as the back-and-forth singing caught you into the flow of sound waves coordinating between dark bodies, bodies bruised and yet buoyed. This communication and connection could not be reduced to words alone. Working inside of and holding these voices of melody, harmony, and reverberation was the drum. The bass came in, then faded, then returned, lifting the voices ever so methodically, never letting them fall flat, like they were bouncing steadily on a trampoline. In between the bass, the voices' movement going 'round and 'round, one voice to the next, on and on, as if this never had to end. Then the dance and the clap began. Dark bodies swaying and circling, feet pitter-pattering, hips twisting and turning, movement that was both performative and prophetic.

The dance, typically the ring shout, was at once an embodiment of art and a liberation of the body from the supremacy of the plantation. On the plantation, beads of sweat dripped from the Black body due to labor not chosen but forced. In hush harbors, the sweat from dark bodies was like a cool rain washing away the heat of trauma and tyranny, giving coolness that felt like rinsing and cleansing and freedom. One enslaved African recalled the experience of dancing, singing, and drumming as if it were flying:

Duh slabes wuz out in duh fiel wukin. All ub a sudden dey git tuhgedduh an staht tuh moob roun in a ring. Roun dey go fastuh n fastuh. Den one by one dey riz up an take wing an fly lak a bud. Duh obuhseeuh heah duh noise an he come out an he see duh slabs riz up in duh eah an fly back tuh Africa. (Harrison 2009, 204)

This ministry of movement in hush harbors was ripe with meaning for enslaved Africans: the Creator and the ancestors were with them in the drum, in the dance, in the singing, enlivening their very bodies and souls. Rhythmic movement in the hush harbor enabled enslaved Africans to fly, if not literally, certainly for their spirits to fly, to soar free from the circumstances of the plantation to have the definitive meaning over their lives. This kind of belief in the divine and the ancestors being present in the fleshy and kinesthetic experiences of daily life and especially in hush harbors was rooted in African cosmologies that did not bifurcate the sacred from the secular and ordinary.

Conjure and Healing

It was this conviction of the sacredness in all life that animated the healing relationship between the natural world and the enslaved. Even today, I (Brandon) can remember how my maternal grandmother, on days that I knew she was in pain, not by her voicing her pain but by how she teetered so tenderly around the house, would hobble her way into the kitchen. She never told me what she was making in the kitchen. I smelled the aroma of the herbs. It was one of her self-care potions to sooth her aching bones that had been passed down to her across generations.

This is the practice of conjure. Conjurers are healers who mediate the sacred through the natural world. They use resources like plants and herbs for potions and rituals to address specific problems an oppressed person or community is facing. Before we knew what medical racism and big pharma was, my grandmother stood in a long lineage of healers, Black people who conjure the spirit world by partnering with the planet to apply sacred medicine to meet the needs of Black communities.

In hush harbors, healing took many forms, but it generally fell into two categories: protection from harm and curing illness.

> Griffin Whittier, a former South Carolina slave, recalled how the adults among the more than sixty slaves on his master's plantation would meet secretly on Saturday nights for a "'lil . . . fun frum de white folks hearin'. . . . They felt especially confident because a 'Conjun Doc' told them he had put a spell on 'ole Marse so dat he will 'blevin ev'y think dat us tole him bout Sa'day night and Sunday morning." (Jones 1990, 140)

Confidence was a spiritual gift, given by the divine through community, when the plantation economy was bent on humiliating African peoples. The use of the spell, often channeled through some resource from the natural world—a root, for example—mediated safety and confidence for the enslaved at the same time it was believed to render confusion for the white slaveholder. These healing practices were also used to treat the physical ailments of the community or to cause physical ailments for the enemies of the community, typically white slaveholders and their families. One story of an enslaved woman, "Aunt" Darkas, a respected conjurer, goes like this:

> She was blind but she could go ter the woods and pick out any kind of root or herb she wanted. She said the Lord told her what roots to get. Before sun-up you see her in the woods with a short handled pick. She listened to what ailed slaves and then, she go out there and draw a bucket of water and set it on the floor. She created a healing substance with the water and certain herbs taken from the woods. After placing the bucket on the floor she waved her hand over it and say something. She called it healing the water. She said the Lord gave her power and vision. (Harrison 2009, 185)

Womanist theologians and practitioners call these leaders mystics, as they mediated a direct encounter with the sacred, the spirit, the transcendent in ways that brought calm, cool, wholeness, and protection (Harding 1981, 14; Harrison 2009, 183). These healers cannot be easily dismissed as superstitious or exceptions. Conjurers were pivotal to the spiritual leadership and practices of hush harbors and the Black prophetic religion it engendered (Harrison 2009, 173–89; Wilmore 1998, 49). Historians attest that the healing practices of these leaders functioned in relationship with Christianity. "The practices of herbalism, divination, and conjuration survived alongside Christianity in the folk culture of southern blacks. . . . Conjuration served as a countercultural protest to the worldview of the dominant society and met needs in the slave quarters that Christianity did not" (Sernett 1999, 76).

Word Power

Whether through the natural environment or through sacred Scripture, enslaved Africans accessed the power of the sacred wherever it was available. The vast majority of enslaved Africans were illiterate and were forbidden by law and custom to learn to read and write. The slaveholder class thought that by keeping the enslaved illiterate, they would keep them subordinate. What they failed to understand was the power of the oral-aural dimensions of knowledge production and spiritual practice that was deeply tied to rhythmic and embodied African worldviews. Enslaved Africans claimed spiritual power through words while they were denied political and economic power through formal education. One of the primary modes of word power was prayer.[11]

11. Word power was also expressed through the Spirituals and preaching. I discuss preaching in chap. 2, biblical interpretation in chap. 5, and the Spirituals throughout. I limit the discussion to prayer here since it hasn't been covered throughout, and because it is one of the practices, like singing, that virtually everyone in the hush harbors engaged in.

In chapters 2 and 5, we discussed the critical interpretation and pedagogy, layered meanings, and coding the enslaved employed to subvert the dominating uses of Christianity by the slaveholder class. This creativity and agency certainly deepened the sense of existential and moral power possessed by the enslaved. Prayer gave the enslaved a unique form of word power because, unlike singing and preaching, praying could be done aloud, silently, or quietly, alone or with others. The prayer life of the enslaved took on an elasticity that gave them even more freedom to say and believe and express themselves exactly how they pleased. Prayer was such a unique spiritual act in hush harbors that it had a special space of its own. One former enslaved African named Amanda McCray states that on her plantation in Florida, there was a special praying ground: "The grass never had a chance ter grow fer the troubled knees that kept it crushed down." Another enslaved African named Andrew Moss describes the hush harbor prayer grounds that were on his Georgia plantation: "My Mammy's was a ole twisted thick-rooted muscadine bush. She'd go in dar and pray for deliverance of de slaves" (Levine 2007, 41).

Prayer in hush harbors served many purposes. One of the most immediate was its practical function. Prayer was a means of well-being, of being at ease, of cooling off. Historian Renee Harrison speaks to this practical dimension of prayer, especially for enslaved women: "This act alone—stepping away and entering nature—connected them to themselves, their bodies, their voices, feet, hands, hearts, souls, and minds. It connected them to the earth, and each other, and their precolonial African past. . . . This act signified their need for connectedness to something human and spirit, real and organic, open and free; a space where they could momentarily clear their heads and cool their faces" (Harrison 2009, 154).

The prayer warriors of hush harbors were prophetic contemplatives, those who saw moments of stillness as a chance to encounter the sacred, to be set free, and for the experience of that spiritual freedom to invoke their deepest conviction in a liberated world. Womanist theologian Barbara Holmes calls this crisis contemplation (Holmes 2004, 59). This was not the privileged meditation that allowed one to escape the suffering and conditions of the world. Enslaved Africans practiced crisis contemplation in the hush harbor as an act of guttural, visceral prayer that involved bodily responses—moans, chants, cries, songs, dance. Often, a large pot or kettle would be turned down to "catch" the sounds of the prayers and responses. This was an act of safety, to keep from being caught by the overseers. It was also a deeply African spiritual act of keeping faith with the ancestors, with the belief that the pot held the prayers for the ancestors to hear and engage. There are very few written prayers of enslaved prophetic contemplatives. This prayer from Frederick Douglass is worth quoting at length:

There with no audience but the Almighty, I would pour out my soul's complaint, in my rude way, with an apostrophe to the moving multitude of ships: You are loosed from your moorings and are free; I am fast in my chains and am a slave! You move merrily before the gentle gale and I sadly before the bloody whip! You are freedom's swift-winged angels that fly round the world; I am confined in bands of iron! O that I were free! O, that I were on one of your gallant decks, and under your protecting wing! . . . The glad ship is gone; she hides in the dim distance. I am left in the hottest hell of unending slavery. O God, save me! God, deliver me! Let me be free! Is there any God? Why am I a slave? I will run away. I will not stand it. Get caught, or get clear, I'll try it. I had as well die with ague as the fever. I have only one life to lose. I had as well be killed running as die standing. Only think of it; one hundred miles straight north, and I am free! Try it? Yes! God helping me, I will. (Douglass 1994, 64–65)

This was a treasonous prayer. A prophetic contemplative uttered prayers that could get them killed. The prayers of hush harbors soothed the soul and troubled the society. And they certainly would have made the church uncomfortable.

Discomforting the church's theology was one of the most powerful ways that prayer functioned in hush harbors. Douglass's prayer called into question any way that the church was well adjusted to the political and economic system of chattel slavery. However, hush harbor prayers also challenged Christian supremacy. One example of how enslaved Africans deployed the syncretistic power of prayer is the prayer-Spiritual "Let Us Break Bread Together."

> Let us break bread together on our knees
> When I fall on my knees,
> with my face to the rising sun,
> O Lord, have mercy on me.

On the surface, this is a common Christian song for the sacrament of Communion. For enslaved Africans, this song functioned as a secret summons to hush harbors, and the third line—"with my face to the rising sun"—was symbolic for some enslaved Africans of Islamic prayer practices (Harrison 2009, 201). By incorporating the diverse African cultural and religious milieu into the prayer practices of the hush harbor, enslaved Africans resisted the dogmatic and purity culture of slaveholding Christianity.

Juzgar (Judge) / So What?

The mixing of theologies and spiritualities in hush harbors troubles my (Brandon's) childhood interpretation of neatly defined Southern Black Christian history. And for many enslaved Africans, religious syncretism was a violation of Christianity as they had come to know it. Here is what some of them had to say:

> "I learned a long time ago dat dey was nothing to charms. . . . De Bible teaches me better 'n dat." One former enslaved man remarked, "I am a great Christian. . . . I don't believe in conjurers. . . . He [God] . . . said, 'There ain't no such thing as conjurers.'" Another recalled . . . "Aunt Jane was the cause of so many on our plantation getting religion. . . . She said them beads and crosses we saw every body have was nothing. She said people must give their hearts to God, to love him and keep his commandments; and we believed what she said. I never wanted them beads I saw others have." (Harrison 2009, 129–30)

African traditional religious ways were disdained not only by enslaved African lay Christians but also by those who were clergy of emerging independent Black denominations. For example, post-slavery, after Bishop Daniel Alexander Payne of the AME Church witnessed a ring shout at a camp meeting inspired by hush harbors, he says:

> About this time [1878] I attended a "bush meeting." . . . After the sermon they formed a ring, and with coats off sung, clapped their hands and stamped their feet in a most ridiculous and heathenish way. I requested the pastor to go and stop their dancing. At his request they stopped their dancing and clapping of hands, but remained singing and rocking their bodies to and fro. This they did for about fifteen minutes. I then went, and taking their leader by the arm requested him to desist and to sit down and sing in a rational manner. I told him also that it was a heathenish way to worship and disgraceful to themselves, the race, and the Christian name. In that instance they broke up their ring; but would not sit down, and walked sullenly away. After the sermon in the afternoon, having another opportunity of speaking alone to this young leader of the singing and clapping ring, he said: "Sinners won't get converted unless there is a ring." Said I: "You might sing till you fell down dead, and you would fail to convert a single sinner, because nothing but the Spirit of God and the word of God can convert sinners." He replied: "The Spirit of God works upon people in different ways. At camp-meeting there must be a ring here, a ring there, a ring over yonder, or sinners will not get converted." This was his idea, and it is also that of many others. These "Bands" I have had to encounter in many places. . . . To the most thoughtful . . . I usually succeeded in making the "Band" disgusting; but by the ignorant masses . . . it was regarded as the essence of religion. (Raboteau 2004, 68–69)

What I have discovered as I have talked to Black elders in my life is that folk religion has always existed alongside Christianity for Black folks in the South. Even the spiritual origins of herbalism and other folk ways and spiritual practices of my own grandmother were never talked about. Old African spiritual ways—from before our people knew the colonizer's religion—have survived even inside these silences about aspects of Southern Black spirituality that do not fit neatly inside respectable Christianity. The extent to which this folk religion is made explicit in Christian spaces of worship and practice is a complicated matter. Hush harbors created a space for Black people to be honest and authentic about the beliefs and practices that guided their lives. Two key conceptual tools help make sense of hush harbor spirit-uality: hybridity and a pedagogy of discomfort.

Hybridity

The colonial project was a practice in the refusal of joining. From the beginning, colonialism thrived on the logics of purity and perfection, a pure-blood race, the perfect doctrine, the pure citizen. And yet since the beginning of the colonial project, no such purity has ever been available. The claim to settle the lands of the Americas was from the beginning shot through with desires and outcomes of conquest and pillage. Though some claim that the motive for slavery and settling the Americas was to spread the Christian gospel, the motive was never about healing the land and bodies of Native and African peoples or caring for their souls. This is the way that hegemony works. Claims to what is true and reasonable and moral can so easily conceal what is really at work. This is also true on the bodily level. The racial scale has never functioned consistently. The stated sexual ethics of the antebellum period say one thing—the "Christian" commitment to monogamy and to sex within the bounds of marriage. The functional sexual ethics tell a different story. The story of Southern ancestry is one of mixture—Black, white, and Native—mixing that was both consensual and forced, and within the chattel slavery economy, force was the norm. White, male, heteropatriarchal sexual ethics of raping Black women and breeding their own forced labor was the status quo.

The interaction of cultures and peoples always results in hybridity. It typically occurs implicitly and organically. Thomas Dorsey did not set out to create gospel music from jazz, blues, and boogie-woogie. He imbibed the sounds of his time and his experience in Holiness churches, and through the inspiration of his own talents in collaboration with others, the world was given the gift of Black gospel music. The question is the politics or ethics of that hybridity. In the case of hush harbor spirit-uality, enslaved Africans hybridized Christianity, Islam, conjure, and other African Traditional Religions into a distinctive theological worldview and spiritual practice. Enslaved Africans engaged in spiritual hybridity in ways that enacted care, survival, and liberation among one another as oppressed peoples (Hopkins 2000, 135–45). White slaveholding Christianity concealed its hybridity in the name of being righteous and having authority. The plantation church wielded its hybrid Christianity to pillage and plunder, to terrorize and torture Black and Native peoples and lands. This is hybridity as concealment and control.

Contemporary leaders seeking to cultivate hush harbor communities will have to be liberated from the logics of purity and perfection that are so often concealed inside God-talk. Claims of being "biblical" and being "Christian" must be interrogated and made plain. We must get curious about their theological and moral sources, and we must confess and abolish those sources that conceal and control. Alternatively, we must claim and reclaim sources that engender care, justice, and love.

A Pedagogy of Discomfort

It takes courage to embody hush harbor spiritual hybridity in a climate of religious hegemony. And courage is a practice in making discomfort normative—not the kind of discomfort that is forced or negative but the kind that is produced through the process of growth and change. The oft-quoted Octavia Butler quip is relevant: "All that you touch you change. All that you change, changes you. The only lasting truth is change. God is change" (Butler 2012, 11). Decolonial theorist Julietta Singh speaks of a pedagogy of discomfort to describe this praxis. Singh draws on the work of Sara Ahmed, who describes discomfort beautifully in this way: "To feel uncomfortable is precisely to be affected by that which persists in the shaping of bodies and lives. Discomfort is hence not about assimilation or resistance, but about inhabiting norms differently. The inhabitance is generative or productive insofar as it does not end with the failure of norms to be secured, but with possibilities of living that do not 'follow' these norms through" (Singh 2018, 151). This is the process of making one's discomforts conscious instead of allowing unconscious discomfort to produce internalized or externalized oppression.

To practice a pedagogy of discomfort is to embody a spirit-uality of truth-telling and vulnerability. From this place, genuine connection and collaboration emerge. What if when they encountered the Native peoples and Africans, the early European settlers normalized the kind of self-awareness and courage needed to name their discomfort rather than enact violence? Hush harbors were sites where enslaved Africans could be honest about the trauma they experienced in their bodies and psyches. They did not have to hide and trick to get by, like they did in the slave quarters and in the plantation church. From the vulnerability exercised in hush harbors, enslaved Africans could freely practice their native folk-religious ways and feel at ease to experiment with mixing these ways with the parts of the Christian tradition that felt like love and liberation. When everyone in a gathering is encouraged to exercise discomfort, we render divide-and-conquer tactics powerless. This reminds me of Jesus's words that those who lose their life will gain it, while those who seek to save or hoard their life will lose it (Matt. 16:25). Singh calls this practice of discomfort "vital ambivalence," which she defines as "a practice of representation that emphasizes, politicizes, and embraces the subject's contradictions and slippages" (Singh 2018, 158).

Actuar (Act) / Now What?

The dominant religious culture operates by a theology and spirituality of concealment, using God-talk to cover fear of and discomfort with change and loss of power and control. To cultivate the spirit-uality of hush harbors, leaders will need to break rank with concealment and get brutally honest about their own needs and the ways that their own neglect of themselves has produced a religion of domination and violence, particularly against women and against Black, Brown, non-Christian, and queer bodies. The following questions will help leaders reponsibly practice hybridity and discomfort:

> **Amos**: What are the spiritual ways of being that your community talks about only in private? How can you normalize those beliefs and practices in your community, adapt them for changing times, and use them as a source of blessing to those outside your community?
>
> **Lydia**: Who were your people before they were in a position of dominance? What foundational beliefs and practices anchored their sense of identity that are not rooted in exclusion and violence? How has the spiritual concealment of your people dehumanized you and others?
>
> **Ruth**: What spiritual practices have you adopted from the dominant culture? Can you trace the origins of those practices? Are they rooted in truth or myths, values you want or lies that render you and your community of origin invisible?

A Spirit-uality of Incarnation

At first glance, the spirit-ualities of BECs and hush harbors were significantly different—strikingly moving and beautiful but distinct. However, deep similarities sit just below the surface, and each holds insights for the twenty-first century in its distinctive responses to particular contexts.

BECs and hush harbors both rest on a vibrant embodiment of faith. The heart of the word *incarnational* (*incarnatio* in Latin) is *caro*, meaning "flesh." BECs and hush harbors were about the Word going deep into the flesh. Whether we are reflecting on the dancing and moaning of hush harbors or the prophetic dramas of the BEC reconciliation practices, we are examining a multisensory experience of a God who is vividly present in every aspect of daily life. A fully incarnational spirit-uality includes the spectrum of all human emotions and all physical movements—as we see in the beautiful stories of hush harbor prayer. It also includes the capacity to see the presence of God in the midst of daily life, to see miraculous options. How did BEC members find peace and joy on the battlefield, and the courage to risk and sacrifice? They took seriously that God was walking beside them, holding them, even carrying them as they entered into danger for justice's sake—and as they struggled with personal and family issues. They took it so seriously that they expressed it openly in symbol and language, both by including the world in their worship and through their acts in the world.

Each movement encountered barriers to fully incarnational spirit-uality, and each drew on different resources to overcome them. Despite the ever-present danger, they were not intimidated or impeded. Holding the divine and the human together is not a simple task. As fallen and broken human beings, we tend to move into the flesh and lose the spirit or move into the spirit and leave our bodies behind. Institutions tend to respond to problems with attempts at control. The impulse to control is, at best, an impulse to preserve what is precious. At worst, it's an impulse to be safe from the disruptive power of the Spirit. Those who persecuted BEC members were Christians. The Catholic leadership initially supported BECs but ultimately withdrew support from the movement, which affected its ability to continue. Those who criticized hush harbors were often Black pastors and other devout Black Christians. Vibrant life is messy. Messiness provokes the impulse to impose control and order, yet we are called not to quench the Spirit even when the Spirit moves in unexpected and uncomfortable ways.

If you commit yourself, as individuals, as leaders, to nurturing vibrant, embodied spirit-uality in your church, you will be criticized. You will not always be sure that you are right. It is rumored that Martin Luther once said, "Perhaps I am the worst sinner in Christendom." He was facing the profound loneliness of disagreement with those whose opinion mattered to him. Both direct experiences of rejection and the corrosive power of that loneliness can serve as real barriers to exploring the fullness of incarnational spirit-uality. Is it worth it?

BEC spirit-uality gave BEC members the power to change their lives and their communities, even when it required risking death in the process. Hush harbor spirit-uality kept enslaved Africans going through terrible pain until there was a chance for liberation. In the midst of all the challenges of our age, this kind of spirit-uality holds out a promise that we cannot afford to ignore.

7

Faith-full Organizing

Alma y Fermenta de la Sociedad

BEC Organizing

> Dios nos manda hacer de este mundo
> una mesa donde haya igualdad;
> trabajando y luchando juntos,
> compartiendo la propiedad. ("Canto de Entrada," verso 3, *Misa
>   Salvadoreña Popular* ["Opening Hymn," verse 3 of the *Misa*])

> God has commanded us to make of this world
> a table without inequality,
> working and struggling together,
> sharing our property.[1]

> He has shown you, O mortal, what is good.
>   And what does the LORD require of you?
> To act justly and to love mercy
>   and to walk humbly with your God. (Mic. 6:8)

Also, seek the peace and prosperity of the city to which I have carried you into exile. Pray to the LORD for it, because if it prospers, you too will prosper. (Jer. 29:7)

1. This is an excerpt from "Vamos al Banquete," the opening song of the *Misa Salvadoreña Popular*—the liturgy created by Guillermo Cuellar for Archbishop Oscar Romero in 1980 and widely used throughout the BEC movement.

In 1965, the Second Vatican Council produced *Gaudium et spes*, a pastoral document redefining the church in response to the signs of the times. BECs took its description of the church as "soul and leaven" as a vocational mandate. The church was meant to be not only *for* the community or *in service* to the community but also an essential *part* of the community, fulfilling the function in the body politic that the soul fulfills in the body. The church was also to be the yeast of the kingdom of God (Matt. 13:33), transforming the society as yeast transforms bread.

Living this out in their context meant ongoing participation in various activities designed to benefit the community. As described earlier, BECs were known for direct service, caring generously, even sacrificially, for their neighbors in need. However, their activities went beyond direct service to community development, community organizing, and advocacy. Their incarnational identification with their communities also led to integration into popular movements. As their work resulted in a new voice and capacity for the people of their communities, powerful leaders and forces reacted with retaliation that reached the point of violent persecution. BECs understood this process through the lens of the cross.

Ver (See) / What?

Community Development

Faith of a People by Pablo Galdámez describes the community development activities of BECs as "signs and wonders" heralding the presence of the kingdom of God (Galdámez 1983, 24–32). These signs and wonders included clinics that combined home remedies from the abuelas (grandmothers) and Western medicine, literacy training, hygiene courses, schools for children, nutritional assistance programs, and cooperative enterprises. Community development work was profoundly integrated with the spiritual formation and leadership development work of BECs.

> The teachers in our communities started organizing literacy courses. We began to build a little school, since the slum didn't have a single one. Every night we would mix cement, lay bricks, and so on. Everybody helped, men, women, and children. I remember Nacho. Nacho had never been to a meeting; he was too busy drinking. When he saw his neighbors doing construction work he felt "called." Nacho was a bricklayer. He knew everything there was to know about it and he pitched right in. And so his alcoholism ran straight into the walls of a school! When we were finished, we named him Builder of the Year, and toasted him with lemonade! (Galdamez 1983, 26)

Separate projects were often linked in a multipurpose cooperative. In the Philippines, the cooperative at the BEC of Santa Teresita sold goods to the members at cheaper prices, provided credit to members for their income-generating projects, sold goods produced by the members, and helped pay for medical expenses and mortuary services for the members (Healey and Hinton 2005, 117).

Community Organizing and Advocacy

Of course, these activities did not happen in a vacuum. Community development projects required electricity and plumbing, which required official access to land. Control of land has been at the heart of inequality and injustice throughout Latin America and the Philippines since the Spanish conquest. Even a small step toward housing could trigger land issues. Dominique Barbe relates such issues in Brazil:

> Our community took form the day when the group, which had been talking together and studying the Bible, decided to reconstruct the *barraco* of a widow with ten children and expecting the eleventh. Her husband had been killed some days earlier on the highway that passes not far from us. So it was decided one Sunday morning all the volunteers would show up with saws, hammer and nails, and axes at seven in the morning to work on the widow's house. . . . Inspectors from the town council came to tear down the hut, which although only partially built was already being lived in, and the widow had to pretend to go into labor—she was so frightened that she almost lost the baby. The next week we had to employ a ruse. The walls of the hut were to be constructed separately, at a distance and then assembled in an instant the next Sunday. We had barely finished when the officials appeared again on the horizon. The widow barely had time to install herself in her new lodging, still unfinished, with a bundle of clothes; for a municipal decree provides that no dwelling whatever may be demolished if it is actually occupied by the person who takes shelter there. So that was a victory. (Barbe 1987, 99–100)

In the Philippines: "Another time they confronted Rosano himself, who had been sent by a landlord to make sure that a piece of land grabbed from a peasant would not be planted by that peasant. Brian, Father Vincente Dangan, a Filipino priest who was an assistant in Kabankalan, and hundreds of community members had gone into the flooded rice patty, and with trousers rolled up had planted the seedlings, defying the watching Rosano and his armed companions. Rosano made no move to stop them and did not come back to Oringao" (O'Brien 1987, 157–58).

Individual struggles naturally morphed into broader efforts that included community organizing and advocacy. "CEBs try to expand the individual

goal of owning a house into a collective project. Most of the slums and poor
neighborhoods are squatter settlements where people do not own the land.
The Catholic Church, through CEBs and other religious groups, such as the
Pastoral de favela, performs an important role in helping poor people fight
for land on which they can build houses or where they already have houses"
(Mariz 1994, 128). Galdámez tells a story about an initially successful effort
to obtain residential services for an entire area, which foundered when the
BEC ran into land issues.

> We appointed a committee to try to get electric lights for the slum. We went to
> the light company and they promised to "study the matter." Somebody came
> up with the idea of going to the papers just in case the company was thinking
> of filing our application away somewhere and forgetting about it. So we wrote
> a long letter to the newspapers. It was a shrewd letter—we thanked the com-
> pany for the attention they had given our request. That did the trick. Shortly
> after, electricity came to the pasteboard shacks. You could have seen us late
> in the evenings putting up light poles. . . . The water problem turned out to
> be more difficult. The only way, it seemed, to get water was to lay a main on
> somebody else's land. And besides, we were afraid our own landowner might
> take advantage of the situation by waiting until the water main was in and then
> evicting our community and renting to people who would be willing to pay
> more. (Galdámez 1983, 30)

BECs would often turn to the joint purchase of land for collective housing, but land was easily subject to land-grabbing by wealthy individuals or
businesses with political patronage. Guillermo Cook describes a long and
partially successful struggle to defend a village from forced eviction by a
land development company owned by a general who was also head of the
government land reform agency that was charged with intervening in such
cases (Cook 1985, 129).

Yet communities were not powerless. Niall O'Brien describes the process
through which BEC members were equipped for successful confrontation.

> I felt that one of the simplest, most powerful, and unusual ways of achieving
> justice was learning to confront the guilty, to speak up and put your case con-
> vincingly. . . . A judge would send a private letter, summoning a poor person,
> who overawed by the letter, would go immediately, borrowing the fare to do
> so. Then in the judge's office, standing in their bare feet, battered straw hat in
> hand, the summoned person would meet his antagonist, and a charade would
> be played out, in which the judge adjudicated the whole matter without a
> trial, to the detriment of the poorer party. We trained the people to know their
> rights, and if they had to meet a judge, a landowner, a *barrio* captain, a lawyer,
> to discuss the whole thing carefully beforehand. They would even act out the

possible reactions of their adversary and in this way get used to absorbing anger. We asked them to sign nothing unless it was in Ilongo and until they had first taken it home to show the community. Victory was in the process more than in the product. In fact, in one sense the process itself was the real product. . . . But too often a bullet cut short that growth-filled process. (O'Brien 1987, 200)

BECs understood these struggles to be spiritual as well as material. The logo of the National Federation of Sugar Workers in the Philippines was of Christ in the temple with a whip overturning the tables of the money changers. I (Alexia) had a personal experience with the federation's work and faith. A group of workers who lived on a plantation (owned by Dole in partnership with a wealthy Filipino) were paid malnutrition wages, and so they began to plant banana trees next to their little huts as a sign of resistance as well as a practical solution. Thugs from the management came one day, while I was present, and dug up the banana plants. The women and children were wailing and crying. I asked the young organizer how they could keep going in the face of the power inequalities, and she told me that they were going to win soon. When I asked how she could believe that could possibly be true, she referred to the exodus story and said that they would win in the generation of her daughter's daughter.

Bishop Dom Hélder Câmara of East Recife, Brazil, would regularly address and exhort BEC members who were fighting land speculators. Cook describes a meeting in which thousands of BEC members in such a battle came together for street theater, a communal meal, and a Mass at which the bishop preached (Cook 1985, 129).

BECs were primarily responsible for some amazing direct victories, including setting up peace zones that have resulted in the cessation of violence in specific areas, stopping logging operations, and engaging in reforestation (Healey and Hinton 2005, 121). However, as conflict intensified in all BEC contexts, broader social movements accelerated, and participation in these movements became a natural next step.

Joining the Movements

Throughout Latin America and the Philippines in the 1970s and '80s, the strongest opposition to government neglect and repression as well as exploitation by elite families and corporations was spearheaded by broad social movements in which multiple organizations joined in national coalitions. These broad movements were often in relationship with political parties or revolutionary forces, but they also maintained a level of independence. That line of separation became increasingly blurry as violent conflict and government repression intensified.

These movements offered the potential for added power and protection in the short term and more comprehensive solutions to poverty and injustice in the long term. At the same time, participating in their activities increased the risk of government or paramilitary persecution.

While the Roman Catholic Church had historically supported the ruling elites, new theological and ecclesiological developments in the 1960s divided leaders of the church between those who accompanied and supported movements for land reform and other justice-related social changes and those who continued to back the large landowners and the governments that supported them. The liberation church assisted the social movements in a variety of ways. The role of BECs was to "mobilize and motivate the poor to organize themselves and to participate in these movements" (Mariz 1994, 115). BECs became the spine of the social movements, providing foot soldiers and leaders whose faith gave them the courage and commitment to risk and sacrifice. Their self-understanding as alma y fermenta de la sociedad, soul and leaven of the society, encouraged participation in movements instead of independent religious action. The community efforts of BECs changed from an organic response to the needs of their communities to uniting several barrios in a common cause, such as the creation of a regional clinic (which created an organization that could then join a broader movement), to engagement in worker-controlled labor unions to participation by the members in political movements (Barbe 1987, 106).[2] BEC members understood this broader participation as a missionary task. According to the pastoral documents that emerged from the Bolivian Episcopal Conference of 1973, BECs were to inspire their members to become "involved in popular organizations, syndicates, and political parties offering testimony of the Christian faith that is oriented by the social teachings of the church" (Healey and Hinton 2005, 13).

BECs' entry into social movements was controversial. Galdámez describes the internal debate:

> About this time, the popular organizations became organized for systematic struggle and conscious-raising. This was a new weapon which would enable the poor to confront the power of the mighty. *Campesinos*, union members, students, teachers, "marketplace women," catechists, community directors—all of us felt the upheaval and challenge of this new movement in El Salvador. The popular organizations looked like the right tool to drive out the demons living in the very root of society—demons more powerful than the ones that burrow

2. Many Latin American countries have official state-sponsored trade union organizations. These are often legally required to focus only on the needs of their particular occupational constituency rather than on common issues across industries. They are known for graft and incompetence. BEC members often joined and supported autonomous workers' movements that challenged these institutions (Barbe 1987, 106; Cook 1985, 129).

into the individual human heart. This network of new organizations raised new questions for us. Were they any business of ours? Would these organizations unite or divide us? Some of the members of our communities were joining them. Others stayed at the level of collaborators, or sympathizers. Still others were paralyzed by fear. . . . Some of us were of the opinion that the first thing to do was to fashion a new heart for the new human being—and only then attempt to renew society. Others "read" in our harsh Salvadoran society that if our society did not have new roots, the new human being would never be born. All of us saw clearly that the option for the poor was the main thing in Jesus' gospel. But where to begin? Gradually we discovered that the dichotomy between personal conversion and social transformation was a false one. . . . The correct solution to this false dilemma, then, was a personal, interior commitment to the social task. (Galdámez 1983, 56)

Cook cites Pablo Richards's analysis of the political participation of BECs: "This 'Christian dimension of political practice' is . . . generated in the ecclesial praxis of the grassroots communities. A CEB, as a popular movement, is the place where Christian activists 'express, communicate, reflect upon and celebrate their faith, hope and charity.' It is no wonder that the military dictatorships of Latin America look upon the CEBs as subversive" (Cook 1985, 74). The activism of BEC members did not take the same shape for everyone. *The Gospel in Solentiname* shows that the BEC members in Nicaragua who participated in the Bible studies were not all in the same position. Some were revolutionaries, possibly even active participants in the guerrilla forces. Others took a strong stance for nonviolence and leaned toward love expressed in local actions of sharing and community support.

However, O'Brien and Galdámez both describe the difficulty of negotiating an independent identity as the neutral ground shrunk. During the civil wars in El Salvador and the Philippines, territories went back and forth between being controlled by the revolutionary forces and being controlled by the government. BECs tried to continue to minister in the midst of this. Government forces and death squads regularly targeted members of BECs, while the revolutionary forces tended to regard them favorably but pushed them to active participation. Moises Escalante describes how a delegation from a BEC in El Salvador went to attend a funeral of two young men who had been members of another BEC and had been killed by the death squads. The funeral was taking place in a "liberated zone," but they had to pass through an army-controlled zone on the way. The local guerrilla commander showed up and offered them guns to protect themselves. The BEC leaders refused the guns, which the commander respected, but he also sent two armed young revolutionaries to accompany and protect them. Father O'Brien eloquently describes the challenge:

Two young men, brothers, who were in the NPA, had got the news that their father was dying down in the lowlands. They pleaded for help. They wanted to say good-bye to their father and receive his blessing, a very sacred moment in Ilongo culture. They were surely absent without leave so they were taking a double risk. They asked us to take them as far as the town where their father was dying. We agreed that I would take them to the rice fields outside the town, arriving as dusk came. I knew that they had weapons and noted that each had a grenade, which they put inside the front of their trousers. For them to be caught alive was worse than death because of the torture which was being used. . . . The dilemma of drawing the line between humanitarian cooperation and military collaboration was becoming more and more difficult. (O'Brien 1987, 207)

Persecution and the Cross

The powerful were keeping an eye on us more and more. It was impossible to get the ministry to give official recognition to our housing co-op, one of the most relevant signs of the growth of our communities. We weren't trusted. The government spied on us to see what "sort" we were, how we thought, where we got our funds. Manolo was called in by the director of his company and questioned about us and about his participation in the community. He was told then and there that he would be fired if he kept up his "subversive" activities. With Arsenio it was worse. They hauled him in and interrogated him about the communities. After three days, they let him go. . . . The community battle to defend those who were behind in their mortgage payments was one of our many conflicts. We were accused of fomenting disorder. It was the same with the literacy campaign. We used the Freire method. But Freire was a "notorious Communist," they said and so they began to keep us under surveillance. Our work was becoming more risky by the day—which made it more Christian. (Galdámez 1983, 42)

We are up to our neck in problems here. The popular organizations are more active than ever and repression has kept pace. A member of one of our Christian groups was kidnapped last Tuesday. He was a schoolteacher. We don't know where he is or what has happened to him, and we don't have much hope of seeing him again. Every day, they uncover more corpses. Yesterday was the saddest day of my life. The teacher's students said they'd seen his body on the way into a village an hour from here. We went to see along with his wife and some relatives. The village justice of the peace had processed ten bodies the day before. He said it happened every day. We were thinking that one of the ten, one who hadn't been identified, might be our friend. He was already buried but we got permission to exhume him, so we got a pick and shovel and went to the cemetery. We dug up the body. It was miserably tortured but it wasn't him. (Galdámez 198, 76–77)

The community transformation work of BECs became increasingly dangerous as time passed. I (Alexia) have a vivid memory from the Philippines.

I was attending a regional planning retreat, and we were waiting for the nun who was the director of the human rights office in Manila to arrive. She never arrived. (We later found out that she was last seen being forced into a car with tinted windows.) When it began to get dark, the group was silent, so depressed that we could not work. Finally, one of the Irish brothers who was connected to the BEC movement suggested that we start our cultural-night sharing. Cultural night was a regular part of every retreat in the BEC movement in the Philippines; any member could share a poem, a song, a dance— any gift that they wanted to offer the community. We thought he was crazy, but we went along. He began to sing in Gaelic a cappella, in a beautiful tenor voice, a song about injustice in Ireland and the hope for justice. Everyone was crying, but we were able to move again and go back to work.

Although BECs increased the risk for their members, they also provided spiritual strength and sustenance. They framed these experiences of horrible suffering in the biblical language of the cross: "In this way, by being so close to death, we discovered a new way of being 'acolytes.' 'Acolyte' means one who accompanies. This new way consisted in accompanying those who were suffering—being their companions along their way of the cross, their way of pain and helping them not to be afraid. . . . Being an acolyte meant risking your life" (Galdámez 1983, 77).

Of course, not everyone stayed. Over five hundred thousand refugees fled Central America for the US during the civil wars. Ana, a leader in a BEC in El Salvador, describes the struggle to continue the community in the face of so much loss—loss from the murders and the departures as well as from betrayals by those who cracked under the pressure and informed on their companions. A young Salvadoran in seminary shares that his experience growing up was of a "great silence" in which the members of his church community, led by those who had been traumatized during the war, stayed away from social engagement (Benavides, May 2019). However, in the Lutheran Church of El Salvador, the BECs' experience of suffering and martyrdom is remembered as an inspiration that has strengthened their current commitment to stand up to organized crime in spite of the risk and danger.

Juzgar (Judge) / So What?

We spoke in chapter 6 about BEC spiritual practices as being incarnate in action. In this chapter, we see from the other side—how their social practices incarnated their faith and spirituality. Those who are seeking to do what God requires have important lessons to learn from BECs. Their engagement in working for the shalom of their communities was holistic, courageous, and profoundly incarnational. Each of these characteristics offers an important yardstick for churches in our current context, particularly as increasing numbers of young people are alienated from churches that they perceive to be hypocritical, exclusive, and indifferent to their experiences of injustice.

Holistic

Most churches offer some form of service to their communities. However, often the depth and/or breadth of engagement with their communities is very limited. They are *for* the community but not *with* the community. BECs took on the problems and struggles of their communities as their own, using every resource and opportunity available to seek solutions that involved and benefited the whole community. Community development, community organizing, advocacy, and participation in social movements were all instruments of God's love to be used for divine purpose. These initiatives were not carried out as purely social activities divorced from spiritual realities. BECs infused all social action with spiritual power, using explicitly Christian language and integrating Christian practices. Conversely, all spiritual activities were rooted in and addressed the reality of the whole person, family, neighborhood, and society.

Churches commonly prioritize either their spiritual life and mission or their commitment to social change and community service. BECs lived their faith on multiple levels simultaneously, not only as individuals but also collectively, providing a vibrant witness to their society of the presence of God's kingdom in their midst.

Courageous

In a society that is increasingly indifferent or hostile toward organized Christianity, many churches are tempted to make faith as easy as possible in order to attract and keep members. Historically, from Jesus onward, the Christian faith has had a stronger impact when being a Christian hasn't been easy. In *The Cost of Discipleship*, Dietrich Bonhoeffer (famous pastor and leader of the resistance against Hitler) warns against cheap grace: "Cheap grace is grace without discipleship, grace without the cross, grace without Jesus Christ, living and incarnate" (Bonhoeffer 1937, 44). The courage of BEC members won the respect of their enemies and gave the marginalized hope. Courage is an act of faith that any loss suffered through a righteous action will be worth the cost. Timidity is not inspiring. Stepping out into the midst of social battlefields may result in losing some members and donations. But not stepping out also has consequences. BECs give us a contemporary image of the meaning of Luke 9:24: "For whoever wants to save their life will lose it, but whoever loses their life for me will save it."

Incarnational

In an exercise in a seminary course on community transformation at Fuller Theological Seminary, students are asked to role-play a one-on-one scenario, pretending they are visiting a neighbor of the church to ask about their perceptions of the neighborhood. Every time the exercise is done, one of the biggest takeaways is the simple realization that they are actually residents of a neighborhood. They don't have to pretend to be members of the community; they are members of the community.

BECs' theological frame placed them inextricably in the heart of the community. They were alma y fermenta, soul and leaven, and they built on the foundation of the Catholic understanding of parish. Just as BECs did not separate body and soul, they did not separate their small Christian community from the broader community. This created an automatic humility that is often missing from Christian participation in political arenas. BECs' struggle to discern their roles in the larger social movements was a family conversation, not an attempt to arrive at a common declaration of a possessed truth. It is possible to be both bold and humble.

Actuar (Act) / Now What?

Amos

If we are part of a marginalized church or community, we may have trouble trusting that real change can occur in our community and society. We have been disappointed so many times. As a result, we may often fall into either cynical passivity or angry self-expression, leaving us disconnected from any constructive strategy. Either way, we may have become an atheist in the public square; we may have stopped believing that God is the Lord of the universe, not just our private life. BECs offer us foretastes of the feast to come. We may not be able to change the whole system—that may require the second coming of Christ—but we can experience precious moments of victory in the struggle, signs of the love of God made manifest in and through us.

I (Alexia) had the great privilege of meeting Bishop Desmond Tutu a few years ago, the Nobel Peace Prize winner and nonviolent warrior for justice in South Africa. He was being interviewed by a young journalist, who asked him how he felt at the last stage of his life seeing South Africa still beset by so many terrible problems. Bishop Tutu winked at him and said, "We are resurrection people."

Our word to you today from the cloud of witnesses in BECs is "persist." Have the faith of the persistent widow, who believed so deeply in the God of the exodus that she bothered the indifferent and cruel judge until he gave her justice.

Lydia

In "Letter from Birmingham Jail," Martin Luther King Jr. chastises well-meaning white Christians for their timidity and their pleas for him to move more slowly. "Justice too long delayed is justice denied," King thundered (King 1963, 292). It is natural to want to be reasonable, to try to see all sides, to be careful when you and your family are not in pain and when you have valuable relationships with people in charge that you want to honor. However, when their child is crying out in pain, most parents will move heaven and earth, cross every boundary, to ease that pain. In the movie *John Q*, Denzel Washington plays a man whose nine-year-old son needs a transplant to survive, and the man does not have the capacity to pay for it. He takes hostage the people in an emergency room in order to force the doctors to save his son's life. That is how it feels when your child is threatened by organized crime syndicates in Central America—you take your child and run desperately toward the promise written on the Statue of Liberty, but you are stopped at the border. "All children are our children," a woman said to me (Alexia) in the Philippines in 1986. She lived in the urban poor squatters' barrio. Take on the pain of other people's children with the same passion and urgency that you would if they were your own; let that carry you into new and bolder actions for justice.

Ruth

We may have learned that we can individually overcome restrictions and obstacles to meet our goals and realize our dreams. It is tempting to recommend that road to everyone—but we know in our hearts that we had the advantage of unexpected opportunities. Hieronymus Bosch (the main character in a detective series by Michael Connelly) says that his personal motto is "Everybody counts or nobody counts." We are not free until everyone is free. "If one part suffers, every part suffers with it; if one part is honored, every part rejoices with it" (1 Cor. 12:26). More than you may know, you need to join in the grand battle. "For whoever wants to save their life will lose it, but whoever loses their life for me will save it" (Luke 9:24).

Hush Harbor Organizing

What, indeed, could have more adequately sanctioned resistance to slavery than the presence of priests who, able to assure supernatural support to leaders and followers alike, helped them fight by giving the conviction that the powers of their ancestors were aiding them in their struggle for freedom. (Wilmore 1985, 28)

Hush harbors shaped revolutionary leaders. Often when we think about social movements, we think of the most visible leaders, those who have the most charisma, who speak the most to the masses. Charismatic leaders certainly rose from hush harbors. The prominence, theology, and strategy of revolutionary leaders like Nat Turner and Harriet Tubman were cultivated and shaped by the syncretistic African Christianity and radical political orientation that the hush harbors engendered. But countless unnamed leaders were the real unsettling force of hush harbors as a movement, and they proliferated widely out of the sight and control of the plantation regime. The oral history passed down through Black families attests to this multitude of leaders taking bold, revolutionary action against the status quo. Rachel Harding, whose late mother is Rosemarie Harding (a revolutionary leader in her own right during the Southern Black Freedom Movement of the mid-twentieth century), said this about a conversation with her formerly enslaved late grandmother: "I asked Mama Freeney if she had ever heard of Harriet Tubman, and she told me, 'Yes, I've heard of Harriet Tubman. Grandma Rye talked about her . . . but there were a lot of Harriets. Women like her, you know. And men too'" (R. Harding 2015, 12).

These prophet-leaders were part of a hush harbor movement rather than an institutional clergy order. Hush harbor leaders were both lay leaders and clergy, a distinction that really held no weight, since everybody could be inspired by the Spirit to speak and act. The revolutionary praxis of hush harbor member-leaders was varied, from mutual aid and community building (discussed primarily in chap. 3) to the more standard activities we now associate with organizing, acts of resistance, and seeking permanent escape from slavery. Because most of what happened in hush harbors is unwritten, there are few explicit ties between hush harbors and the organization of strategies like the Underground Railroad and the abolitionist movement. Most of what we know is indirect; the references visible leaders made to faith speak to a version of Christianity not proliferated on the plantation but instead found in hush harbors. In this way, the formation of hush harbors was itself an act of resistance. Hush harbor organizing can be explored as direct actions and strategic campaigns.

Ver (See) / What?

Direct Actions

Hush harbors were a demonstration of collective power. They catalyzed other forms of action to protest the slavocracy system of the plantation and institutional church. These actions were numerous and varied, with running away and becoming literate being the most popular. But several other types of actions are noteworthy, even if not as popular: aesthetic actions, trickery, strikes, attacks, and mercy killings.

Aesthetic actions were deeply informed by and were expressions of the cultural gifts of enslaved Africans. Given the primacy of religion to the survival and communalism of enslaved Africans, many of the aesthetic actions were religious in character. Elsewhere, I (Brandon) have discussed how the Spirituals, drumming, and conjure were at the same time spiritual practices, tools for raising consciousness, and also coded and straightforward ways to resist. Another form of aesthetic action was rooted in the African spiritual principle of *itutu*, or coolness. The principle derives from the spiritual principles of many African people groups like the Ashanti and Akan, who say, "It is the calm and silent water that drowns a man" (Harrison 2009, 155). Historian Renee Harrison says, "The harshness of slavery called forth their intuitive coolness (*itutu*)—an inner resolve and outward persona of grace under pressure. Such a persona of coolness was an act of resistance. . . . Coolness (*itutu*) allowed them to contain their strength in order to speak, protest, or act at the right moment" (157). Coolness as a protest act also related to how enslaved Africans viewed Jesus, as seen in the lyrics of the Spiritual "He Nevuh Said a Mumbalin' Word":

> They nailed him to a tree,
> and he never said a mumbalin' word;
> they nailed him to a tree,
> and he never said a mumbalin' word.
> Not a word, not a word, not a word. (Moses Hogan Singers 2011)

Itutu as protest action invokes the imagery of young Black activists in the sit-in movement of the 1960s who demonstrated ease and restraint as drinks, condiments, and food were dumped on their heads and bodies. Or BLM activists chanting "We gon' be alright" as though they have no care in the world while police are in full riot gear face to face with them on the front line of a protest.

Another form of protest was the use of trickery. Whether disguising themselves as white folks or freed Black people or playing tricks on white folks to get unsupervised time away from the plantation, enslaved Africans used their wit and cunning to fool white folks into getting temporary or permanent freedom. Historian William Loren Katz explains, "Blacks pretended to be free or white, men became women, and women men. Some, dressed as sailors, took jobs on ships. Runaways threw off the scent of bloodhounds with pepper, dead fish, or by rubbing graveyard bones on their clothes. Some pretended to ask whites for directions, then headed along another road. Others escaped on rafts built from fence posts and across bridges built from sleds" (Katz 1990, 92).

Trickery tactics often looked different between enslaved men and women. Given the prominence of the image of a fugitive as a strong Black man, it is critical to reveal the many ways enslaved women used their cunning to protest the white supremacist, patriarchal slavocracy system. Harrison says, "Enslaved women impersonated white women, disguised themselves as white male slaveholders, posed as black male soldiers, faked physical and mental illnesses, served as spies. . . . They risked their lives in creative and subversive ways because they believed they had a right, as one former enslaved man stated, 'to own your own body'" (Harrison 2009, 170). Additionally, many enslaved women used the power of their bodies to seduce or engage in sexual interplay with slaveholders, who were almost always men, as a form of resistance to free themselves or their families (Frederickson and Walters 2013, 58).

Often, trickery was utilized to disrupt production on plantations as one among several kinds of strike tactics. Katz says that "against strict orders, gates were left open and bars let down, rails removed from fences, mules injured, tools broken. Everywhere was careless workmanship, boats left to drift away, heavy items moved, dangerous embankment holes not filled but thinly patched on top. Workers failed to perform jobs and then lied. . . . Production on some plantations varied as much as 100 percent due to slowdowns and sabotage. Slaves pretended to be too sick or lame to work, women pretended they were pregnant, and illness soared when work was hardest" (Katz 1990, 48). Enslaved Africans would also escalate their strikes by destroying the property of slaveholders, often through setting property on fire or vandalizing it (Harrison 2009, 161). Other forms of striking were specifically enacted by women, such as refusing to have children in order to prevent the ongoing forced labor of the plantation economy. These strikes slowed down or completely disrupted production, therefore giving enslaved Africans control, however temporary, over their time, and on rare occasions enough time to run away entirely.

The final two forms of actions are related in that they both used physical violence: attacks and mercy killings. Enslaved Africans would sometimes use force against slaveholders to seek freedom. Attacks would look like poisoning or arson, getting into fistfights and wrestling matches, and when there was access to weapons, shootings or stabbings. Sometimes these acts were done to defend themselves against rape, hanging, whipping, beating, verbal abuse, and much more. Sometimes enslaved Africans plotted these acts as offensive tactics, catching slaveholders and the plantation regime off guard. Mercy killings by enslaved Africans included suicide and taking the life of a child by abortion or infanticide. These acts happened as early as when Africans threw themselves overboard to drown in the Middle Passage on their way to the Americas. A mercy killing is portrayed in the well-known book *Beloved* when Sethe kills her young daughter rather than let her be taken back to the plantation. Many enslaved Africans believed it was more honorable and loving to die by taking one's life or to take the life of one's child than to be subjected to the terrorism of plantation life. There is need for a word of caution for those who uncritically and hastily call into question the moral and theological basis of riots and mercy killings. One must first call into question a system that produces desperate people who must make the choice between slavery and death.

Strategic Campaigns

Organized protests against slavery, in addition to taking the form of direct action, often carried out by individuals, also took the form of strategic campaigns, most notably armed rebellions, Christian abolitionism, the Underground Railroad, the purchasing of freedom, maroon communities, and the coordination of fugitive groups, families, and networks. The more prominent rebellions in the US are those of Nat Turner, Denmark Vesey, and Gabriel Prosser. However, there were many rebellions. In fact, so many rebellions were attempted that this became a source of paranoia for slaveholders.[3] Many times armed rebellions were done in coalition with Native Americans.[4] Natives knew the landscapes and had access to resources that many enslaved Africans did not have. These intercultural campaigns were a threat that caused white backlash. In the Pontiac Rebellion of 1763, one white leader complained about Natives joining forces with Africans, saying, "The Indians are saving and caressing all the Negroes they take. To prevent solidification of a force that could spell their doom, British officials heated up ancient rivalries and ignited new ones. . . . Divide and rule became British Colonial policy. Africans were armed to fight Indians and Indians bribed to hunt runaways" (Katz 1990, 101). White backlashes like this one expose, again, that violence is only a problem when enacted on white people. Violence is acceptable when used against Black and Brown bodies, and especially when used as a divide-and-conquer tactic between oppressed communities in order to keep the white elite in power. This is why it is key to lift up the proliferation of armed rebellions, not because they were violent but because they demonstrate Black agency and

3. "According to many historians, the first 250 years that followed the conquest of the Americas were interspersed with conspiracies and slave revolts. . . . In reality, many of those rebellions only existed in the frightened imaginations of colonial elites and numerous whites" (Helg 2019, 82).

4. In the earliest slave rebellions, Black people often united with Native peoples. In 1526, the two groups joined in a North Carolina coastal revolt that sent the surviving European colonists packing for home. When Native Americans besieged Jamestown in 1622, whites died, but Africans were spared. In 1657, Africans and Native Americans invaded Hartford, Connecticut. In 1727, the two peoples threatened Virginia settlements (Katz 1990, 101).

organization and the commitment to liberation. Table 7.1 lists rebellions over an eight-year period in Virginia and Massachusetts alone.

Table 7.1 Slave Conspiracies and Revolts in Which Enslaved Women Participated (Harrison 2009, 164)

Date/Location	Revolts/Insurrections	Outcome
1722/Virginia	Slave conspiracy was uncovered. Slaves planned to revolt in two or three Virginia counties.	Leaders were sentenced and some members imprisoned. Others escaped. Stricter laws were enacted limiting movement of slaves and clergy, requiring slaves to carry passes. Secret meetings among slaves were prohibited.
April 1723 / Boston, MA	Slaves accused of setting a dozen fires in one week.	Curfew laws were enacted. Also various laws prohibited slaves meeting on Sundays independent of master.
1730/Virginia	Slave conspiracy involving over two hundred slaves. Arose after enslaved Africans heard that whites covered up an order by King George II to free Christian slaves.	Laws enacted. One Virginia law ordered white males to carry arms to church to protect themselves. Other laws prohibited slaves from testifying in court against whites, but not against nonwhites.

These rebellions attest to the role of religion in organizing. That slaveholders launched or reinforced bans on secret religious meetings bears witness to the role that hush harbors played in shaping a liberationist faith that animated bold action against the slaveholding regime.

Both Christianity and African Traditional Religions were sources from which enslaved Africans drew inspiration for their rebellions, especially biblical stories such as the exodus and conjurers' wisdom from invoking harm through spells and natural objects. One of the most vivid examples of the way enslaved Africans derived inspiration from the religious syncretism of hush harbors is Gabriel's Rebellion. Historian Albert Raboteau says this about the rebellion:

"Preachings," or religious meetings, served as occasions for the recruitment of slaves and for plotting and organizing the insurrection. Gabriel's brother Martin, one of the plot's leaders, was known as a preacher. He used the Bible to argue that their plans would succeed even against superior numbers. In one discussion of the rebellion Martin contended that "their cause was similar to the Israelites," and that in the Bible God had promised "five of you shall conquer an hundred & a hundred a thousand of our enemies." Significantly, African religious beliefs were also referred to in the conspiracy. One organizer, George Smith, proposed that he travel to the "pipeing tree" to enlist the "Outlandish people" (born outside this country) who had the ability "to deal with Witches and Wizards, and thus [would be] useful in Armies to tell when any calamity was about to befall them." (Raboteau 2004, 147)

Nonviolent campaigns, most notably Christian abolitionism, also drew on the liberative religious ideas of hush harbors. The abolitionist movement relied heavily on the proliferation of the written word to disseminate antislavery biblical arguments. For those enslaved Africans who could read and write, gaining access to this literature by word of mouth or physical copies became a powerful tool for educating the enslaved population on the plantation and through hush harbors. "Attentive to any weakening of division among slave owning powers, slaves knew how to exploit existing tensions to advance the cause of their own liberation. As writing and Christian abolitionism developed, slaves used petitions, the publication of manifestos, and the pulpit to demand their freedom" (Helg 2019, 113). David Walker's *Appeal* and Henry Highland Garnett's *Call to Rebellion* were critical sources for raising the consciousness of enslaved Africans to collective struggle. These works, along with Frederick Douglass's speeches and writings, initially meant to counter Garnett's *Call to Rebellion*, contributed to the development of abolitionism as a highly organized movement with national conventions and periodicals, such as *Freedom's Journal*, especially among formerly enslaved Northern Black communities.

The Underground Railroad was another movement that quenched the longing of enslaved Africans for freedom. The Underground Railroad required incredible planning, coordination, and commitment all through covert and subversive channels of communication, building on the culture of hush harbors. One conductor on the Underground Railroad covertly named "Ham and Eggs" sent a message to Philadelphia abolitionist leader William Still, saying, "I want you to know that I feel as much determined to work in the glorious cause, as ever I did in the all of my life, and I have some very good hams on hand that I would like very much for you to have" (Katz 1990, 95). For enslaved Africans, most of the immediate planning for embarking on the Underground Railroad centered on the arduous task of determining the most effective routes to take. The routes were varied:

While slaves who lived along the East Coast used land and ocean to escape to freedom in the northeast, those who lived in the interior states utilized rivers and lakes as a source of transportation. At night, when the plantation owners were sleeping, many slaves would slip away on the UR [Underground Railroad], leaving neither a trace nor track. In many instances, conductors would lead a group of eight-to-twelve slaves to a river where another conductor was waiting in a small boat. The passengers would quickly board the boat and away they went into the darkness of the night. This type of get-away was useful and it was sometimes repeated two times each night, as slaves were being unshackled. (Wiggan et al. 2014, 13)

Not everyone made the trek, whether due to physical limitations or fear of being captured. Conductors on the Underground Railroad had to display agility and creativity so as to be responsive to conditions that might change at any given moment.

The Underground Railroad required the covert organizing of allies—safe houses, church buildings, fugitive communities, hush harbors—that gave a sense of stability to the Underground Railroad when unpredictability characterized the trek and the mission to keep every passenger safe to the end of the trip. Conductor Harriet Tubman was known for using a variety of tools to keep her train well organized: "Tubman found a calling to help others and for the next ten years returned nineteen times to Atlantic seaboard slave states. She aided three hundred men, women and children—loved ones and perfect strangers—to escape. She carried a pistol for enemies and the faint of heart, and potions to quiet crying infants. She proudly claimed, 'I never lost a single passenger'" (Katz 1990, 98).

Tubman was but one example of various styles of leading on the Underground Railroad. The Underground Railroad was a big tent operation that gave space for leaders to deploy a variety of techniques of planning and communication and strategizing, all in service to delivering precious cargo to that destination called freedom. Tubman and Margaret Garner were two women leaders who depict the diverse and genius ways to escape: "The lives of Margaret Garner and Harriet Tubman, two very different women widely associated with escape and the Underground Railroad, lay at opposite ends of the spectrum in the quest for liberation. Their life experiences are indicative of the numerous liberation strategies and the divergent roles women actively undertook. The escape of Margaret Garner with her extended family required forethought, planning, and organization, while Harriet Tubman escaped alone, finding help along the way" (Frederickson and Walters 2013, 54).

Not every emancipation strategy was tied directly to national movements. The fire for emancipation was not fueled by one way of escape. A few of the other ways that enslaved Africans escaped were smaller in scope but were nonetheless collective actions. Many enslaved Africans purchased their own and their loved ones' freedom. They earned the money for this act in a number of ways, often through joining the armed forces or in rare cases being paid by slaveholders for their work.

When some slave owners agreed to let their slaves work for pay, and then use the money to purchase loved ones, many women jumped at the chance. They worked for decades, first to buy their own liberty and then to ransom children and spouses. President Jefferson's servant Alethia Tanner purchased her freedom in 1810, and by 1828 saved enough to buy her sister, ten children, and five grandchildren. In 1836, she bought more grandchildren. In that year 476 of Cincinnati's 1,129 free blacks had purchased their own freedom. . . . The practice of taking in children changed the meaning of the word parents in the slave community to mean all adults. "'Parents' means relations in general . . . family," explained Robert Smalls. A black community expression was, "If you hurt one of the family, you hurt them all." (Katz 1990, 36)

The theme of kinship is present in this act of purchasing the freedom of other enslaved Africans. Enslaved Africans engaged in acts of resistance not by blood but by a bolder vision of family rooted in their African identity of interconnectedness. This also informs the other collective actions enslaved Africans took to get free.

Enslaved Africans knew they were better together. Escaping in groups, families, and networks was a strategy that ensured that everyone brought their skills and talents and knowledge to the action. Women especially used the strategy of groups, families, and networks for escape, often linking it with other forms of resistance, all of which required very measured commitment and meticulous planning.

To secure freedom, women often devised measured solutions that went beyond the bold actions of their male counterparts. Black women used the chaos of the American Revolution, the War of 1812, and the Civil War to forge alternative and expanded paths to self-liberation. They effected emancipation through the courts, escaped with and to family members, or reunited with relatives once freedom was realized. Whenever possible, women escaped within groups or relied on networks. When the opportunity presented itself, they often purchased their freedom or the freedom of loved ones and combined these purchases with escape strategies. (Frederickson and Walters 2013, 51)

Forming maroon communities also required organizing. Maroon communities were an effective strategy for resistance not only because they were highly organized but also because they attracted other enslaved Africans. "The most radical strategy available to slaves was to escape to territories that had not yet been conquered by whites and in which they could establish maroon communities. Those fugitive groups incidentally constituted a permanent threat to several slaveholding societies due to both their ability to attract defiant slaves and their raids on plantations" (Helg 2019, 82). Some maroon communities were interracial, including both abolitionist whites, who were often poor, and Native Americans. Abolitionists Frederick Douglass and Sojourner Truth both were temporarily members of an interracial community that harbored fugitives called the Northampton Association of Education and Industry, which functioned as an intentional and utopian community in the Midwest (Nembhard 2014, 35). Both Black and interracial maroon communities maintained their own schools and economic infrastructure where enslaved Africans learned trades and skills.

Through a combination of reinterpreted Christianity and African Traditional Religions, hush harbors gave enslaved Africans the theological, existential, and moral basis for struggling by direct action and strategic campaigns against the tyranny of chattel slavery. There is much to learn from their organizing genius. Two themes stand out to put into conversation with contemporary faith justice organizing: abundance and base building.

Juzgar (Judge) / So What?

Abundance

I (Brandon) was in an organizing training at the historic Highlander Research & Education Center. The trainer was from an organization called Momentum.[5] He was explaining their theory of change, that our movements needed to go beyond our siloed organizing approaches. Direct actions, like the occupations we saw with the Occupy Movement and protests we saw with Black Lives Matter, are inspiring and catalytic and bring the masses to the movement, but on their own, they cannot build the kind of long-term organization to wield the power that's needed to make far-reaching policy changes. These are the kind of changes that can fundamentally shift the political weather and radically transform the material conditions of people's everyday lives: to no longer have to choose between paying a medical bill or rent, for a mental health crisis in a low-income neighborhood to be met with a medical professional and not the police. These and many other kinds of sweeping policy changes require large-scale organization and governing political power across geographical and social locations. The trainer shared a vision of how different organizing approaches can serve alongside each other to build this kind of power for long-term sustainable change. The training hit home with our large, ragtag group of faith-rooted activists and organizers from across the country.

At the time I was forming a community development organization in a white, rural, mixed-class neighborhood in the mountains of western North Carolina. This was half of my work; the other half was as an appointed clergy to a declining rural United Methodist congregation. I'd just started working on that project in July of 2013. I watched the news of George Zimmerman being acquitted in a place foreign to how Black people felt in that moment. The trainer that day at Highlander spoke to the need I had during my time

---

5. Learn more about Momentum at their website: https://www.momentumcommunity.org/.

organizing in that rural community for bridging the lament and rage in my soul as a Black man with the congregational and community development work I was doing with white people. One way to look at my situation was that I was in the wrong place at the wrong time. Or that I was in a place and doing work that was not relevant to the Movement for Black lives. What I heard from that trainer, though, is that the white rural community needed to be organized to believe that Black lives mattered as much as any other community across the globe. Whose job it was to lead that work was another question. But the work of racial justice organizing was critical there. That trainer called into question the politics of purity and perfection in social movements that can betray the justice we seek.

An organizer colleague of mine, Sendolo Diaminah, commenting on the need for bringing together various organizing approaches, says, "We come from different organizing traditions, but when you combine them all, experience with workplace or labor organizing, experience with community organizing, and experience with electoral, and each of those actually has powerful strength . . . and there are limitations, . . . [so] we need the systematic [labor], the relational [community], and the scale [electoral] in order for our people to wield the power that they need to address things at the scale of the economy" (Diaminah 2021). The three approaches that Sendolo outlines only touch the surface of the many organizing traditions that have propelled international movements for social change.[6] Still, Sendolo drives home the point that it serves the interests of the ruling class, which is committed to keeping the existing domination system in place, for the masses to fight over crumbs. We must leave any table or room that forces us to see only crumbs. Instead, we must come to our own tables to see the strengths and limitations of the various approaches to social change, to better coordinate and collaborate for impact at the scale of bringing down the racialized capitalist economy and reconstructing a system of shared wealth and dignity.

Antebellum organizing that was shaped by the hush harbors used various organizing tactics and strategies for social change. Scarcity was too risky a belief for enslaved Africans who'd been reborn through the hush harbors' liberation message. They had to believe that all things were possible. What did they have to lose? Harriet Tubman is quoted as saying, "There are two things I've got a right to, and these are, Death or Liberty—one or the other I mean to have. No one will take me back alive; I shall fight for my liberty, and when the time has come for me to go, the Lord will let them kill me." This is faith-full organizing! Laying it all on the line. This abundance approach to organizing invites us to be open to collaborating with any person and perspective that aligns with the path of freedom, of real liberation. Alexia says it this way in

6. For a recent survey of organizing traditions see Pyles 2021.

her book *Faith-Rooted Organizing*: "The broader movement for justice will be strongest when each sector does what it does best, contributing its unique gifts rather than using the same talking points and participating in the same activities regardless of context or giftedness" (Salvatierra and Heltzel 2013, 146).

Base Building

Context is queen! That's why in this particular moment we have to reexamine what organizing even is. When extreme right-wing ruling-class forces have come to see themselves as oppressed and use the tools and tactics of organizing to fight for their "rights," we have to reexamine the playing field. After over a decade of door-to-door conversations for community organizing in rural and urban front-line communities, the overwhelming majority of residents I have talked with respond with some version of "I stay to myself. I go to work and come home. I don't really know my neighbors." The majority of my organizing has been in the South. I have come to expect a lie or two covered by Southern hospitality. So at first I was suspicious of these responses. Perhaps them telling me this was their way of keeping me out of their and their neighbors' business. Or maybe they wanted me to work harder before getting any kind of access to their network and the news on the street. Corporate media might traffic in fake news, but the neighborhood press is filled with the real and raw. Occasionally, I was right about these barriers being in place. But in most cases these neighbors were being straight up with me.

Once, I was knocking doors in my neighborhood in Greensboro, North Carolina, for a housing injustice campaign. I met Ms. Wallace, an elder who has been in the neighborhood for decades. Ms. Wallace and I discussed the housing injustice we saw in the community. I learned that she's a homeowner and active with her local church's Christian education department. In the midst of that conversation, Ms. Wallace shared with me that she hadn't seen anyone knocking on doors to organize neighbors like I was doing since the days of Mr. Troy Jackson. The street Ms. Wallace lives on is named after Mr. Jackson. On a different occasion when out knocking doors, I met Mr. Simpson, another elder in the community who'd been in the neighborhood their whole life, raised their children there, and seen the neighborhood change from a place where kids could play out in the street into the night to a place where leaving your kids out to play during the day could mean them being hit by the regularly speeding cars. Letting them play past dark could result in them not coming home. It was near dusk when I knocked on Mr. Simpson's door. My family was out knocking on doors with me that day. Mr. Simpson said he only opened the door because he heard my kids' voices. He was timid when he first opened the door for us. Then he invited us to come in to talk because he was afraid for us, and himself, being out on the porch as the sun made its descent. When I asked Mr. Simpson what could be done to change the gun violence in the community, he said that it would take an army of neighbors. Then I agitated Mr. Simpson by asking him what he was willing to do to see that army come to life. Mr. Simpson was hesitant to get involved. Both of these residents have long-standing status and memories in this place. They're connected to old institutions, like Black churches and families. Yet both of them were largely isolated in their own communities, from their neighbors and from the problems they identified.

Community was one of the foundations of Southern organizing during the civil rights movement. Organizers like Ella Baker would bring young folks from across the country, wet behind the ears to the movement, into a Southern community, and find a place for them to stay with a host family that would avail that new young organizer to all of their relationships and give them access to their networks and institutions. From this foundation, new young organizers launched their social change projects with the Black community. The social fabric of Black communities at that time was thick. That is no longer the case. My countless experiences with the Mr. Simpsons and Ms. Wallaces attest to this. There are varied explanations for the destabilization of Black communities and institutions: gentrification, voter suppression, state surveillance, and sabotage (e.g., COINTELPRO), big money control of the two-party system, and so on. Voter suppression is so invasive in these communities, for example, that some describe it as if it were done with surgical precision (see Associated Press 2021). These forces and many others are outcomes of global racialized capitalism that has enacted a modern form of colonization in Black and low-income communities. Organizations, institutions, and the very social fabric of informal networks of families and neighbors in these communities have been made fragile and fragmented. The relatively permanent bases of organization, leadership, and community that reach the masses, across generations, in Black and low-income communities from days past are no more.

Faith-full organizing in the contemporary moment requires new base building in Black, Brown, and low-income communities. A base is the furthest reach among a constituency that an organization can mobilize, which includes more than the membership of an organization. Base building, then, is the systematic process of bringing into our movements, congregations, and organizations the majority of the people who are not yet members but are in our constituency. To bring into the movement these people who are part of the same constituency because of a common condition or social or geographical location means going to the base, going to the people rather than assuming these people will come to the movement. It means developing the leadership of these people so that they wage collective struggles against the systems of tyranny from a deep consciousness. The Carolina Federation, a statewide organization I work with, describes base building this way: "Being a base-building organization means that we don't wait for people to come to us and take whoever shows up—that's an activist group. We go to where our people are and actively work to recruit people who do or can actually lead others in their neighborhoods. In fact, we develop plans that try to reach each household in our clearly defined neighborhoods" (Carolina Federation 2021, 19).

The church calls this the work of evangelism. The "E"-word is out of favor with most progressives. Those of us who believe social justice is at the heart of the gospel message and ministry must take back evangelism from the white church industrial complex, which has turned it into a marketing scheme and reduced it to the afterlife and individual salvation. When enslaved Africans were recruited into the hush harbors, this wasn't proselytizing. It wasn't about saving their souls from hell. Hush harbors recruited members to transform the whole lives and conditions of the world right in front of them. Evangelism was organizing, building a base of freedom fighters among the enslaved population, most of whom had to be agitated out of their conditioning to depend on the very culture and system that was killing their souls and bodies.

Those who want to learn from hush harbors how to be faith-full organizers will need to sit at the feet of movement organizations like the Carolina Federation. Secular justice organizations and movements will have to teach the church how to be faith-full. These organizations are borrowing from the church growth movement, reading books like Rick Warren's *Purpose Driven Church*, to learn the mechanics of reaching the inactive masses to build powerful organizations and movements for social change. Not in a copycat way. These organizations and leaders are looking for the best ideas from wherever they can be found, vetting the materials in alignment with justice values and principles. They are eating the meat and spitting out the bones, as Southern elders often say.

Both church-based and secular social change work has always identified the distinction between organizing and mobilizing. Mobilizing is the work of preaching to the choir, galvanizing those who are already on your side. Organizing is reaching those people who are persuadable but are not yet part of the work. There has not been radical honesty about the wide-scale destabilization of our once permanent bases in oppressed communities. This challenges our social change work to be overwhelmingly about organizing the majority of Black, Brown, and low-income neighbors into our movements and organizations. In the same way that secular movement organizations have no other choice but to reorganize Black and Brown and low-income communities, the church and faith-full organizers of modern hush harbors must talk to more than just clergy, congregations, and elected officials in our organizing.[7]

7. This framework challenges both the traditional faith-based model of organizing and the newer model of faith-rooted organizing. While faith-rooted organizing shares more in common

It will take us implementing a strategy and a plan to reach and persuade the majority of the oppressed in our communities to join the struggle for justice. The concrete strategies for doing that in local communities will look different based on the particular contextual factors that have caused destabilization of bases in those communities. Base building is not a solo sport. No one leader or organization can or should go into low-income communities to cold-turkey knock on doors without seeking a point of entry into those communities through coalition and local leadership. Still, we must go! We cannot expect that because there are Black and Brown faces in positions of authority and influence in multiracial institutions, that the masses of the oppressed, especially low-income folks, will follow these figures. We cannot expect that long-standing institutions in Black and Brown communities will draw the oppressed masses. We cannot wait for neighbors to show up to our worship services and rallies and demonstrations. The church can no longer make the assumption that it has the kind of relationship to have these expectations of the masses in our low-income, Black, and Brown neighborhoods. We must do the work of bringing a revival of prophetic, revolutionary faith to the masses of unchurched, dechurched, and inactive folks in our neighborhoods to organize the majority of them into modern sacred-secular hush harbor spaces and the wider movement for justice.

Actuar (Act) / Now What?

Fresh energy is emerging related to the possibilities of local politics to bring a democratic revival in the US with victories like those in the Georgia runoff of 2021, resulting in the election of the first Black and Jewish senators respectively, Senators Raphael Warnock and Jon Ossoff. The organizing prowess of movement groups like the New Georgia Project and leaders like Stacey Abrams have captured the attention of justice workers everywhere to rethink our organizing strategies. Conversations are sparking like wildfire about co-governance, base building, building new progressive political majorities, and working collaboratively rather than in our silos. It is a good thing to have cultural moments like this to revitalize commitment to justice and organizing.

with the faith-full organizing of hush harbors, both faith-based and faith-rooted approaches focus most of their energies on talking to the church. Faith-rooted organizing does not prescribe that faith leaders only need to talk to congregations and clergy, but it functionally describes the church as talking primarily to the church. The assumption is that there is a broader movement of organizing (not only mobilizing) that is happening in local communities. Salvatierra and Heltzel say in their book, "Faith-rooted organizing, for example, is not meant to be implemented when organizing neighborhoods, unions or students; it is designed instead to organize faith communities to contribute our unique gifts to the larger whole" (Salvatierra and Heltzel 2013, 146).

Yet there must be clarity about our political analysis amid all the excitement. The two-party system is still controlled by big money, the ruling class that has no interest in radically sharing God's abundant creation among the poor and working class. So even as it is exciting to see and participate in these fresh conversations, we must ask, Toward what end? Toward what end is our base building, our collaboration, our building political majorities, our election of political candidates with whom we can co-govern around shared values? What political vision guides our faith-full organizing? Revolutionary organizer Nijmie Dzurinko says this about how we must be clear about our political vision:

> Though they are related, Elections are only a part of Politics. It's in the interest of the ruling class to limit our understanding of Politics to Elections. They pour billions every election cycle into the illusion of conflict. TV ratings soar, as pundits and the two mainstream parties carve up our communities before our eyes, dividing us by geography, race, age—all the identities we're told make us fundamentally different. This is Politics, they tell us, presenting us with a false choice between bad and worse. The choice between two arms of the same ruling class is disguised as an exercise of our autonomy—an expression of our "free will." They depend on us believing them, believing that Politics is all about the one day a year that we order off their menu. But we'll never get what we need if we limit ourselves to what a few billionaires want us to think is possible. To structure our society around meeting our human rights, we need organization, unity, and the power to make our own future. That is Politics. Politics is the process of uniting around our needs and learning to fight for them. It's the process of identifying, developing, and uniting everyday leaders. It is building permanently organized communities. We need organization of the poor and dispossessed working class in every county, in every state in this country, building a politically independent program across race, age, ability, religion, region, nationality, language, sexuality, and gender 365 days a year. It is difficult work, but not as difficult as the future we are facing if we don't organize now. The biggest mistake we could make, as we face up to the reality of what is in store, is falling into disillusionment, cynicism, and despair. We are not naive or unrealistic. We have the vision, we have the numbers. We [the working class and poor] are 140 million strong. (Dzurinko 2020)

Our goal is the abolition of the political and economic system of racial capitalism as we have come to know it, from its inception with colonization of the Americas through its shapeshifting across generations into its present forms of gentrification, global imperialism, and gross inequality, to name only a few.

Abolition is the north star of hush harbor organizing. Nijmie calls this "revolutionary organizing": "A *revolutionary* is someone who is working toward a fundamental change in the economic structure of our society. In the way I'm defining it, a revolutionary *does not believe that we will be able to legislate our way beyond capitalism using the existing two-party system*. We cannot use the existing mechanisms of the state, which function at the behest of the ruling class, to overthrow that class" (Dzurinko 2021). But we are not only committed to what we are against. As faith-full organizers we are committed to the reign of God, the beloved community, and the radical reversal of the present order—a vision where justice flows like a river and righteousness like an ever-flowing stream (Amos 5:24). Where everyone experiences wholeness and dignity because everyone has what they need and freely shares any overflow. Where our shared life of abundance is co-governed by the laws of love and justice. And where our creator is among us, the love that holds us all in balance with one another and the planet.

This constructive vision will be realized by a power that is not of the state but is also not blind to the state's power. A power that is not of the institutional church but is not blind to the institutional church's power. To realize this vision will take spiritual and moral power that is not beholden to the present order of racial capitalism and slaveholder religion. No politician or clergyperson, no organizer or missionary, is forcing or manipulating our time and talents and motivations for the interest of money or status. Spiritual and moral power can only be organized by breaking rank with the forces of domination so love and justice are truly the forces that bind us together. Where political and religious status were denied them, prophetic leaders in the antebellum hush harbors wielded spiritual and moral power to wage their struggles for abolition. The opportunities abound in our time to ascend the ranks of the status quo for a political and religious system that is a death dive of the soul. Hush harbors organized for a revolution of the soul and systems of this nation. Those who will build modern hush harbors will need to be faith-full organizers to this revolutionary tradition. Several questions are relevant based on your social location:

Amos: Who are the informal elder leaders in your community? What stories can you learn from them about the victories of the community? About the community's sufferings? What do they believe are the most pressing needs of your community, and what solutions do they have to address them? What do they believe it would take to organize your community block by block to pursue these solutions? Then, go to a young person in your community to ask the same questions.

Lydia: Have a conversation with trusted people in your inner circle of privilege. What are the local institutions that produce inequality between you/your families and the Black and low-income folks in your community? How is that inequality produced? What would it mean for you and your families to abolish these institutions? What would it mean for those inequalities in your community? What next faith-full step can you and your friends take? How can you do this in ways that are accountable to Black and low-income folks in your community?

Ruth: Have the systems of organization you've learned from the institutions you've ascended shaped you to mistrust the leadership and knowledge of your community of origin? If so, what do you mistrust, and what experiences of privilege shaped that mistrust? Who is a grassroots leader and grassroots organization(s) in your community of origin or an oppressed community close to you that you can build a relationship with and seek to follow? Ask them if there are resources from your sphere of influence that you could take leadership in divesting from the elite and redistributing as an act of solidarity to that leader and the grassroots organizing work they are doing in their community.

Faith-full Organizing: Catalyzing Change

Hush harbors happened in a place and time when the heart of the hope of the enslaved was freedom. BECs grew in a moment and context where the hope of the people was the right to economic justice and a voice in the public decisions that impacted their lives. While the ultimate vision of the kingdom of God is all of the above and more, in each time and place, the hunger for abundant life takes a different form, comes up against particular barriers.

What is the common call and the common gift across centuries and continents? How do these long-ago struggles speak to your church and community?

Catalytic Power

John Lewis, iconic civil rights leader and congressional representative, said, "The church must be the headlight not the taillight" (Lewis 2015). The church has often historically been pulled along reluctantly by broader movements for justice rather than being at the forefront illuminating the way. In comparison, the faith of the leaders and members of BECs and hush harbors was a catalytic faith; it propelled them to action and gave them power. It inspired change. The word *inspiration* comes from the Latin word meaning "to breathe"; breath and wind are cousins. Anyone who has seen a hurricane knows the power of wind to move, to flatten obstacles in its path. It is that kind of power that moved members of BECs and hush harbors to take risks to change their lives and their societies against daunting odds.

What would it mean for you to expect that the people in your ministry would be propelled by the Spirit into courageous action for justice? To expect that the people in your ministry can connect with and offer a winsome message of hope and change to neighbors in your community? Our assumptions affect our perceptions. When I (Alexia) was growing up in Los Angeles, we would go to the beach and watch the surfers catch the waves. They looked out toward the ocean expecting the wave to come. They had to be ready when it came to move boldly, fearlessly, to catch it and ride it to its destination.

Open to Evolve

Jesus said, "The wind blows wherever it pleases. You hear its sound, but you cannot tell where it comes from or where it is going. So it is with everyone born of the Spirit" (John 3:8). BECs' engagement in social justice often started with the response to an individual family's unjust suffering. The attempts to solve the problem moved organically from one level to another, from community development to community organizing to advocacy to participation in broader social movements, led by a passionate drive toward an effective resolution of the problem. Hush harbors used the tools at hand to respond to slavery, moving from one tool to another as the opportunity and need arose. Churches often make plans that are limited by a narrow imagination and then doggedly implemented. We hand out food at the food bank as we have always done; we do not ask why people are hungry or whether there is more that can be done. We are afraid that the answer would lead us into risky and costly places. Dom Hélder Câmara once said, "When I give food to the poor, they call me a saint. When I ask why the poor have no food, they call me a communist" (Câmara 2009, 11). What would it mean for us to walk through the world open to evolve, to be led by the Spirit past our fears into uncomfortable and unknown places for the glory of God?

In the Beatitudes, Jesus uses the phrase "hunger and thirst for righteousness" (Matt. 5:6). That is the hunger and thirst that often come more naturally to people who eat the bread of affliction on a daily basis. Those of us who are less directly affected often need to connect intimately enough with those on the firing line to feel the pain as our pain and to get hungry. However, the hunger for justice can be suppressed by despair or desperation, leading oppressed people to become passive or to struggle only for their individual benefit. On the other hand, that hunger and thirst for justice can take us past the internal and external barriers to try every door until we find one that opens. To learn from the examples of BECs and hush harbors is to be relentless in stoking the fire of the hunger and thirst for righteousness and being open to the movement of the Spirit to lead us to new methods, strategies, alliances, and opportunities—even to new ways of being the church!

Persistence

Reverend James M. Lawson Jr., the African American pastor whom Dr. King called his theologian of nonviolence because of his role in the development of the theory and practice of nonviolence in the civil rights movement, was the chair of the board at Clergy and Laity United for Economic Justice (CLUE) when I (Alexia) was the executive director. He used to share with the new interns and staff his interpretation of 1 Kings 18:20–39. In the passage, Elijah is competing with the false prophets. They each build an altar of wood and pray for divine fire to come down. The fire comes down for Elijah but not for the false prophets. The wisdom that Jim would draw from the story was that Elijah's success came from three elements—the fire, the prayer, and the wood. The fire is analogous to what happens in a movement when suddenly the number of people engaged multiplies and floods of human beings break down previously impenetrable barriers. The element of prayer is always critical. But the fire could not come down if there were no wood for it to burn. The building of the wooden altar is the slow, daily process of movement building, the endless conversations and meetings, the actions that seem to have no impact, the multiple defeats of initiatives and proposals. No human being can control when the fire comes down, but we can and must pile up the wood.

BECs and hush harbors were not a Hollywood fantasy of an easy and assured path to justice and shalom. The ambiguities were constant. Not everyone was in support of bold action; different leaders pursued distinct strategies. The constant moral balancing acts needed to collaborate with broader social movements were as necessary and difficult then as they are now. Yet the wood was built up and the divine fire came down both in the form of individual transformations through empowerment and in the form of objective social change.

To learn from BECs and hush harbors about faith-full organizing is to lean into the catalytic power of faith, to be open to evolve into new forms of struggle, and to persist. Imagine how these fundamental commitments could change your church and local justice movements.

8

Catch the Fire

An Integrated Vision for the Twenty-First Century

> When the day of Pentecost came, they were all together in one place. Suddenly a sound like the blowing of a violent wind came from heaven and filled the whole house where they were sitting. They saw what seemed to be tongues of fire that separated and came to rest on each of them. (Acts 2:1–3)

n early 2021, Biola University's Center for Christian Thought organized a summit of national faith leaders to discuss the findings of a number of sociologists and scholars of religion regarding the growing number of young people who want nothing to do with organized religion. The deidentified (or the "dones") and those without a religious background or interest (or the "nones") make up a rapidly growing percentage of the US population. This is particularly true of emerging generations. The statistics hover around 30 percent for millennials and Generation Z. The scholars had studied the reasons for these statistics; the faith leaders brought their own experiences to the table. One scholar stated his perspective on the problem bluntly: religion is not relevant in the modern world; there is nothing that a young person needs from religion that they cannot get from somewhere else—and more conveniently.

As I (Alexia) listened, I remembered Manuel. A group of primarily immigrant workers and other workers of color had been employed at a luxury airport hotel for many years under a union contract. Over time, as their wages rose, they had been able to buy small homes and send their children to college. They had pride in their work and considered each other family. Then the ownership of the hotel changed hands. and the new owner closed the hotel for a long renovation, with the express purpose of getting rid of all the workers and their union contract. The workers were devastated. The union wanted them to fight back, but it was crystal clear that the fight would be long and protracted, the outcome unsure, and the economic situation of the workers precarious.

Clergy and Laity United for Economic Justice (CLUE) stepped in to inspire and support the workers. As chaplains on the battlefield for justice, the faith leaders engaged the workers in spiritual activities that fanned the flame of their hunger for justice and turned their grief into determination. Manuel was the young union organizer in charge of the campaign. He had grown up on a spiritual battlefield of another sort, with a Jehovah's Witness mother and a Catholic father. He despised religion. He allowed CLUE's engagement because he was willing to try anything that might help. Halfway through the campaign, a national team of researchers came to interview the workers about the role that their faith played in the struggle. Manuel was at the union hall and listened. After all the workers had spoken, he asked to speak as well. He said that he had started the campaign as a committed atheist but that he had changed. He had seen the power of God in the lives of the workers, and he had found himself beginning to believe. He added that he didn't know what kind of Christian he was but that he had realized he had become a Christian and that he wanted to live a life of faith, in communion with his brothers and sisters.

Faith was no longer irrelevant to Manuel. He had caught the fire. Building a campfire in the wilderness can be a frustrating process. The flames start and die out. When the fire catches suddenly, the wood blazes with energy and light. In 1738, John Wesley had an experience that started the Methodist movement. He was listening to Martin Luther's "Preface to the Epistle to the Romans" when he felt his heart "strangely warmed." I think of the common expressions "on fire for a cause" and "having a fire in the belly." When we read the stories and the accounts of BECs and hush harbors, we see the light and feel the heat of the fire reaching us across decades, centuries, miles. How can our churches and ministries in the twenty-first century catch the fire? How can emerging generations share Manuel's experience?

BECs and hush harbors had in common a vibrant spirit-uality, a fully embodied faith, and an encompassing consciousness—all of which culminated in members' capacity to act together to transform their lives and their communities. In this final chapter, we focus on what we can learn from their experiences that can help us today. We also lift up some stories of twenty-first-century faith communities that are seeking and struggling to incorporate some of these practices in their common life.

Kinship

Every reasonably healthy church is a community in which people care for each other, right? How were BECs and hush harbors different?

The inspirational power of BECs and hush harbors was rooted in the depth, breadth, and length of members' connection and commitment to each other. The depth of their commitment—the extent to which people with scarce resources shared them generously, assuming equal ownership over their personal and private time and goods—is shocking and echoes the early Christian community in the book of Acts. This commitment included the willingness to take risks in the name of love, to stand so close to the person being shot at that the blood spatters all over you.[1] The breadth of their commitment is troubling for those of us who claim to share their faith. BEC members contributed sacrificially to other BECs whose members they would never meet and went together in teams to take care of neighbors who were not part of their fellowship. Members of hush harbors fought for abolition for all, welcomed newcomers, and sheltered runaways who could potentially expose them. Finally, the length of their commitment was impressive. In contexts in which heartbreaking tragedy was a daily bitter root and dear ones could be taken without warning at any moment, they practiced active reconciliation to renew and maintain relationship over time. A shameful aspect of most of the churches we have helped lead (as well as the social justice movements we have known) is the long-term personal conflicts that are accepted as facts of life. Christians, by and large, in our experience do not fully believe in or practice the healing of relationships. We excuse rather than forgive.

Poor people have to take care of each other in order to survive. Members of BECs and hush harbors went a step beyond, seeing their relationships as core to their spiritual identity and living this care with intentionality and courage. It is important to note that BECs and hush harbors were small enough for people to know one another intimately and proximate enough for them to share life together. Deciding to organize in that way is itself a decision to risk control and the economy of scale for the sake of creating real kinship.

Are acts of radical and dangerous generosity a habit in your church? To the extent that the answer is no, the examples of BECs and hush harbors can

1. This phrasing is from Rev. Nelson Johnson of Beloved Community in Greensboro, North Carolina.

call you forward to a new way of being together that will amaze the world and give glory to God.

Leader-full

Every church relies on the volunteer energy of its members, right? What can we learn from BECs and hush harbors?

Remember the story (from chap. 5) of the puentes-led immersion trips across the Mexican border? Shifting the guide from a middle-class white expert to a young brown person with direct experience of the immigration crisis is a change in the protagonist or lead agent of change. BECs and hush harbors changed the "hero," which then changes the way that the work is organized, ensuring that everyone's full contributions are solicited and appreciated.

The potential contribution of people on the margins is often invisible to those who make the decisions—particularly with respect to sharing in the decision-making process.[2] Even when churches are committed to the full inclusion of people from the margins, they often continue to think of people from the centers of power and privilege as the protagonists of God's action. Missionary accounts that describe the beautiful work of the Spirit in a distressed community assume that the people guiding that work come from outside the community and are usually white and/or higher class than the community members. BECs and hush harbors were led by a critical mass of the oppressed. While some BECs were started by a pastoral agent from outside, the ones that succeeded transferred over all the central leadership roles and responsibilities to people from the community.

Both of these communities did leadership differently. They changed the perception and structure of leadership. Roles were intentionally rotated, recognized callings were diverse and varied, and participatory democracy was the process used to make decisions. Facilitated dialogue, consensus, and reflection-action cycles with group evaluation and planning were the rule. Women and youth were intentionally centered in the process. Mystical gifts with no relationship to formal education or training were honored and valued. Social justice tasks were seen as acts of spiritual service, as equally valuable as more traditional forms of church service.

At the same time, people from the margins were not romanticized, patronized, or set up for failure by the assumption that their capabilities would not require formation and training. BECs recognized that their structural changes,

2. I (Alexia) have often heard from seminary students in my courses that their churches or ministries are inclusive because some of the people served end up volunteering. When I ask, however, if they are on the steering committee or board making the decisions about the program, the response is an awkward silence.

because they were so profoundly countercultural, required intensive formation for everyone. The practical strategies of Paulo Freire were essential in that process. BECs and hush harbors also understood that everyone's gifts had to be developed through coaching, accompaniment, or mentoring processes.[3] In BECs, the gifts and skills of privileged people were also valued and utilized. However, those gifts and skills did not confer decision-making power. A lawyer's capacity to interpret the law was respected, but they did not retain the ultimate decision about how that interpretation fit into the broader strategy.

Who volunteers in your church? Who leads? We are often a body of Christ with many sleeping members because their potential contribution is unrecognized and undeveloped. How can the examples of BECs and hush harbors awaken you to the radical potential of marginalized people?

Consciousness

Many churches have a midweek Bible study and a Christian education team. What makes the formation that happened in BECs and hush harbors different?

"The whole truth and nothing but the truth . . ." Witnesses in a court of law swear that oath before testifying. Yet we so often shy away from uncomfortable truths. In 1974, the poet Carole Etzler wrote a song with the following line in the chorus: "Sometimes I wish my eyes hadn't been opened." Once we know that unjust suffering is not inescapable but instead can be changed if we love the victims, we cannot sit idly by. Yet in this complex world of ours, there are many barriers to action, both internal and external. Consciousness is the process of facing the human truth and the divine truth fearlessly, with the end result that we have the wisdom, humility, and energy to take on all the problems, small and large, that keep us from abundant life. BECs and hush harbors not only give us examples of that fearless faith and dedication but also bequeath a host of techniques for how to overcome internalized oppression and equip marginalized Christian communities to be effective change-agents.

Sunday school classes are not necessarily in high demand. The last time I (Brandon) checked, getting the seats of religious education spaces filled required clever marketing strategies, salacious titles, and well-known pastors. Learning, connecting, analyzing, and planning together touched a deep hunger and thirst in oppressed people who could not find this kind of agency elsewhere. The formation that happened in BECs and hush harbors touched the deep call of the people.

---

3. BECs also offered formal training; the context of hush harbors did not allow for that kind of structure to be developed.

Theirs was a formation for bodies, souls, and minds. It was not enough to talk about the Bible. BECs and hush harbors conscientized the Bible. They asked questions of the sacred text, interrogating the power dynamics and inequalities and social-emotional needs of the people and communities in the text. They were playful with the sacred text, going beyond a scholarly approach to a story in service to the meaning-making that can be done only by the Spirit and the community together. A Black Spiritual says, "Oh Mary, don't you weep, don't you mourn, / Pharaoh's army got drowned / Oh Mary, don't you weep." Hush harbors connected the lament of Mary of Bethany over her dead brother Lazarus (and also of Mary the mother of Jesus over the brutalizing of her son Jesus) to the victory of the Israelites over Pharaoh's oppressive regime. BECs and hush harbors exercised their agency by seeing all of the sacred text and all of life through the lens of their belief in the healing and liberating power of God and the teaching and ministry of Jesus. They incorporated dance, singing, physical touch, and role-playing that moved what they learned intellectually into the type of formation that comes from the body entering into practice. And then they had the audacity to actually believe what they discovered and to put it into practice in their daily lives. They didn't apply these lessons uncritically from text to their context. A member of a BEC in Nicaragua, in light of the slaughter of children ordered by Herod in Matthew 2, said, "The revolutionary conscience in these countries [Nicaragua and Costa Rica] is still a child. It's still tiny. And they persecute it so that it won't grow" (Cardenal 1976, 38). BECs and hush harbors contextualized the messages and lessons from their study for their own cultural contexts of oppression.

Contextualization was rooted in a commitment to formation that produced concrete social and spiritual change. Take the interpretation of Matthew 2 as an example. BEC members would commonly move from connecting the moral injury of the slaughter of children to a place's premature revolutionary consciousness to analyzing how this moral injury takes place and constructing and executing a plan for resisting it, while simultaneously using that resistance to mature and grow the revolutionary consciousness of the people. This is no typical midweek Bible study. The theological and political consciousness shaping that took place in BECs and hush harbors let the Bible catch fire to spread through the lies and stoke the truth through people who otherwise had no access to the formal education and upward social mobility the dominant society wrongly assumed was the only path to real knowledge and change.

Are just a few people in your church active in working for shalom? Take inspiration and wisdom from these movements to galvanize a conscious, healthy, active, well-coordinated body of Christ in your context.

Vibrant Spirit-uality

> Now Moses was tending the flock of Jethro his father-in-law, the priest of Midian, and he led the flock to the far side of the wilderness and came to Horeb, the mountain of God. There the angel of the LORD appeared to him in flames of fire from within a bush. Moses saw that though the bush was on fire it did not burn up. . . .
>
> God said, "Take off your sandals, for the place where you are standing is holy ground. . . . I have indeed seen the misery of my people in Egypt. I have heard [my people] crying out because of their slave drivers, and I am concerned about their suffering. So I have come down to rescue them from the hand of the Egyptians and to bring them up out of that land into a good and spacious land, a land flowing with milk and honey. . . . So now, go. I am sending you to Pharaoh to bring my people the Israelites out of Egypt." (Exod. 3:1–10)

Where do we meet the living God? In BECs and hush harbors, God came to the people where they were. They did not have to leave behind their bodies, their cultural identities, or the complicated, painful reality of their daily lives and their common life to go and meet God. As God met Moses in the midst of his daily struggle and called him to action that would lead to freedom from oppression, so the God of BECs and hush harbors met the people in the midst of their real, daily circumstances and called them to be active agents of liberation. And just as God promised Moses, "I will be with you," BECs and hush harbors trusted and experienced that God accompanied them intimately as they struggled to survive and overcome. Matthew 1:23 echoes the prophet Isaiah in speaking of Jesus as Immanuel, God with us. For BECs, Jesus was daily bread of sustenance and wine of mystical joy, the ever-present companion who gave them the courage to fight for a better world. The liberating Word of God confirmed and nurtured their deepest hopes, calling them to sacrificial love with and beyond each other. In hush harbors, the people danced and sang their anguish and their joy, moving from fear to faith in the process. Their faith was bursting with life even in the midst of a battlefield where death was always a step away.

Learning from their examples requires the willingness to create communities in which people can choose to be emotionally naked before God and each other, pouring out and facing the full realities of their individual and common lives together. It also means expecting God to show up with foretastes of the feast to come. It means dancing with joy when the Spirit moves, persisting faithfully in prayer and dialogue for days with someone who is battling with the call to change their life, and acting on plans for social justice that depend on God's active agency in the process. To learn from the examples of BECs and hush harbors is to create communities in which people experience in *carne propia*, in their own flesh, the cross and the resurrection—to experience their suffering as redemptive and their joys as a foretaste of resurrection.

The dance with God that is not limited by the walls of a church building but expects the Holy Spirit to move with power throughout our communities and societies—that is the secret sauce of BECs and hush harbors. I (Alexia) remember being asked to preach in a Pentecostal Hispanic megachurch in the middle of an immigrant workers' struggle. When I proclaimed victory in Jesus, I received a chorus of loud amens. When I continued to praise God for accompanying us in our fight for a living wage, the congregation was confused. It was not the message they were accustomed to hearing. After the service, members of the congregation were waiting in a line to speak to me. They spoke in hushed tones, so timid but so excited at the thought that God might care about whether they were being mistreated in their workplaces and that God might actually bring his power to bear in changing the injustices they bore on a daily basis.

It is every bit as important to name, though, that their faith in the present power of God was not limited to God's accompaniment in the pursuit of social justice. After my daughter came back to faith at a Hispanic Pentecostal church led by redeemed OGs (original gangsters) and deeply committed to a fully integral mission, she returned to college in western Massachusetts. She went to a church the next Sunday with a rainbow flag in the window because she took that as a sign that they were committed to social justice. She called me afterward baffled. "Mama, I don't understand what was happening there. It was a liberal political club of old white people. They didn't talk about Jesus, and no one got healed." In BECs, God was as vibrantly present in overcoming addiction, healing broken marriages, and giving hope in the midst of despair as in building a school, starting a cooperative, or fighting exploitative landlords and corrupt judges. In hush harbors, God was vibrantly present in their fight to hold on to their cultural sources of strength and in the long duration of their passionate prayers. To learn from BECs and hush harbors is to create communities with a living faith without limits or boxes, rooted and centered in the living God.

Do you know any burned-out activists? BECs and hush harbors knew the secret of spirit-uality that fuels liberation and heals the wounds of the struggle. It's a spirit-uality that goes deep in the flesh and embraces an unbroken line from earth to sky—enabling people to move from mourning to dancing. Patty Van Cappellen is a scholar of religion at Duke University. Her recent research shows that worship that creates self-transcending emotions and includes bodily expression draws people back to church (Van Cappellen 2018). BECs and hush harbors would confirm that truth but add that when those who are worshiping together also share a Holy Spirit–imbued life and struggle, the joy of the Lord becomes their strength (Neh. 8:10).

Be encouraged. Draw from the wells that BECs and hush harbors offer for deepening and broadening the spiritual life of your church and movements.

Faith-full Organizing

The majority of churches help those in need, usually through the simplest and most direct form available, such as a food pantry or visiting the sick and elderly. Some churches go beyond direct services to community development—working with the community and not for them—on projects that benefit the whole community, such as a community health clinic, a community garden, or an affordable housing development. Some practice community development as incarnational work, intimately sharing the suffering of the community and joining with the community in realizing its dreams.

However, in most community development work, there comes that moment when community development runs up against the wall of an unfair system. Then church members engaging in the work often begin to ask what they need to do in order to change the system that is blocking their way and impeding the attainment of their goals. For example, it is common for churches at the community development level to work on employment and housing. However, what happens when those working to get homeless people off the street learn that getting clients into low-wage, full-time work will not help them enough to pay rent? Or when a community job-preparedness and job-training program runs headlong into the unwillingness of employers to hire an ex-offender or a young adult who was brought to the US as a baby and is not a citizen? Or when the locally run small businesses in a small business incubation program cannot get the capital they need to grow because the banks are not providing loans to people who live in a low-income area? These problems have proven public policy solutions. The questions facing the church at that moment of realization that more can be done to solve these problems are these: Can we help make those solutions happen? Can we influence public policy? Should we participate in the process of influencing public decision-making?

Members of BECs and hush harbors did not hesitate to work for solutions that went beyond mercy to questions of justice. They understood their faith as calling them to live out the relentlessness of divine love in its pursuit of abundant life for the beloved—to love as intelligently and effectively as possible—integrating direct service, community development, community organizing, and advocacy as needed. They followed the incarnational principle all the way into full identification with and advocacy for those who were suffering and struggling against injustice. Their mission was holistic. At the same time, their participation in broader movements for justice was not only spurred on by their faith but also guided by their faith.

Faith-full organizing ensures that every aspect of the struggle for justice is guided and shaped by faith—from the assumptions about power and human nature on up. And a faith that can include and incorporate the fullness of the cultural and spiritual heritages of marginalized peoples. Faith-full organizing contributes all the unique gifts of faith to broader struggles. What does it mean to participate in broader collaborative efforts for justice in a way that is guided by faith, that is shaped in every way by faith?

"I am sending you out like sheep among wolves. Therefore be as shrewd as snakes and as innocent as doves" (Matt. 10:16). This is a wonderful instruction from our Lord and Savior for faith-full organizing. To be as shrewd as a snake is to take seriously the carnal and sinful nature of human beings. There are wolves out there—BECs and hush harbors suffered terribly from the attacks of human wolves. Even when people do not act in horribly cruel ways, they often prioritize their narrow self-interest and the quest for power. To be as shrewd as a snake is to respond effectively to reality as it is. However, human nature goes beyond the animal impulses. Everyone is made in the image of God, capable of sudden acts of sacrificial love and moral courage. The Holy Spirit is alive and well, working on everyone's heart to fan the flame of divine motivation. To be as innocent as a dove is to respond effectively to reality as it can be—to live into the kingdom of God.

Members of hush harbors developed a number of effective strategies for faithful serpent shrewdness. They learned to keep their cool. They learned to be as tricky as the midwives who saved Moses's life by telling the Egyptian overseers that the Hebrew babies were born too quickly to need midwives. Members of BECs were known for their dove power, for their courageous and creative initiatives to convert enemies to friends by calling on their faith. Hush harbors also knew how to rely on the power of prayer, and BECs knew how to build a critical mass of pressure to get an authority to release a political prisoner. Both movements practiced the dance of serpent wisdom and dove power.

Both movements also contributed a number of additional gifts to the broader movements for justice in their contexts. They took God's agency seriously, the dance with God that brings an extra measure of hope and valor to any action. Their commitment and faith had catalytic power and inspired others to persistence and to greater courage.

How far are you willing to go to use every gift and opportunity you have to work with those in your community who are suffering from and struggling with injustice? What are all the ways in which you can contribute the unique gifts of your faith to the process?[4]

---

4. Alexia is the coauthor of a book on faith-full organizing, *Faith-Rooted Organizing: Mobilizing the Church in Service to the World*, that contains more detailed information about such strategies.

Embracing the Contradictions

Jesus did not confuse accountability with punishment. He rendered prophetic critique, but he did not cancel people. I (Brandon) see Jesus as a model for abolition, for transformative justice. He used many metaphors to describe the work of transformation, to depict the complicated and tragic relationship between the way things are and his vision of wholeness and righteousness. Yeast, salt, and light were among the most prominent. Each of these is a transformative agent. Yeast works inside the dough to make the bread rise. Salt works to preserve or season food to prevent waste and cultivate taste. Light creates visibility where previously there was darkness. These agents are not meant to destroy. Yeast does not destroy the bread. Salt does not destroy food. Light does not destroy darkness. The same applies to the relationship between BECs and hush harbors with the institutional church. The prophetic witness of BECs and hush harbors is not to destroy the institutional church.

The best of any prophetic tradition seeks transformation, to abolish the characteristics and systems that do not constitute life and love and justice, and to replace them with characteristics and systems that do produce these virtues of shared abundance. Black pastor and theologian Raphael Warnock describes the distinctions between the hush harbors and the institutional Black church: "The invisible institution [hush harbors] represents the formation of a liberationist faith, and the rise of independent black churches and denominations constitutes the founding of a liberationist church, then King's movement, under the auspices of the SCLC [Southern Christian Leadership Conference], signifies the fomenting of a church-led liberationist movement" (Warnock 2020, 32). Warnock admits to what he calls the Black church's "theological double-consciousness" as a vehicle of both liberation and assimilation (29). Even as Warnock summons King for bringing a revival of a liberationist church-led movement, it was King who called the church, including the Black church, to task in his "Letter from Birmingham Jail" when he said,

> In deep disappointment I have wept over the laxity of the church. . . . How we have blemished and scarred that body through social neglect and through fear of being nonconformists. There was a time when the church was very powerful in the time when the early Christians rejoiced at being deemed worthy to suffer for what they believed. In those days the church was not merely a thermometer that recorded the ideas and principles of popular opinion; it was a thermostat that transformed the mores of society. Whenever the early Christians entered a town, the people in power became disturbed and immediately sought to convict the Christians for being "disturbers of the peace" and "outside agitators." But the Christians pressed on, in the conviction that they were "a colony of heaven," called to obey God rather than man. . . . Things are different now. So

often the contemporary church is a weak, ineffectual voice with an uncertain sound. So often it is an archdefender of the status quo. Far from being disturbed by the presence of the church, the power structure of the average community is consoled by the church's silence and often even vocal sanction of things as they are. . . . If today's church does not recapture the sacrificial spirit of the early church, it will lose its authenticity, forfeit the loyalty of millions, and be dismissed as an irrelevant social club with no meaning for the twentieth century. . . . Is organized religion too inextricably bound to the status quo to save our nation and the world? Perhaps I must turn my faith to the inner spiritual church, the church within the church, as the true ecclesia and the hope of the world. But again I am thankful to God that some noble souls from the ranks of organized religion have broken loose from the paralyzing chains of conformity and joined us as active partners in the struggle for freedom. (King 1963, 292)

King was not as optimistic about the existence of a liberationist church that was the same as the "independent black churches and denominations." Instead, he spoke to the other reality of "the church within the church" not tied to organized religion. Warnock and other Black prophetic leaders laud hush harbors as the origin of liberationist faith. I (Brandon) agree with this claim. However, I also view hush harbors as at the same time a liberationist faith *and* a liberationist church.

A similar breakdown exists when trying to understand the relationship between the Black church and contemporary Black liberation movements such as the Movement for Black Lives. This question is typically asked: Where is the Black church in this movement? Religion professor Nyle Fort challenges this question by asking, "What if, in our search for the church, we miss the spirit erupting beyond its walls?" (Fort 2022). Fort and others stretch the imagination of what church is and can be. Street memorials, protests, teach-ins, strategy sessions, and other social movement activities have become church for many Black people and their allies. For so many of the spiritually underserved these activities are "a makeshift spiritual practice rooted in a love of justice and a reverence for the sanctity of Black lives" (Fort 2022). Fort likens the spirituality of contemporary activism to the hush harbors.[5] He connects Baby

5. Fort is one of many leaders and scholars explicitly connecting the Movement for Black Lives and the hush harbors. In her article "A Black Church Proposition for Radical Human Flourishing," Dr. Oluwatomisin "Tomi" Oredein distinguishes between *the* Black church and Black church. The former is the institutional form. Even though the founders of BLM (and many Black activists) do not claim ties to *the* Black church, Oredein says that they are still Black church. She says,

Black church is not aligned with the spiritual-institutional practice alone, but it is an aura of freedom and liberation grounded in an understanding of one's self in the divine (the Creator God), ultimately turned toward a total, holistic lived liberation that invites human flourishing. . . . Many within the traditional institution stop short of liberation as the end goal assuming that freedom to be (Black) church unburdened from the white

Suggs[6] and Black Lives Matter saying that they "make a road we can all travel" (Fort 2022). Hush harbors are not something ancient that we appreciate but that must mature to institutional forms to be seen as legitimate, organized, or successful. Often what it really means to be organized and successful in a racialized capitalist society is an approximation of whiteness and supremacy, of mimicking colonized structures.

In a similar way that hush harbors cannot be reduced to the institutional Black church, BECs and the Catholic Church are not one and same. One historian captures the tension that the Catholic Church held toward the BECs:

> Concern in the Vatican, even before the death of Paul VI, over what was per-
> ceived as an ecclesiastical transformation that had moved too far and too fast,
> prompted Paul to convene that third general assembly of the Synod of Bishops
> (1974). . . . While promoting "generous dedication to the service of all men—
> the poor especially and the oppressed" in order "to eliminate the social conse-
> quences of sin"—the synod warned against remaining "with the mere political
> and social [consequences], however important." . . . On the debit side, one can
> perceive strong hints of Vatican fears that it was beginning to lose control of
> events. (Cook 1985, 242)

BECs and hush harbors constitute all that it means to be the church, the ecclesia, the called-out ones who are the body of Christ in the world. They are the church within the church, to invoke King once again. They represent a particular tradition that overlaps with the institutional Black church and the Catholic Church but cannot be reduced to them. BECs and hush harbors rendered sharp critiques of both of these institutions for not living fully into the highest ideals of the reign of God manifest on earth, especially the call to healing, solidarity, and justice in the social, economic, and political order. These critiques were not so much written as they were lived, a witness to a radically different way of being church with a commitment to what my organizing colleague Casey Thomas calls a left-bottom ethic, a commitment

---

supremacist version of Christianity is the epitome of an emancipated existence. . . . The Black Church is found in the songs, chants, mannerisms, and even ideologies toward a divinely recognized and full existence. . . . Black Church pursues liberation and thinks beyond white supremacist Christianity as its only foe. Its aim is to join the idea of Black worth and the right to thrive with dismantling white supremacist systems at large. Black Church believes with their actions that Black people should be free in totality. Black Church centers all living complexities and intersections such as gender identity, sexuality, disability, colorism, classism, misogyny, and environmental injustice as critical to the vision of the divine affirmation of Blackness. Black Church is a pursuit of a full life, not merely a practice of gathering alone. (Oredein 2022)

6. Suggs (who Fort calls an "unchurched" preacher) was a Black woman that Toni Morrison depicts in her book *Beloved* as an example of the kind of radical preaching done in hush harbors—what she calls "the clearing."

to the least of these, the oppressed, the poor, the marginalized as the center of their organization, leadership, and practice.

The hush harbors and BECs challenge us to grapple with many contradictions. With the exception of their liberation-theological traditions, the institutional Black church and the Catholic Church have been chaplains of the status quo that keeps women, queer kin, and the poor and working class at the bottom. The institutional church, across race and denomination, has largely become an accomplice of state violence, stripping the Bible and the gospel of their ancient liberationist roots and contemporary revolutionary potential. Instead, the institutional church individualizes and spiritualizes the gospel as a cover for idolatrous worship of flags, cash, or the preservation of their own institutions. Howard Thurman captured the idolatry of the institutional church: "To those who need profound succor and strength to enable them to live in the present with dignity and creativity, Christianity often has been sterile and of little avail. . . . Too often the price exacted by society for security and respectability is that the Christian movement in its formal expression must be on the side of the strong against the weak" (1976, 1).

Even the liberation-theological strains of the church hold serious contradictions. Liberation and womanist theologies are more proliferated in the academy and among the professional class. Many of my clergy colleagues struggle to find congregations that embrace and desire to embody these theologies. Most walk away from the church, remain closeted about their differences, or keep their heads down until they can ascend to bigger and more educated churches where they feel they can be more open about their real theological commitments.

These are false choices. The ruling class and dominant religion want to keep the masses from studying and (re)membering liberating truths (Dillard 2021). Septima Clark, popular educator during the Southern Black Freedom Movement, said it this way: "I believe unconditionally in the ability of people to respond when they are told the truth. We need to be taught to study rather than believe, to inquire rather than to affirm" (Watson-Vandiver 2021, 111).

BECs and hush harbors were training grounds for studying and embodying the gospel of liberation among the most disenfranchised and within social movements. BECs and hush harbors are a remnant that bears witness to the reign of God rather than the reign of the nation-state. This remnant is in solidarity with and led by the poor, working class, women, and all those who are outcasts of the ruling class and dominant religion. And yet BECs and hush harbors had their own contradictions. Neither BECs nor hush harbors were powerful enough to prevent betrayal and infiltration within their ranks. Neither movement was able to fully dismantle the culture and systems of inequality and injustice in their midst. Neither movement was able to grow to such a scale that made its legacy and ongoing impact permanent in church and society.

Holding in tension these contradictions across and within different parts of the church raises another of Jesus's metaphors—the one most resonant with this book: the seed. Jesus is especially fond of the mustard seed, which he compares to the reign of God (Matt. 13:31–32; Mark 4:30–32; Luke 13:18–19). He explains that the mustard seed, though small, grows into a large tree, and the birds and other life in the ecosystem benefit from its presence. Not only does this vulnerable seed have the potential to grow, but the mustard plant also has the potential to be one of the most invasive and proliferated weeds in its habitat, able to grow in the sun or shade and to inhibit other plants from growing. Mustard plants produce thousands of seeds that are viable in soil for several years.

Decolonial theorist Julietta Singh uses the metaphor of a garden to depict the work of decolonization. The garden is the society, the complex ecosystems that make up our physical and social lives. The gardeners are us, humans. Singh reminds us that past gardeners have cultivated the garden with colonization and its afterlife, treating the garden as object and themselves as the only agent. The garden is a site of futurism that is always already haunted by the past. The gardener is an agent in this drama, and yet in terms of the future, the gardener, no matter their skill level or desires, always stands in an ultimate place of wonder related to the garden's future. The garden is also an agent, acting on the gardener and a dynamic partner in the uncertain, and at times unwanted, possibilities of how nature will act through it for what harvest, or lack thereof, is to come. The garden ultimately cannot be reduced to the gardener's will. Singh states that the "garden—rife with unexpected visitors and 'willful' species—reveals the entanglements of the past, the present, and the future as it uncovers not only the gardener's vulnerability but her fraught constitution as a porously bounded subject. . . . Not knowing 'what to do' . . . leads us toward emergent conceptions of being . . . that we might uproot our masterful subjectivities, dwelling within our devastated landscapes alongside other dynamic agencies that are making up the future with us" (Singh 2018, 170).

A good garden, and its relationship with gardeners, is not a project of mastery but a project of fellowship and transformations. Because, like Singh says, mastery is elusive anyway. There is no politically pure or moral high ground on which any of us can ultimately stand. This does not mean we forfeit our hopes and actions toward change. It does mean that we are bound to one another and to the histories of our communities, no matter what "sides" we claim. The only future we have is together, whether we like it or not. What a sobering and challenging invitation for us to seek change with more truth and grace! Building contemporary hush harbors and BECs is not a strategy to save the church or to take it back from the institution. BECs and hush harbors are with us. They've never left. They are always already here: on the edge, the margin, off the grid, hidden in plain sight. No matter what has been built or grown on top of or around them, BECs and hush harbors cannot stay buried. They will always rise because they are seeds. Let the mustard seeds of BECs and hush harbors do their unique, vibrant, invasive work to proliferate small witnesses to the reign of God.

Case Studies

The following ministries are twenty-first-century examples of faith communities that have a sensibility similar to BECs and hush harbors and that are trying to meet similar goals and manifest the same Spirit in their contexts. We share these case studies with you to encourage you and stimulate your imagination.

La Fuente Ministries

Founded in 2013, La Fuente Ministries started as the Hispanic Ministry of the First Church of the Nazarene of Pasadena (commonly known as PazNaz) as an initiative to connect with and minister to the various Latinx surrounding communities. Since its inception, it has been led and carried out bilingually (Spanish and English). Pastor Marcos Canales shares that the desire to minister bilingually was birthed out of a desire for Latinx families and generations to worship together (given that immigrant generations tend to prefer the language of their country of origin and their offspring tend to prefer the language of their new country) as well as the opportunity to offer a Latinidad name with a complex social and cultural location as a gift to deepening people's understanding of God (Canales, October 16, 2020).

During the first year, the group of founding members met once a week for Bible study and once a month for *convivio*—a gathering of testimony, food, and fellowship.[7] This time served to fortify interpersonal relationships and create a familia culture of mutual commitment and care. As one of the founding members of this ministry states, "Formamos esta comunidad de fe en el amor, pues si nos amamos los unos a los otros, y si Dios es amor, pues no hay duda que Dios habita entre nosotros." ("We founded this community of faith in love, for if we love one another, and if God is love, then there is no doubt that God is going to be present.") While the second year of the ministry involved weekly worship gatherings, it was not until the third year that the leadership team decided to enter into a three-month process of prayer,

7. Taken from La Fuente Ministries' DNA, values, and leadership orientation document (internal document, La Fuente Ministries 2021).

discernment, and consensus to name the ministry La Fuente Ministries. This step also helped to clarify the identity and purpose statements attached to the name, which is based on Psalm 36:9: "For with you is the fountain of life; in your light we see the light." While *fuente* means "fountain," "wellspring," "font," and "source," in Spanish *la fuente* also has other connotations; since the name was given three years into the ministry's existence, members were able to attach meaning to experiences lived in the community. Cristina, a poet and songwriter from the community, mentioned to the pastoral team, "La Fuente también significa el arribo de un bebé; cuando se rompe 'la fuente' una criatura está por nacer. Esto quiere decir que La Fuente Ministries es el vientre donde Dios está creando algo nuevo!" ("La Fuente also reminds me of the arrival of a baby; when your water [*fuente*] breaks, a new baby is going to be delivered. This means that La Fuente Ministries is a womb-like space where God is birthing something new!")

Because the ministry is bilingual, people of many cultures have been able to participate, and it has been a welcoming place for a number of mixed families. It is a church designed for people who live in the intersections between communities and as a result are often marginalized. As described on La Fuente's website, this ministry "is willing to dwell and celebrate the intersection between the Latina community and the Latina church; between first generation and second generation; between the realities of race and culture; between Christian evangelism and God's justice; and between Spanish and English. God has called and established La Fuente Ministries as an alternative space for the already existing variety of ways of doing church . . . so that those in these intersections not be rejected, erased, assimilated or be put to competition" ("Que Hacemos" 2021).

Over the years, La Fuente has also been a refuge for people who have been wounded and marginalized by other church communities. In some cases, congregants have said that La Fuente was the last faith community they wanted to check out before giving up on church altogether. During a regular time of Stories of God's People (the time in the worship service when participants share testimonies or personal stories), one member mentioned that "after the 2016 election, we were embarrassed to use the name Christian because of all the connotations that it carried in a polarized political reality. We said there has to be a place where Jesus's politics, social justice, and the church intersect. Once we experienced La Fuente's commitment to God's heart of justice for the immigrant, the orphan, and the widow, we found Jesús and we started to use the term *Christian* again" (Canales, October 16, 2020).

La Fuente Ministries' congregational culture is fostered by the collaborative work of a pastoral team and a leadership team. Reverend Rosa Cándida Ramírez, Dr. Andrea Canales, and Rev. Marcos Canales make up the pastoral team. They regularly preach and teach the liberating Word, intentionally inviting people into holistic reflection on their individual and common lives, their mental and spiritual health, and their radical discipleship. Newcomers are immersed in the ministries' culture: a holistic understanding of the gospel, "announcing the good news of God's ongoing action in the world and denouncing all that goes against God's will for everyone to have abundant life," and seeking the intersection between their reality and God's promise and call. La Fuente's pastoral team integrates Latin American liberation and Latina theologies, Misión Integral, Black theologians, activist church leaders, and psychoeducation resources into the preaching, an approach that seeks to follow the hermeneutical circle of ver, juzgar, and actuar. Pastor Marcos's goal is to preach the whole Bible, not just proof texts, which leads the pastoral team and the leadership team to embody the liberating gospel. In fact, this process of concientización through teaching the Word informs the initiatives and experiments carried out by the leadership team and various others leaders in the congregation. La Fuente Ministries' leadership team is intentionally mixed—men and women, older immigrant leaders and second-generation leaders born in the US, laborers and professionals. It is not an easy mix to manage. They find their way into consensus through ongoing contemplative prayer, deep dialogue, a requirement to practice mutual respect, and an atmosphere that grants permission for each one to follow the voice of the Spirit, who speaks to their hearts. Dissenting voices are welcome.

The permissive atmosphere is not an empty promise. Every member of the congregation learns that their daily work is a ministry and has dignity. At the same time, La Fuente encourages people to dream big about the kingdom of God. Members often start their own mission and ministry projects, inviting others to join them and receiving the blessing of the pastors and church. A favorite saying of Pastor Marcos is "Do less. Trust people more." A mission of accompaniment and evangelical outreach for people who spend their days in a local barrio park, a set of families who obtained foster care licenses to care for unaccompanied migrant children, participation in support circles and advocacy for families seeking asylum—every project grew out of the vision of specific members who were encouraged and supported in making their dreams into reality. None were professional social workers or volunteers with years of experience in community development.

La Fuente Ministries grew slowly and organically, building relationships first, bathing their early activities in prayer before making plans. Even though ideas might come to individual families or friends for specific forms of mission and ministry, these ideas grew out of the ongoing conversation and were connected to a common vision. Their most passionate ministry projects came out of a shared experience with specific families who were particularly affected by the social injustices in their community. An undocumented family with a son with special needs broke open a powerful dialogue about health care and immigration. Members of the congregation who were essential workers in hospitals and others who died of COVID-19 continued to provoke the reflection-action cycle. They expect the Spirit to speak to them in the moment about opportunities and needs; they have experienced God as an active agent, dancing with them and guiding them. The focus is never to create programs but rather to accompany people and see what emerges. These catalytic conversations often happened in home Bible studies with the members. The early church gatherings rotated from home to home, like the BEC meetings, and they broke bread together, shared stories and testimonios, and reflected on the Word. La Fuente's pastoral team particularly lifts up women and young people with gifts for teaching and preaching. They use various traditions such as the church year and arts in worship in ways that are adapted to their needs and reality.

La Fuente intentionally stays small—about 80 members, 120 with the children—so that they can share life together. Leaders have already left to found sister churches. While financial self-sufficiency is not assured given their priorities and constituency, after eight years of ministry, La Fuente is characterized by generosity, as they have also partnered financially with the Immigration Resource Center of San Gabriel Valley and offered rental assistance to those impacted by COVID-19.

La Fuente is not the garden of Eden. They have had many disappointments— partner organizations that didn't come through, deaths of beloved members— some through an unjust lack of access to quality health care and some from the tension between the desire to go slow and follow the Spirit and members' real need for formal leadership development. They are interested in using the examples of BECs and hush harbors to see how much more they can do and be, but they are already steadily drawing young people who were nones and dones into a new and vibrant experience of Christian community.

Mission House Church and the Good Neighbor Movement

Both Mission House Church (MHC) and the Good Neighbor Movement (GNM) are based in North Carolina, MHC in Salisbury and GNM in Greensboro. MHC began in 2015 and GNM in 2017, though both began with small groups entering ministry together prior to these official launch dates. Both faith communities are small, around fifty to seventy-five members who are multiracial but majority Black, led by multigendered Black ministry teams. GNM is explicitly a queer-affirming faith community. Both communities are from the Wesleyan tradition, with GNM affiliated with the United Methodist Church (UMC) and MHC affiliated with the Wesleyan Church. Both explicitly identify the influence of BECs and hush harbors on the way they are organized, gather, and do community outreach. Anthony Smith and Toni Smith are the pastors of MHC. They are both bi-vocational pastors who work full-time jobs in the marketplace while also serving MHC. I (Brandon) am currently a full-time minister and organizer with GNM. GNM has also had part-time staff that support the ministries of care, door-to-door canvassing, and coordinating small groups.

GNM serves the spiritually and socially marginalized—diverse people searching for or open to a spiritual community doing social justice who have struggled to find it in mainstream spaces within the church and society (people of color, queer and trans persons, the underserved, allies, seekers and doubters, the spiritually and theologically eclectic and interspiritual). An anchor Scripture passage for the identity and mission of GNM is John 1:14, which can be paraphrased as "God became human and moved into the neighborhood" (influenced by The Message version). This Scripture inspires GNM to see no divide between the sacred, secular, profane, and ordinary. God connects all things and people. GNM seeks to be a faith community that lives this incarnational reality by doing justice, loving mercy, and walking humbly in everyday life, in homes, coffee shops, bars, the outdoors, on the internet, in the streets—in the neighborhood ("Mission & Values" 2018). GNM does not have its own building, and it rarely gathers in one centralized location. GNM's stated mission is to be an alternative spiritual community inspired by the life and ministry of Jesus and drawing from diverse religious and wisdom traditions to cultivate intentional relationships, work collaboratively, and seek justice with diverse neighbors in Greensboro and beyond. GNM's goal is to create inclusive, local communities that are abundant, just, and whole. GNM's values are framed as questions to its members and community:

- Belong: How will we practice authenticity and care in a way that demonstrates we value our neighborhoods?
- Be still: How will we develop and nurture practices of accountability and rootedness that keep us present to God within us, our neighbors, our enemies, and the world?
- Become: How will we listen for the hospitality and solidarity needed to transform ourselves, our neighborhoods, and our cities?
- Be bold: How will we take transformative actions with neighbors in our communities that seek justice and innovation? ("Mission & Values" 2018)

GNM lives out its identity, mission, and values primarily through contemplative activist groups, believing that it takes a village to develop and sustain disciples. GNM has several groups across Greensboro. Being leader-full is a core characteristic of GNM. GNM embodies being leader-full through three kinds of contemplative activist groups: city villages, self-care collectives, and active neighbors groups. City villages are small groups that gather weekly or biweekly in homes, outdoors, online, and in community spaces for spiritual practices and collective action. Self-care collectives are large groups that meet twice a month to engage in a spiritual practice together. Active neighbors groups meet monthly to coordinate grassroots community building where neighbors take collective action to learn about and make changes to issues and needs that are widely and deeply impacting neighbors. All of GNM's groups are organized based on geographic or social location, or a particular theme or type of practice. These groups are designed to be relationally centered, contextually driven, nimble, decentralized, and replicable ("Contemplative Activist Groups" 2018).

GNM holds space for its groups, the wider community, and its virtual constituency at Good Neighbor Rally, a pop-up hybrid collective gathering on the first Sunday of each month that is characterized by a Black folk mysticism with movement, silence, a cappella congregational singing, chanting, drumming, conversational messages, sitting in circles, and breakout small groups for processing and planning. Good Neighbor Rally is organized around four pillars: Black Prophetic Fire (drawing from revolutionary words and witness, starting with Black ancestors), Bound Together (solidarity across differences), Transformative Justice (change at the roots, in our souls and the society), and Play Your Part (everyone participates, no one spectates). GNM cultivates a rhythm of shaping the interior life of its members and constituency in order to unleash these persons into the community for the public ministry of social change and community organizing. This ministry is done in solidarity with the oppressed to address the root causes of injustice and to contribute the unique gifts of spirituality and faith.

MHC's mission is to mobilize an army of love for the good of its neighborhoods and city. Doing this "is more than having church, more than having a common belief system. This is a Jesus-movement of the kingdom of God, alerting and inviting everyone to be mobilized for the good of their neighborhoods and cities" ("Who We Are" 2015). MHC sees this work with Jesus shaped by reconciliation, renewal, and renaissance in their neighborhoods and city. They live out their mission through what they call the three elements of their DNA: incarnation, mission, and reconciliation. They describe these as follows:

- In Incarnation, we are sent into our community as Christ was sent into the world.

- In Mission, we are sent by the Holy Spirit to join in God's renewal of our neighborhoods and city.
- In Reconciliation, we seek to be agents of peace in the midst of a long history of division and disunity. ("Our Mission" 2021)

MHC is organized in Mission Labs (regular spaces of theological and missional formation), Mission Bands (groups of two to three people who provide care and accountability to one another), and Mission Kids (groups of spiritual formation for the youth of the community). MHC gathers weekly on Sunday for worship, which they call a Worship Rally, characterized by casual attire and Pentecostal-like expression with speaking in tongues, prophecy, dance, and laying on of hands.

GNM and MHC never do the work of activism to the neglect of their faith. A lay member bursts out speaking in tongues at a direct action to hold elected officials accountable because they feel the powerful Spirit of justice fall heavy on them as another church member is speaking the truth with might and conviction. A small yet fierce choir of carolers gathers on a cold December night outside the home of a developer who is displacing many low-income neighbors to sing "Away with the Mangers" (a revolutionary remix of "Away in a Manger"):

> Away with the mangers
> No crib and no bread
> Though houses are plenty
> Kids caged 'n' found dead
> Some heat exhaustion
> Some frozen to death
> And Marcus Deon Smith[8]
> died gasping for breath
>
> ARCO got off easy
> Jerry Wass gets a pass
> Developers winning
> City Council gets cash
> Hiatt Street left scrambling
> Refugees burned to death
> Evictions skyrocket
> While no ERAP is left.[9] (Wrencher 2021)

8. Marcus Deon Smith was a houseless, unarmed Black man who was killed by Greensboro Police Department in 2018 by their use of the deadly hog-tying tactic. Find out more about this situation at https://triad-city-beat.com/?s=marcus+deon+smith.

9. ERAP refers to the COVID-19 Emergency Rental Assistance Program. ARCO and Jerry Wass are developers in Greensboro, NC, who have been the cause of housing injustice for

Both communities draw from prophetic hush harbor faith as they fight for justice in the public square. They are especially focused on those most marginalized taking leadership and giving voice to what issues and needs are prioritized in the work. Both communities' ministry leaders model and live what they proclaim the gospel message asks of their congregations: to embody the gospel through spiritual practices and acts of mercy and justice with the most marginalized. MHC and GNM have struggled to live out their ministries through contested relationships with their denominational bodies' conservative views and anti-activism orientation; capacity issues due to being small in size with a lack of infrastructure, such as staffing and funding; and natural challenges that come from internal conflict and the death and transitions of members. Still, both communities draw on the wisdom of BECs and hush harbors to inspire and sustain their shared life together through the victories, obstacles, and setbacks.

---

immigrant families, including those in the Hiatt Street community. See more about each here: ARCO (https://tinyurl.com/2p9fxxnc) and Jerry Wass and Hiatt Street (https://triad-city-beat .com/hope-for-hiatt/).

La Fuente Ministries

MARCOS CANALES

As I read through the pages of this book, I saw how the Spirit was up to something in our explicit intent of being a bilingual ministry from our inception, especially to decenter both colonial languages (Spanish and English) and not give precedence to one over the other. In waiting for translations, the Spirit was re-forming our inclination toward dominance in "moving things along" to reach a conclusion or decision. Even to this day, this value of waiting for one another in bilingual contexts has paved the way in our leadership processes, nurturing a sense of familia and attentiveness to Scripture and context.

The prolonged COVID-19 season forced us to implement live-streaming capabilities and to recognize that everything we had done or established pre-pandemic needed to be (re)assessed. Prior to regathering in person in the summer of 2021 (after fourteen months online), the leadership of La Fuente Ministries spent two months discerning and reengaging the Spirit's promptings in our congregation through the practice of lectio divina via Zoom. After several sessions and conversations, leaders identified the abundance of gifts, graces, and grit present in our congregation amid the loss, grief, and pain of the pandemic—at both the personal and the collective level. New leadership emerged in pastoral care and accompaniment (not part of the pastoral team); neighborhood engagement continued through podcasts, protests, and the accompaniment of asylum seekers from Central America; a sense of belonging had increased even while we were apart; and new members joined our La Fuente Ministries community.

I believe that much of the Spirit's work in this season was catalyzed by the foundational and nurturing sense of familia. La Fuente Ministries seeks to be a space where we don't replicate dysfunctional family systems that are often romanticized or that leave patriarchy and oppressive relational dynamics intact. Rather, the guiding value that forms our *vínculos* (bonds) is the reconstituted familia: "an *hermandad* [kinship] of equals, called to imitate the life, work and dynamics of our Triune God" (Maldonado Perez 2013, 71).

Eva, one of our members, explained it best in our weekly Zoom meeting: "Yo a ustedes los amo literalmente como mis hermanos y hermanas, más que mis hermanos y hermanas de sangre. Ustedes me han ayudado a navegar mi ansiedad que sufrí por años." ("I love you like my brothers and sisters, even more than my blood siblings. You accompanied me in navigating my anxiety, which I was unable to control for years.") Eva's affirmation prompted Alberto to reflect: "It's so true! Here in La Fuente, I can say no, and that is respected." "Formamos una verdadera familia. Aquí se busca el bienestar de mis relaciones y nos cuidamos como personas y no como números." ("We form a true family. Here, you all desire that my relationships thrive, and we mutually care for one another as persons, not as a number.")

In fact, a reconstituted familia mirrors the común-unión (common union) of the triune God by fostering mutual care, dialogue in conflict, consensus decision-making practices, and healing experiences of relational trust. Our leadership processes and nurturing sense of familia derive from our attentiveness to God in Scripture. We are constantly reminding one another that "cuando leemos las Escrituras, las Escrituras también nos leen." ("When we read the Scriptures, the Scriptures are also reading us.")

Luz, an influential neighborhood leader and member of our congregation, shared with me, "One of the things that keeps me in La Fuente is that we are able to embrace both the suffering and death of our lives and world as well as the hope and joy of the resurrection." In one of our membership classes, Toni reflected, "Intentionality is a word that gets thrown around nowadays; yet in La Fuente intentional means connecting Scriptures to what is happening in our world [especially when other churches are silent] and God's heart for justice."

One of the practices that has recently shaped us to be more attentive to God in the Scriptures and in our contexts is the practice of congregational lectio divina. This practice has fostered a democratization of the interpretation of the Scriptures: a commitment that diversifies interpretive voices and returns the text to the life of the community. This is often done in place of a sermon or during our weekly connect group,[1] and it requires the active listening and participation of those present in person and online. We consider that these

---

1. During the season of Advent, we also practiced visio divina, a time that allowed us to reflect on the mystery of the incarnation through art, imagery, and symbolism.

times affirm our trust that the Spirit is already ahead of us, ready to reveal the next season of our congregational life. Recently, we experienced a time of congregational lectio divina around Jeremiah 29:1–14.[2] When the letter to the exiles of Jeremiah 29 was read and processed in small groups, identifying common words in connection to their own personal experiences, themes of exile, deportation, forced displacement, economic migration, survival of civil war and military dictatorships throughout the Americas, seeking the shalom of the city, and instructions for inhabitants in a foreign land emerged. This shifted all our imaginations as one of our leaders reminded us, "The fact that so many of us have been or are exiles makes me wonder how many of our neighbors in our city are exiles or are feeling like exiles? Perhaps that's a gift that the Spirit gives us to connect with our neighbors!" We have processed and will continue to process this text, for it continues to prompt our own concientización processes of trauma, loss, and migration that are often unattended amid survival tactics. That Sunday I learned that the depth of processes of concientización at the emotional, psychological, relational, and systemic levels promotes and enables us to pursue God's desired shalom.

Eight years ago, at the start of this church planting journey, Rev. Rosa Cándida Ramírez, Dr. Andrea Canales, and I could not have imagined La Fuente Ministries as a BEC. We knew we needed to be shaped by the values and principios embodied by our Latin American or Latina ancestors' legacy and witnesses of faith across the Americas. At the same time, we did not want to be an ethnic enclave that limited missional engagement with Christ in our neighborhoods across languages, cultures, and racial realities. We knew that Latin American theology and Latina theology, from both Protestant and Catholic streams, had often been dismissed or overlooked in contemporary church-planting movements and that recentering such experiences, wisdom, reflections, and accompaniment processes of ecclesial formation would be essential in the reimaging of following Jesus *en el camino* (along the way). I believe that if we had set out to plan step-by-step how to create a BEC from the start, we would have failed; I think we would have defaulted to our modern, Western, capitalist thirst for control, power, and productivity. All of these would have been the weeds, thorns, and toxic fertilizers that would have choked the "buried seeds" wanting to die to give way to the ancient and subversive practices and fruits of Jesus's third way.[3]

2. Throughout the latter part of our summer preaching series, the preaching team and I identified Jeremiah as a timely text that created space for lament, grief, repentance, hope, and processing collective trauma by giving words to wounds. For an exceptional interdisciplinary commentary on biblical, theological, and trauma studies, see O'Connor 2011.

3. Jesus's third way usually refers to the unique path taken by Christians in relationship to the world's standard political categories of right and left or economic categories such as capitalism and communism.

Ultimately, God's message to the buried seeds in the Babylonian exile and a desolated Jerusalem begs for our attention:

> Deténganse en el cruce y miren a su alrededor;
> pregunten por el camino antiguo, el camino justo, y anden en él.
> Vayan por esa senda y encontrarán descanso para el alma.[4] (Jer. 6:16
>   Nueva Traducción Viviente)

As we stand at the crossroads of an eroded witness of US American evangelicalism (due to its entrenchment in the supremacy of whiteness and violent theologies of coloniality) and the rise of the dones and nones, Jeremiah's impetus to ask for directions and discernment from "los caminos antiguos y justos" (the ancient and just ways) beckons the church to urgently consider both BEC and hush harbor movements as liberating and transited pathways of Jesus's third way. The shalom that we so desperately long for in our ecclesial, relational, and economic realities may indeed be nurtured by the wisdom and subversive hope that these communities embodied. While our temptation lies in importing BEC and hush harbor practices into our current context and imposing them, we must enter the ongoing process of translating and dialoguing with these movements as interlocutors in our processes of spiritual, congregational, and missional (re)formation. In other words, the work that Alexia and Brandon have curated is not a how-to manual or a copy-paste format to attract millennials of color to church; rather, it is an invitation to converse with our ancestors, appreciate the liberating resilience of the base, and envision the pathways and possibilities for a faithful church in the twenty-first century.

---

4. "Stop at the crossroads and look around. Ask for the old, godly way, and walk in it. Travel its path, and you will find rest for your souls" (Jer. 6:16 NLT). The Spanish translation uses the phrase the "justice-oriented way" as equivalent to the "godly way." Based on the witness of the Hebrew Scriptures, the way of the Torah as God's justice-oriented way (after Egyptian captivity) for the people of God to be organized as a society opting for the inclusion and participation of widow, orphan, and immigrant clarifies the implications of the ancient and godly way.

Mission House Church

ANTHONY SMITH

The transformative image of the mustard seed that Jesus uses to point to the invasive and landscape-changing reign of God resonates deeply with me and our liberating church expression at Mission House Church. Such buried seeds are watered and cultivated by our shared life together and our dance with the Holy Spirit. They are lovely and wild, and they raise our consciousness so we can reflect on the harm and injustices done on a systemic level in our neighborhoods and cities. Buried seeds appear in our ring shouts when the mothers of the church pull on the rope of heaven, expressing prophetic utterances with insurgent tongues of fire to build up our most holy allegiance to love.

There are buried seeds of children playing, making film shorts, telling stories that are from the invisible voices in our community. Buried seeds are organizing, mobilizing, and popular-educatin' folks into a critical mass to make reversals of power and to shape a people to be a holy irritant to the status quo.

Buried seeds are in the soil of a community trapped in a history they do not know. A history that is always hunting us, breathing down our necks—history in need of an exorcism. Buried seeds are in acts of exorcism of powerful symbols of white supremacy in the heart of our city.

Buried seeds are there when we taste the bitter cloud of tear gas for being boldly present in our Black humanity in the streets of our city. Buried seeds are there when we attune our shared life together to the dangerous, world-remaking red letters of Jesus in the Gospels, when we break bread together, when we play together, when we prayer-walk the streets together, when we sing with joy, when we lament the latest tragic act of policy and inflicted violence on poor bodies.

When our tears become our manna, they are the sustenance we need to keep on keeping on in the wilderness of the American South. We are bodies in need of resources that bring life and health but are blocked by systems gone satanic.

May these seeds grow. May they sprout. May they spread like the wild and invasive mustard plant. We are a liberating church, a hush harbor inspired by BECs in Latin America. May the liturgical acts of sankofa, ubuntu, and listening to the talking book bring about the revolutionary and undomesticated characteristics of the reign of God in our city as it already is in heaven.

Surely, we are in a watershed moment in the church. The COVID-19 pandemic has laid bare the deep, twisted wickedness of the powers as expressed by the disproportionate number of deaths among historically marginalized groups. Social misery is laughing its way to the bank.

In this moment, we hear the prophetic call of our ancestors from hush harbors of old calling us back to a *kairos* when they embodied a faith deeply rooted in mutual aid, shared moments in the Spirit, ring shouts, prayer meetings, and an open table to eat at. A call that pulls us away from the neoliberal spell of hyper-individualized, branded, and anxiety-ridden lives. A call that breaks the hypnosis of the swinging pendulum of shrinking publics, a growing authoritarianism, whitelash, transphobia, and xenophobia.

As we practice sankofa, may Mission House Church, your hush harbor, and your BEC go back and get that incarnational, sacred wisdom born in the sojourn of a people kissed by the sun.

Asé and amen.

Afterword

To Become a Place

WILLIE JAMES JENNINGS

All the believers were one in heart and mind. No one claimed that any of their possessions was their own, but they shared everything they had. (Acts 4:32)

"Therefore I want you to know that God's salvation has been sent to the Gentiles, and they will listen!" For two whole years Paul stayed there in his own rented house and welcomed all who came to see him. He proclaimed the kingdom of God and taught about the Lord Jesus Christ—with all boldness and without hindrance! (Acts 28:28–31)

These two texts from the book of Acts, one from early in the book of Acts and the other near the end, capture the radical hospitality that is fundamental to the gospel. The second text also captures the frustration of Paul. His frustrations are part of his ongoing conversations with his own people over what he believes God is doing. There in the heart of the Roman Empire, Paul is trying to explain to his folk the revolutionary new thing that the God of Israel has done and is doing through Jesus—the old order in all its manifestations (social, political, religious, and economic) has been overturned and is now beginning to crumble from within. But Paul's people understand and seem to appreciate (more than Paul does) where they are—they are in Rome, in the heart of the old order, and no one seems to have gotten this memo about this new order created in Jesus of Nazareth. As far as Paul's people in Rome are concerned, there is no room in Rome for theological experimentation or new political projects, unless you want to end up like Paul: incarcerated. If the frustrations are old yet expected for Paul, so too is his incarceration—he has been jailed before (a Roman citizen yet incarcerated). This one who has traveled everywhere now cannot go anywhere.

Paul is living under constrained conditions. On the one hand, he has not yet broken through to his people, not yet convinced them that a new order is here—a new order of life together in which all the different Jews and all the different gentiles could be joined together in a life of discipleship and communion. And on the other hand, he is being held captive because of a political system and a judicial system being used to destroy him. He cannot break through, and he cannot leave. Yet Paul, in the midst of his constrained condition, enacts a future for himself in which he becomes a place. He decides to open up where he is—open his story, share his journey, announce the new thing that God is doing and wants to do in the world—to all who come to him. He will, with courage and conviction, open his life.

What does it mean to become a place? I don't mean to *have* a place, but to *become* a place. It may seem odd to refer to a person as a place, but I am referring here to a kind of becoming through which one becomes a place of meeting, a place of gathering that opens up for people new possibilities of thriving life together even in, especially in, confined and confining spaces. These pandemic days, these Black-lives-matter days, these grotesque-inequities-in-everything days require a new vision of what we might become collectively and what each of us might become individually. I am reminded of the 1963 Martin Luther King Jr., not the harmless image he has become in our time but the one who became a lightning rod of controversy by drawing diverse people together in a shared project of Black abolition, who from a jail cell in Birmingham, Alabama, wrote those famous words that many of us know so well: "We are caught in an inescapable network of mutuality, tied in a single garment of destiny. Whatever affects one directly affects all indirectly. Never again can we afford to live with the narrow, provincial 'outside agitator' idea" (King 1963, 290).

King saw connection and sought to build connection. That is what is required to become a place of meeting where new possibilities can be seen and imagined. To become a place of meeting is not to envision yourself in that fictive middle position between liberal and conversative. For so many of us, our social vision has collapsed into that mindless duality, that stupefying binary of liberal or conservative, and so we are pressed to imagine that the heart of our moral work now is to get liberals and conservatives to talk respectfully to one another. That is not being a place of meeting, that is becoming a place of confusion.

Everything comes down to how we see and build connection. Especially in the Western world we have inherited, we have one way of seeing and building connection—it is a vision in which we are all connected by being competitors, struggling over the same resources, bent on exploiting and on guarding against being exploited. Through this vision, we build connection to profit and to secure ourselves against threats. Much of Western life is captured in this vision of connection, and it aims to turn our lives toward the individual quest for thriving and to collapse that work of thriving down to your body and the bodies of those whom you love.

Alexia Salvatierra and Brandon Wrencher reverse that vision of connection by overturning one way of connecting bound by greed and exploitation and hatred and fear and living toward another way of connecting bound by the Spirit's desire to build thriving life, to see it made real. They give material content to holy subversive desire, a desire to become a place where people thrive, a desire that moves us beyond simply being those who are not impediments to people's thriving. That is such a low bar for living—simply not being an impediment—where people are free to pursue their individual quest for thriving. That low bar for living will not meet this moment. This moment requires people who wish to place their bodies as living conduits, who make their lives bridges where knowledge, and ideas, and resources, and opportunities, and hopes, and dreams flow back and forth between peoples and communities that have refused connection and resisted collaboration. This moment will require people who will turn not only their resources but their lives toward building the common, the shared, the joined.

This moment requires people who will refuse gated communities, resist gated lives, and attune to the wisdom of Martin Luther King Jr., place their lives in the midst of others, in the midst of a distressed environment, in the midst of segregated neighborhoods, in the midst of class division, in the midst of grotesque economic inequalities, and say to themselves, "I will be a place that connects. I will be a place of thriving in a place where thriving is a distant memory."

We who name the name of Jesus are all faced with a decision that grows in urgency with each passing day, whether we will live in places in ways that are inconsequential to the gospel we say guides our lives or whether we will root ourselves in a place and decide to become people whose very name becomes synonymous with a meeting and with a thriving together that others never thought possible. Such people who become a place will also become synonymous with another name that gathers together hopes and dreams rooted in a life that overcame death and promises an overcoming.

References

Abbott, Sherry L. 2003. "My Mother Could Send Up the Most Powerful Prayer: The Role of African American Slave Women in Evangelical Christianity." MA thesis, University of Maine. https://digitalcommons.library.umaine.edu/etd/187/.

Acappella. 1993. "Everybody Talkin' 'bout Heaven." *Acappella Spirituals*. The Acappella Company.

Albert, Octavia V. Rogers. 2012. *American Slaves Tell Their Stories: Six Interviews*. Mineola, NY: Dover.

Albert, Octavia V. Rogers, and Cairns Collection of American Women Writers. 1988. *The House of Bondage; or, Charlotte Brooks and Other Slaves*. The Schomburg Library of Nineteenth-Century Black Women Writers. New York: Oxford University Press.

Alexander, Torin, Stephen C. Finley, and Anthony B. Pinn. 2009. *African American Religious Culture*. Santa Barbara: ABC-CLIO.

Alinsky, Saul D. 1971. *Rules for Radicals: A Pragmatic Primer for Realistic Radicals*. New York: Vintage.

American Spiritual Ensemble. 2006. "Follow the Drinking Gourd" and "I Want Jesus to Walk with Me." *The Spirituals*.

Andrews, William L., ed. 1986. *Sisters of the Spirit: Three Black Women's Autobiographies of the Nineteenth Century*. Bloomington: Indiana University Press.

Angelou, Maya. 1994. *Wouldn't Take Nothing for My Journey Now*. New York: Bantam Books.

Associated Press, The. 2021. "N.C. Judges Strike Down a Voter ID Law They Say Discriminates against Black Voters." NPR, September 17, 2021. https://www.npr.org/2021/09/17/1038354159/n-c-judges-strike-down-a-voter-id-law-they-say-discriminates-against-black-voter.

Barbe, Dominique. 1987. *Grace and Power: Base Communities and Nonviolence in Brazil.* Maryknoll, NY: Orbis Books.

Barber, Leroy, with Velma Maia Thomas. 2014. *Red, Brown, Yellow, White: Who's More Precious in God's Sight?* Bangor, PA: Jericho.

Bedford, Nancy. 1998. "La Misión en el Sufrimiento y ante el Sufrimiento." In *Bases Bíblicas de la Misión: Perspectivas Latinoamericanas,* edited by C. René Padilla, 319–34. Grand Rapids: Eerdmans.

Benavides, Martinez. 2019. Interview by Alexia Salvatierra. May 2019.

Black Emotional and Mental Health Collective. 2017. https://www.beam.community/healing-justice.

Boff, Leonardo. 2011. *Church, Charism and Power: Liberation Theology and the Institutional Church.* London: SCM.

Boles, John B., ed. 1988. *Masters and Slaves in the House of the Lord: Race and Religion in the American South, 1740–1870.* Lexington: University of Kentucky Press.

Bonhoeffer, Dietrich. 1937. *The Cost of Discipleship.* Cambridge, UK: Touchstone. Reprinted in 2012.

Bonner, Raymond. 1987. *Waltzing with the Dictator: The Marcos's and the Making of American Policy.* New York: Times Books.

Brafman, Ori, and Rod A. Beckstrom. 2006. *The Starfish and the Spider: The Unstoppable Power of Leaderless Organizations.* New York: Portfolio.

Branson, Mark Lau, and Alan J. Roxburgh. 2021. *Leadership, God's Agency, and Disruption: Confronting Modernity's Wager.* Eugene, OR: Cascade Books.

Brooke, Samuel. 1846. *Slavery and the Slaveholder's Religion: As Opposed to Christianity.* Cincinnati: Self-pub.

brown, adrienne maree. 2017. *Emergent Strategy: Shaping Change, Changing Worlds.* Chico, CA: AK Press.

———. 2019. *Pleasure Activism: The Politics of Feeling Good.* Chico, CA: AK Press.

Bryant, Jamal Harrison. 2020. "Jamal Bryant calls out Christians who burn sage." Twitter, March 5, 2020, 3:50 p.m. https://twitter.com/jamalhbryant/status/1235669059473203200.

Busse, Fr. Brendan, and Robert Bustillo. 2021. Interview by Alexia Salvatierra. January 15, 2021. Zoom.

Butler, Octavia E. 2012. *Parable of the Sower.* New York: Grand Central.

Cade, John B. 1935. "Out of the Mouths of Ex-Slaves." *Journal of Negro History* 20 (July 1935), https://www.jstor.org/stable/2714721.

Callahan, Dwight Allen. 2008. *The Talking Book: African Americans and the Bible.* New Haven: Yale University Press.

Câmara, Hélder. 2009. *Dom Helder Camara: Essential Writings.* Maryknoll, NY: Orbis Books.

Canales, Rev. Marcos. 2020. Interview by Alexia Salvatierra. October 16, 2020. Zoom.

Cardenal, Ernesto. 1976. *The Gospel in Solentiname*. Maryknoll, NY: Orbis Books.

Carolina Federation, The. 2021. "Path To Power: The Carolina Federation Organizing Model v2.1." https://docs.google.com/document/d/1jP9XEekQ2HWifAW0t 4wJIEd3CYEs4Bfh9J2Ys7RVxkc/edit?usp=sharing.

Chakraborty, Ranjani. 2019. "When White Supremacists Overthrew a Government: The Hidden History of a North Carolina Coup." Vox, June 20, 2019. https://www.vox .com/2019/6/20/18693018/white-supremacists-overthrew-government-north-carolina.

Christianopoulis, Dinos. 1978. "The Body and the Wormwood." In *Poems*. Translated and with an introduction by Nicholas Kortis. Athens, Greece: Odysseas. Reprinted in 1995.

Cone, James H. 1992. *The Spirituals and the Blues*. Maryknoll, NY: Orbis Books.

"Contemplative Activist Groups." 2018. The Good Neighbor Movement. https:// www.goodneighbormovement.org/what-are-city-villages.

Cook, Guillermo. 1985. *The Expectation of the Poor*. Maryknoll, NY: Orbis Books.

Cornelius, Janet D. 1999. *Slave Missions and the Black Church in the Antebellum South*. Columbia: University of South Carolina Press.

Creel, Margaret Washington. 1988. *"A Peculiar People": Slave Religion and Community Culture among the Gullahs*. New York: New York University Press.

Cuellar, Guillermo. 1980. *Misa Popular Salvadoreña*. Recorded in 1980. https://open .spotify.com/album/79u2AxazF73BSQ2dLv3iu8.

Diaminah, Sendolo. 2021. "How to Weave Organizing Traditions Together to Advance Systemic Change." Rebuild the Economy Webinar Series. *The Nonprofit Quarterly*. 3:05, video. https://fb.watch/alC6iLJ9iX/.

Dillard, Cynthia B. 2021. *The Spirit of Our Work: Black Women Teachers (Re)Member*. Boston: Beacon.

Douglass, Frederick. 1994. *Autobiographies: Narrative of the Life of Frederick Douglass, an American Slave*; *My Bondage and My Freedom*; *Life and Times of Frederick Douglass*. Edited by Henry Louis Gates. The Library of America 68. New York: Literary Classics of the United States.

Dubois, W. E. B. 1903. *The Souls of Black Folk*. Reprint, New York: Barnes & Noble Classics, 2003.

Dunkley, Daive A., and Stephanie Shonekan, eds. 2019. *Black Resistance in the Americas*. New York: Routledge.

Dzurinko, Nijmie Zakkiyyah. 2020. "From Elections to Politics." Put People First! PA. March 19, 2020. https://www.putpeoplefirstpa.org/from-elections-to-politics/.

———. 2021. "Revolutionaries and Electoral Politics." University of the Poor. https:// universityofthepoor.org/revolutionaries-and-electoral-politics/?fbclid=IwAR1xB c3pZjcmCuYIUSs-PkGzMPR5nghl_JjSZ7i9YpzNoTqctp7oTy4gyj4.

Earl, Riggins Renal. 2003. *Dark Symbols, Obscure Signs: God, Self, and Community in the Slave Mind*. Knoxville: University of Tennessee Press.

Erskine, Noel. 2014. *Plantation Church: How African American Religion Was Born in Caribbean Slavery.* Oxford: Oxford University Press.

Escalante, Moises. 2020. Interviews by Alexia Salvatierra. October 8 and 10, 2020. Zoom.

Escobar, Samuel. 2019. *In Search of Christ in Latin America: From Colonial Image to Liberating Savior.* Downers Grove, IL: IVP Academic.

Etzler, Carole. 1976. "Sometimes I Wish." In *Sometimes I Wish.* Sisters Unlimited.

Evans, Freddi Williams. 2008. *Hush Harbor: Praying in Secret.* Minneapolis: Carolrhoda Books.

Faulkner, William J. 1993. *The Days When the Animals Talked: Black American Folktales and How They Came to Be.* Trenton, NJ: Africa World Press.

Fort, Nyle. 2022. "The Religion of Protest." The Cut. January 31, 2022. https://www.thecut.com/2022/01/black-lives-matter-religion-spirituality.html.

Frederickson, Mary E., and Delores M. Walters. 2013. *Gendered Resistance: Women, Slavery, and the Legacy of Margaret Garner.* The New Black Studies Series. Urbana: University of Illinois Press.

Freire, Paulo. 1992. *Pedagogy of Hope: Reliving Pedagogy of the Oppressed.* London: Bloomsbury.

Frey, William H. 2018. "The US Will Become 'Minority White' in 2045, Census Projects." Brookings. September 10, 2018. https://www.brookings.edu/blog/the-avenue/2018/03/14/the-us-will-become-minority-white-in-2045-census-projects/.

Fulop, Timothy E., and Albert Raboteau. 1997. *African-American Religion: Interpretive Essays in History and Culture.* New York: Routledge.

Gage, Royal. 1848. *A Treatise on Resistance and Nonresistance: In Which Is Included a Scriptural Distinction between the Church of Christ and the Civil Government of the World. Slavery, Abolition & Social Justice.* Brattleboro, VT: J. B. Miner.

Galdámez, Pablo. 1983. *Faith of a People.* Maryknoll, NY: Orbis Books.

Gates, Henry Louis. 2021. *The Black Church: This Is Our Story, This Is Our Song.* New York: Penguin.

Gilkes, Cheryl Townsend. 2001. *If It Wasn't for the Women: Black Women's Experience and Womanist Culture in Church and Community.* Maryknoll, NY: Orbis Books.

Glaude, Eddie, Jr. 1999. *Exodus! Religion, Race, and Nation in Early Nineteenth-Century Black America.* Chicago: University of Chicago Press.

———. 2012. "The Black Church Is Dead." HuffPost. Updated August 23, 2012. https://www.huffpost.com/entry/the-black-church-is-dead_b_473815.

Gleeson, Scott. 2020. "The Power of Virtual Group Therapy during a Time of Quarantine." *Counseling Today.* July 1, 2020. https://ct.counseling.org/2020/07/the-power-of-virtual-group-therapy-during-a-time-of-quarantine/.

Golden Gospel Singers, The. 2007. "Oh Freedom!" In *A Capella Praise.* Blue Flame Records.

Gomez, Bishop Medardo. 2012. Interview by Alexia Salvatierra. May 14, 2012. Headquarters of the Iglesia Luterana de El Salvador, San Salvador, El Salvador.

González, Justo. 1997. *Tres Meses en la Escuela del Espiritu*. Nashville: Abingdon.

Gutiérrez, Gustavo. 1981. "The Irruption of the Poor in Latin America and the Christian Communities of the Common People." In *The Challenge of Basic Christian Communities*, edited by Sergio Torres and John Eagleson, 108–30. Maryknoll, NY: Orbis Books.

Haggerty, Richard. 1990. *El Salvador: A Country Study*. Washington, DC: Federal Research Division, Library of Congress.

Hannah-Jones, Nikole, Caitlin Roper, Ilena Silverman, and Jake Silverstein, eds. 2021. *The 1619 Project: A New Origin Story*. New York: One World.

Harding, Rachel. 2015. *Remnants: A Memoir of Spirit, Activism, and Mothering*. Durham, NC: Duke University Press.

Harding, Vincent. 1981. *There Is a River: The Black Struggle for Freedom in America*. Orlando, FL: Harcourt, Brace.

———. 1997. "Religion and Resistance among Antebellum Slaves." In Fulop and Raboteau, *African-American Religion*, 107–32.

Harrison, Renee K. 2009. *Enslaved Women and the Art of Resistance in Antebellum America*. New York: Palgrave Macmillan.

Healey, Joseph G., and Jeanne Hinton, eds. 2005. *Small Christian Communities Today: Capturing the New Moment*. Maryknoll, NY: Orbis Books.

Hebblethwaite, Margaret. 1994. *Base Communities: An Introduction*. Mawah, NJ: Paulist Press.

Helg, Aline. 2019. *Slave No More: Self-Liberation before Abolitionism in the Americas*. Translated by Lara Vergnaud. Chapel Hill: University of North Carolina Press.

Herskovits, Melville J. 1990. *The Myth of the Negro Past*. Boston: Beacon.

Hoeffel, Paul Heath. 1981. "The Eclipse of the Oligarchs." *New York Times Magazine*, September 6, 1981. https://www.nytimes.com/1981/09/06/magazine/the-eclipse-of-the-oligarchs.html.

Holmes, Barbara A. 2004. *Joy Unspeakable: Contemplative Practices of the Black Church*. Minneapolis: Fortress.

hooks, bell. 2009. *Belonging*. New York: Routledge.

———. 2014. *Sisters of the Yam: Black Women and Self-Recovery*. New York: Routledge.

Hopkins, Dwight N. 2000. *Down, Up, and Over: Slave Religion and Black Theology*. Minneapolis: Fortress.

Howard-Pitney, David. 2005. *The African American Jeremiad: Appeals for Justice in America*. Philadelphia: Temple University Press.

Huerta, Dolores. 2008. Interview by Alexia Salvatierra. August 30, 2008. Los Angeles.

Iriarte, Gregorio. 2006. "¿Que es una comunidad eclesial de base?" Redes Cristianas. http://www.redescristianas.net/¿Qué-es-una-comunidad-eclesial-de-base?-gregorio-iriarte.

Ismet, Fanany, Aswar Hazan, and Sue Kenny. 2021. "Sustainable Livelihoods in Indonesia." In *The Routledge Handbook of Community Development*, edited by Sue Kenny, Brian McGrain, and Rhonda Phillips, 144–58. Milton Park, UK: Routledge.

Jackson, Mahalia. 1955. "Walk over God's Heaven." In *The World's Greatest Gospel Singer Mahalia Jackson*. Columbia Records.

Jennings, Willie James. 2010. *The Christian Imagination: Theology and the Origins of Race*. New Haven: Yale University Press.

———. 2020. *After Whiteness: An Education in Belonging*. Grand Rapids: Eerdmans.

Johnson, Clifton H. 1993. *God Struck Me Dead: Voices of Ex-Slaves*. Cleveland: Pilgrim.

Johnson, Paul E., ed. 1994. *African-American Christianity: Essays in History*. Berkeley: University of California Press.

Jones, Norrece T., Jr. 1990. *Born a Child of Freedom, Yet a Slave: Mechanisms of Control and Strategies of Resistance in Antebellum South Carolina*. Middletown, CT: Wesleyan University Press.

Joyner, Charles W., and Norman R. Yetman. 1971. "Life under the 'Peculiar Institution': Selections from the Slave Narrative Collection." *Journal of American Folklore* 84, no. 334 (1971): 453.

Katz, William Loren. 1990. *Breaking the Chains: African-American Slave Resistance*. New York: Atheneum.

Kaye, Anthony E. 2007. *Joining Places: Slave Neighborhoods in the Old South*. Chapel Hill: University of North Carolina Press.

Kenny, Sue, Brian McGrath, and Rhonda Phillips, eds. 2018. *The Routledge Handbook of Community Development*. New York: Routledge.

King, Martin Luther, Jr. 1963. "Letter from Birmingham Jail." In *A Testament of Hope: The Essential Writings and Speeches of Martin Luther King Jr.* Edited by James M. Washington. New York: Harper & Row, 1986.

———. 1998. *A Knock at Midnight: Inspiration from the Great Sermons of Reverend Martin Luther King, Jr.* Edited by Clayborne Carson and Peter Holloran. New York: Warner Books.

Kolokotronis, Alexander. 2018. "Participatory Democracy: A Tool for Social Change." Truthout. July 13, 2018. https://truthout.org/articles/participatory-democracy-a-tool-for-social-change/.

La Fuente Ministries. 2021. Accessed October 15, 2020. https://www.paznaz.org/lafuenteministries.

Lawrence, Chris. Interview by Alexia Salvatierra. October 6, 2015. Training course at Federation of Protestant Welfare Agencies, New York.

Levine, Lawrence W. 2007. *Black Culture and Black Consciousness: Afro-American Folk Thought from Slavery to Freedom*. 30th ed. New York: Oxford University Press.

Lewis, John. 2015. Quoted by the Very Rev. Mike Kinman, Christ Church Cathedral, St. Louis, MO. Sermon delivered December 13, 2015. http://yourcathedral.blogspot.com/2015/12/the-church-must-be-headlight-not.html.

Madonado Perez, Zaida. 2013. *Latina Evangélicas: A Theological Survey from the Margins*. Eugene, OR: Cascade.

Marins, José. 1981. *Base Ecclesial Community: Church from the Roots*. Bangalore, India: Biblical Catechetical and Liturgical Centre.

Mariz, Cecília Loreto. 1994. *Coping with Poverty*. Philadelphia: Temple University Press.

Martinez, Juan Benavides. 2019. Interview by Alexia Salvatierra. May 3, 2019. Fuller Theological Seminary, Pasadena, CA.

Menser, Michael. 2018. "Participatory Democracy: A Tool for Social Change." Truthout. July 31, 2018. https://truthout.org/articles/participatory-democracy-a-tool-for-social-change/.

Mesters, Carlos. 1981. "The Use of the Bible in Christian Communities of the Common People." In *The Challenge of Basic Christian Communities*, edited by Sergio Torres and John Eagleson. Maryknoll, NY: Orbis Books.

"Mission & Values." 2018. The Good Neighbor Movement. https://www.goodneighbormovement.org/values.

Mohamed, Besheer, Kiana Cox, Jeff Diamant, and Claire Gecewicz. 2021. "Faith among Black Americans." Pew Research Center. February 16, 2021. https://www.pewforum.org/2021/02/16/faith-among-black-americans/.

Morrison, Toni. 2004. *Beloved*. New York: Vintage Books.

Moses Hogan Singers, The. 2011. "Oh Mary Don't You Weep" and "He Nevuh Said a Mumbalin' Word." In *La Magie des plus beaux Negro Spirituals*. Bayard Musique. April 28, 2011.

Murphy, Jeannette Robinson. 1899. "The Survival of African Music in America." *Popular Science Monthly 55*.

Murray, Hannah-Rose. 2020. *Advocates of Freedom: African American Transatlantic Abolitionism in the British Isles*. Slaveries Since Emancipation. Cambridge: Cambridge University Press.

Nembhard, Jessica Gordon. 2014. *Collective Courage: A History of African American Cooperative Economic Thought and Practice*. University Park: Pennsylvania State University Press.

Noel, James A. 1994. "Call and Response: The Meaning of the Moan and Significance of the Shout in Black Worship." *Reformed Liturgy and Music* 28, no. 2 (Spring 1994): 72–76.

Nunley, Vorris L. 2011. *Keepin' It Hushed: The Barbershop and African American Hush Harbor Rhetoric*. Detroit: Wayne State University Press.

O'Brien, Niall. 1987. *Revolution from the Heart*. Oxford: Oxford University Press.

O'Connor, Kathleen M. 2011. *Jeremiah: Pain and Promise*. Minneapolis: Fortress.

O'Halloran, James. 1990. *Signs of Hope: Developing Small Christian Communities.* Maryknoll, NY: Orbis Books.

Oredein, Oluwatomisin. 2022. "A Black Church Proposition for Radical Human Flourishing." Berkely Forum. January 6, 2022. https://berkleycenter.georgetown.edu /responses/a-black-church-proposition-for-radical-human-flourishing.

Ortiz, Ana. 2020. Interviews by Alexia Salvatierra. October 8, 10, and 12, 2021. Zoom.

"Our Mission." 2021. Mission House Church. http://missionhousenc.com/about-us /our-mission.

Padilla, C. Rene, and Tetsunao Yamamori. 2004. *The Local Church, Agent of Transformation: An Ecclesiology for Integral Mission.* Buenos Aires, Argentina: Kairos Ediciones.

Parker, Priya. 2018. *The Art of Gathering: How We Meet and Why It Matters.* New York: Riverhead Books.

Peck, Scott M. 1987. *The Different Drum: Community-Making and Peace.* New York: Simon & Schuster.

Pew Research Center. 2019. "In U.S. Decline of Christianity Continues at Rapid Pace." October 17, 2019. https://www.pewforum.org/2019/10/17/in-u-s-decline -of-christianity-continues-at-rapid-pace/.

Polleta, Francesca. 2002. *Freedom Is an Endless Meeting: Democracy in American Social Movement.* Chicago: University of Chicago Press.

Potter, Laurel. 2021. Unpublished presentation on the third wave of CEBs. American Academy of Religion, San Antonio, TX.

Powery, Emerson B. 2016. *The Genesis of Liberation: Biblical Interpretation in the Antebellum Narratives of the Enslaved.* Louisville: Westminster John Knox.

"Public Worship." 2018. The Good Neighbor Movement. https://www.goodneigh bormovement.org/worship.

Pyles, Loretta. 2021. *Progressive Community Organizing: Transformative Practice in a Globalizing World.* New York: Routledge.

"Que Hacemos." 2021. La Fuente Ministries. https://www.paznaz.org/lafuentemi nistries/que-hacemos/.

Raboteau, Albert J. 1995. *A Fire in the Bones: Reflections on African-American Religious History.* Boston: Beacon.

———. 2001. *Canaan Land: A Religious History of African Americans.* Oxford: Oxford University Press.

———. 2004. *Slave Religion: The "Invisible Institution" in the Antebellum South.* Oxford: Oxford University Press.

Randolph, Peter (an emancipated slave). 1855. *Sketches of Slave Life, or Illustrations of the "Peculiar Institution."* Boston: n.p.

Rawick, George P., ed. 1979a. *The American Slave: A Composite Autobiography.* Supplemental Series 2. Vol. 2, *Texas Narratives, Part 1.* Westport, CT: Greenwood.

———. 1979b. *The American Slave: A Composite Autobiography*. Supplemental Series 2. Vol. 5, *Texas Narratives, Part 4*. Westport, CT: Greenwood.

———. 2006. *Unwritten History of Slavery*. Vol. 18, *Unwritten History of Slavery*. Westport, CT: Greenwood.

Romero, Archbishop Oscar. 1980. "God Calls Us to Construct Our History Together with Him." Homily delivered February 10, 1980, at the Cathedral San Salvador, El Salvador. Printed in Romero Trust Archives. http://www.romerotrust.org.uk/sites /default/files/homilies/ART_Homilies_Vol6_185_GodCallsUsConstructOurHis toryTogetherWithHim.pdf.

Saint-Exupéry, Antoine de. 1943. *The Little Prince*. New York: Reynal & Hitchcock.

Salvatierra, Alexia. 2019. "Latinx Millennials in the U.S. and Theological Education." Research completed through Centro Latino, Fuller Theological Seminary.

Salvatierra, Alexia, and Peter Heltzel. 2013. *Faith-Rooted Organizing: Mobilizing the Church in Service to the World*. Downers Grove, IL: InterVarsity.

Sampson, Melva L. "Digital Hush Harbors: Black Preaching Women and Black Digital Religious Networks." *Fire!!!* 6, no. 1 (2020): 45–66.

Sernett, Milton C. 1999. *African American Religious History: A Documentary Witness*. Durham, NC: Duke University Press.

Sharp, Christena. 2016. *In the Wake: On Blackness and Being*. Durham, NC: Duke University Press.

Singh, Julietta. 2018. *Unthinking Mastery: Dehumanism and Decolonial Entanglements*. Durham, NC: Duke University Press.

Smith, Venture, James Mars, William Grimes, G. W. Offley, and James L. Smith. 1971. *Five Black Lives: The Autobiographies of Venture Smith, James Mars, William Grimes, the Rev. G. W. Offley, and James L. Smith*. Documents of Black Connecticut. Middletown, CT: Wesleyan University Press.

Solivan, Samuel. 1998. *The Spirit, Pathos and Liberation: Toward a Hispanic Pentecostal Theology*. Sheffield, UK: Sheffield Academic Press.

Squires, Catherine R. 2002. "Rethinking the Black Public Sphere: An Alternative Vocabulary for Multiple Public Spheres." *Communication Theory* 12 , no. 4 (2002): 446–68.

Swift, David E. 1989. *Black Prophets of Justice: Activist Clergy before the Civil War*. Baton Rouge: Louisiana State University Press.

Thurman, Howard. 1975. *Deep River and the Negro Spiritual Speaks of Life and Death*. Richmond, IN: Friends United Press.

———. 1976. *Jesus and the Disinherited*. Boston: Beacon.

Tobin, Jacqueline L., and Raymond G. Dobard. 1999. *Hidden in Plain View*. New York: Doubleday.

Torres, Sergio, and John Eagleson. 1981. *The Challenge of Basic Christian Communities*. Maryknoll, NY: Orbis Books.

UNECLAC (United Nations Economic Commission for Latin America and the Caribbean). 2019. "The Social Panorama of Latin America 2019." https://www.cepal.org/en/publications/44989-social-panorama-latin-america-2019.

Van Cappellen, Patty. 2018. "The Embodiment of Worship: Relation among Postural, Psychological, and Physiological Aspects of Religious Practice." *Journal for the Cognitive Science of Religion* 6, nos. 1–2 (2018): 56–79.

Walker-Barnes, Chanequa. 2017. "Why I Gave Up Church." Bearings Online. https://collegevilleinstitute.org/bearings/why-i-gave-up-church/.

Warnock, Raphael. 2020. *The Divided Mind of the Black Church*. New York: New York University Press.

Washington, Joseph R., Jr. 1966. *Black Religion: The Negro and Christianity in the United States*. Boston: Beacon.

Watson-Vandiver, Marcia J., and Greg A. Wiggan. 2021. *The Healing Power of Education: Afrocentric Pedagogy as a Tool for Restoration and Liberation*. New York: Teachers College.

Webber, Thomas. 1978. *Deep Like the Rivers: Education in the Slave Quarters Community, 1830–1865*. New York: Norton.

West, Cornel, and Eddie S. Glaude Jr. 2003. *African American Religious Thought: An Anthology*. Louisville: Westminster John Knox.

White, Deborah Gray. 1999. *Ar'n't I a Woman: Female Slaves in the Plantation South*. New York: Norton.

"Who We Are." 2015. Mission House Church. http://missionhousenc.com/about-us/who-we-are.

Wiggan, Greg A., Lakia Scott, Marcia Watson, and Richard Reynolds. 2014. *Unshackled: Education for Freedom, Student Achievement, and Personal Emancipation*. Rotterdam, Netherlands: Sense.

Wilkinson Arreche, Whitney. 2019. "Places of Power and Promise: A Pilgrimage into the Enslaved African Hush Harbor." Unpublished paper. http://liberatingchurch.org/wp-content/uploads/2019/05/Places-of-Power-and-Promise.pdf.

Wilmore, Gayraud S., ed. 1985. *African American Religious Studies: An Interdisciplinary Anthology*. Durham, NC: Duke University Press.

Wilmore, Gayraud S. 1998. *Black Religion and Black Radicalism: An Interpretation of the Religious History of African Americans*. Maryknoll, NY: Orbis Books.

Wrencher, Brandon, Lauren Cunningham, and Erica Wrencher. 2021. "Away with the Mangers." https://docs.google.com/document/d/10xnD58CrviwpRmRJet9vy1tNcLM_CWYdmh3NJJIUG28/edit?usp=sharing.

Wrencher, Brandon, and Vennekia Williams, eds. 2022. *Liberating Church: A 21st Century Hush Harbor Manifesto*. Eugene, OR: Wipf & Stock.

Yambasu, John K. (United Methodist Bishop of Sierra Leone). 2015. Interview by Alexia Salvatierra. November 5, 2015. Learning Retreat, Lake Junalaska, NC.

Index